CHALLENGES TO LAW AT THE END OF THE 20th CENTURY

I: RIGHTS

ARSP BEIHEFT 67

ARCHIV FÜR RECHTS- UND SOZIALPHILOSOPHIE

ARCHIVES DE PHILOSOPHIE DU DROIT ET DE PHILOSOPHIE SOCIALE

ARCHIVES FOR PHILOSOPHY OF LAW AND SOCIAL PHILOSOPHY

ARCHIVO DE FILOSOFÍA JURÍDICA Y SOCIAL

FRANZ STEINER VERLAG STUTTGART
1997

CHALLENGES TO LAW
AT THE END
OF THE 20th CENTURY:

RIGHTS

PROCEEDINGS OF THE 17th WORLD CONGRESS
OF THE INTERNATIONAL ASSOCIATION
FOR PHILOSOPHY OF LAW AND SOCIAL PHILOSOPHY (IVR)
BOLOGNA, JUNE 16–21, 1995

VOL. I

EDITED BY
REX MARTIN & GERHARD SPRENGER

FRANZ STEINER VERLAG STUTTGART
1997

Die Deutsche Bibliothek - CIP-Einheitsaufnahme
ARSP-Beiheft : Archiv für Rechts- und Sozialphilosophie. - Stuttgart
: Steiner
Früher Schriftenreihe. - Früher angezeigt u.d.T.: Archiv für Rechts- und Sozialphilosophie / Beiheft
Reihe ARSP-Beiheft zu: Archiv für Rechts- und Sozialphilosophie
ISSN 0341-079X
Nr. 67. International Association for the Philosophy of Law and Social Philosophy: Proceedings of the ... world congress of the International Association for Philosophy of Law and Social Philosophy (IVR) ...
17. Challenges to law at the end of the 20th century Vol. 1. Rights. - 1997
International Association for the Philosophy of Law and Social Philosophy:
Proceedings of the ... world congress of the International Association for Philosophy of Law and Social Philosophy (IVR) ... - Stuttgart : Steiner
(ARSP-Beiheft ; ...)
Bis 15, Bd. 4 (1994) u.d.T.: International Association for the Philosophy of Law and Social Philosophy: Verhandlungen des ... Weltkongresses der Internationalen Vereinigung für Rechts- und Sozialphilosophie (IVR) ...
17. Challenges to law at the end of the 20th century : Bologna, June 16 - 21, 1995
Vol. 1. Rights / ed. by Rex Martin & Gerhard Sprenger. - 1997
(ARSP-Beiheft ; Nr. 67)
Beitr. teilw. dt., teilw. engl., teilw. franz., teilw. span.
ISBN 3-515-07071-0

ISO 9706

 Gedruckt auf alterungsbeständigem Papier.
Druck: Druckerei Proff, Eurasburg.
Printed in Germany

Preface

It is a great pleasure and an honour for me to present the proceedings of the 17th World Congress of the International Association of Legal and Social Philosophy (IVR) held in Bologna from 16th to 21st June, 1995. Over seven hundred scholars from all five continents took part in the Congress, which was structured in four plenary sessions, six parellel sessions, a special session devoted to document logistics (legal and civic computer science applications), and 81 working groups.

The IVR was founded in 1909 and now counts over three thousand members in 44 sections located all over the world. Forthcoming congresses will be held in La Plata/Buenos Aires (Argentina) in 1997, New York (USA) in 1999, and Amsterdam (The Netherlands) in 2001. As current President of the IVR, and a member for 30 years, I am happy to see that by 2001 the Association will have reached its 20th official World Congress.

The goal of the 17th World Congress was to focus on the major legal, political and social issues currently addressed by legal and social philosophy. This was reflected in its far-reaching, stimulating title, "Challenges to Law at the End of the 20th Century".

Congress papers were grouped under four main topics: "Rights and other legal protections"; "New forms of sovereignty and citizenship"; "New and ancient sources of law"; "Technology and the environment". The debate focussed on the latest issues tackled by the legal and social philosophy milieu. First and foremost, a strictly formalist concept of law no longer fulfills the need to safeguard equality and protect basic human rights. In addition, the notions of sovereignty and citizenship have been reassessed in relation to the crisis of the nation state and the globalisation of economic and cultural problems alongside the tension between the idea of sovereignty and the inviolability of human rights.

The wide-ranging topic of the sources of law was also handled by many speakers, as was the relation between the theory of interpretation and the theory of sources, weighing "sceptic" theories against "cognitive" theories of interpretation and comparing different legal systems in historical terms and from a comparative law standpoint.

Last but not least, a number of speakers discussed the problem of the protection of rights with a view to revising traditional cultural categories in the wake of burgeoning technological development. Topics ranged from bioethics to environmental protection, the problems of computer science applications to law and the issue of legislative technique in relation to the computerization of law.

The Proceedings of the Bologna Congress are published in part by *Archiv für Rechts- und Sozialphilosophie* (Franz Steiner Verlag, Stuttgart/Germany), in part by *Rechtstheorie* (Duncker & Humblot, Berlin/Germany), and in part by The *European Journal of Law, Philosophy and Computer Science* (Clueb, Bologna/ Italy).

ARSP publishes four volumes: "Rights" – Beiheft 67 (eds. Rex Martin and Gerhard Sprenger, introduction by Zenon Bankowski and Burkhard Schaefer),

"Law, Justice and Culture" – Beiheft 68 (eds. André-Jean Arnaud and Peter Koller, introduction by Tom Campbell), "The Sources of Law and Legislation" – Beiheft 69 (eds. Elspeth Attwooll and Paolo Comanducci, introduction by Joxerramon Bengoextea), and "Legal Systems and Legal Science" – Beiheft 70 (eds. Marijan Pavčnik and Gianfrancesco Zanetti, introduction by Hendrik Ph. Visser't Hooft).

Rechtstheorie publishes three volumes: "Rule of Law – Political and Legal Systems in Transition" – Beiheft 17 (eds. Werner Krawietz, Enrico Pattaro, Alice Erh-Soon Tay, introduction by Ota Weinberger), "Changing Structures in Modern Legal Systems and the Legal State Ideology" – Beiheft 18 (eds. Eugenio Bulygin, Burton M. Leiser, Mark Van Hoecke, introduction by Aulis Aarnio), and "Consequences of Modernity in Contemporary Legal Theory" – Beiheft 19 (eds. Eugene E. Dais, Roberta Kevelson, Jan M. Van Dunné, introduction by Dieter Wyduckel).

The *European Journal of Law, Philosophy and Computer Science* publishes three volumes: "Practical Reason. History of deontics. Computer Law", "Legal Computer Science" – Volumes 1 and 2 (eds. Alberto Artosi, Manuel Atienza, Hajime Yoshino, introduction by Neil MacCormick), and "Law and Politics Between Nature and History" – Volume 3 (eds. Ralf Dreier, Carla Faralli, Wladik. S. Nersessiants, introduction by Roberto Vernengo).

On behalf of the International Association of Legal and Social Philosophy, I would like to thank all those who have worked on the editing of these Proceedings.

Enrico Pattaro

Contents

Contents of all proceedings of the 17th World Congress of the IVR in Bologna, June 16–21, 1995

Law I: Law, Justice and Culture (ARSP-Beiheft 68)
ed. by André-Jean Arnaud and Peter Koller

Law II: Sources of Law and Legislation (ARSP-Beiheft 69)

ed. by Elspeth M. M. Attwooll and Paolo Comanducci

Legal Systems and Legal Science (ARSP-Beiheft 70)
ed. by Marijan Pavčnik and Gianfrancesco Zanetti

Political and Legal Systems in Transition (Rechtstheorie, Beiheft 17)
Eds: Werner Krawietz, Enrico Pattaro, Alice Erh-Soon Tay

Changing Structures in Modern Legal Systems and the Legal State Ideology (Rechtstheorie, Beiheft 18)

Eds: Eugenio Bulygin, Burton M. Leiser, Mark Van Hoecke

Consequences of Modernity in Contemporary Legal Theory (Rechtstheorie, Beiheft 19)

Eds: Eugene E. Dais, Roberta Kevelson, Jan M. Van Dunné

European Journal of Law, Philosophy and Computer Science

Volume I: Practical Reason. History of Deontics. Computer Law. Eds: A. Artosi, M. Atienza, H. Yoshino. Introduction by N. MacCormick

European Journal of Law, Philosophy and Computer Science

Volume II: Legal Computer Science. Eds: A. Artosi, M. Atienza, H. Yoshino. Introduction by N. MacCormick

European Journal of Law, Philosophy and Computer Science

Volume III: Law and Politics between Nature and History. Eds: R. Dreier, C. Faralli, W. S. Nersessiants. Introduction by R. Vernengo

Zenon Bankowski and Burkhard Schaefer

Introduction

Rights talk has always been important but with the collapse of the communsim as a practical ideological force it becomes more important since it seems to be one of the few alternatives for governance that is left after the final break up of the Soviet Union and the final end of the communist hegemony.

Two of the articles in the collection seek then to justify universal human rights from a liberal, Kantian, discourse point of view. Robert Alexy redefines the Kantian conception of human rights by refining Habermas's weak transcendental argument for the justification of universally valid discourse rules. What is important about Alexy's argument is how he shows that the rules of discourse that he establishes will justify the acceptance of basic human rights outside the discourse situation. He shows that the denial of autonomy for all men, and with this the general right of freedom, a denial of equal rights for all, and a denial of the value of democracy outside the discourse, would make the discourse itself impossible.

Following on from these sorts of arguments and also taking on board Dworkin's principle based theories of justification, J.-R. Sieckmann argues for an a priori or basic rights, that is those which are a necessary prerequisite of making valid rules. Since the weighing of principles is an open and not cognitively determined process, it requires the recognition of autonomy rights of those weighing the principles. These can be broadly categorised as the right to moral autonomy (to live according to one's accepted norms); the right to personal autonomy (to live one's own life) and the right to take part in decision procedures on what norms are legally valid.

Campbell and Holmstrom-Hintikka take an analytical view of the notion of rights based on the seminal analysis of hohfeld, the former arguing that Hohfeld vreated an 'overflow' of rights, while the latter argues that besides rights we must recognise an irreducible concept of responsibilities with a conceptual logic of its own. Matsuo on the other hand advocates that ownership of external things, rather than the ownership of one's own body as proposed by Locke, should again become the fixed point in our conception of "right". Pavcnik shows how violation of a right and abuse of a right can be analytically distinguished and how that tells us something about the concept of right.

Having analysed the possibility of rights and the way they are to be understood we can now turn to look at what sort of ontologies are necessary in connection with right. In other words what sort of things can be classified as being able to hold rights. Gould says that in some respects the decision is a normative one. Thus in trying to see minority rights as those of a group one should avoid seeing groups as objects independent of individuals and at the same time avoid seeing all group rights talk to be something to be reduced to talk of right of atomistic individuals. One should see groups as constituted by "individuals-in-relation". The individual is ontologically prior to the group, but what makes her an individual is the relation to other individuals. As a more concrete corollary, individual rights necessarily trump group rights in case of conflicts. Here also belongs Mallen's essay dealing with belonging to a sect as a possible limit to the right of choosing the education of one's child. Christodoulidis in a sceptical paper shows how law is the wrong medium for producing these collective identities.

We can here also deal with more esoteric ontological entities and their putative rights. Here then we find essays dealing with the rights of the environment by J and LP Francis and Tallachini and also with the right of the unborn by Lang. Lang deals with, as it were, the standard case while Meyer deals with a more unusual case of future people having a right to non-existence. He argues that children can have a right to non-existence, which can be violated by parents who decide to procreate in the light of a high probability that the child would have a life not worth living. To defend this conclusion, he analytically distinguishes actual from possible future persons. In the next step, he distinguishes in the same way three different meanings of the notion "to harm". The decision to procreate results in an actual future person who can be relevant bearer of a right – unlike a mere possible future person, a person before the decision to procreate that person. It is now not possible to cause harm to such a person if harm is understood as an action which now worsens the position of someone else, or an action which, ceteris paribus, results in a person being worse off at a future point in time then he would have been without this action. But if we understand causing harm in the sense that it makes a person worse off in the future than that person should have been, we can cause harm to an actual future person in, procreating a person whose life is not worth living. To avoid this might be by not bringing him into existence in the first place. The rights of aliens and outsiders from the point of view of the USA and Canada are explored by McBride and Galloway.

Since in this collection the arguments for the possibility of rights have used discourse theory it is appropriate that some of the essays deal with free speech and Communication rights Peonides tries to refute the sceptical position of Fish and Husak concerning the possibility to justify the right of free speech. He argues that far from being anti-theoretical, both authors rely on developed philosophical theories to reach their conclusions. A full theory of free speech however must go beyond Husak's "attribution of blame" and answer such questions as the justification of affirmative action by the state to enhance free speech. In analysing Hegel's philosophy as an example of a hostile and dangerous approach to free speech, he develops conditions for a positive theory. Crum, using a British and German example, also argues against Fish's sceptical conclusions. Tom Campbell shows how rights do not only deal with undue state interference. He argues that the classical position regarding the right of free speech focuses unduly on state interference. Today, freedom of speech is endangered more by large media enterprises which make the possibility of expression dependent on economic power. As a result state intervention against the media might be necessary to secure freedom of speech. His chosen example is defamation. The traditional position resulted in an unfortunate antagonism between defamation law and free speech. This could be overcome by a law which, instead of awarding damages after prohibitively costly proceedings, would force publishers in defamation cases to print extensively the reply of the defamed party. This would provide a true "market of ideas". In addition, it could be up to a special commission or panel to find the “truth” in these cases and make accordingly an declarative statement. Shiner argues against using the right to free speech as a way of protecting commercial advertising.

So far we have been looking in the main at how rights can be seen as normatively necessary in governing states and at other papers give more concrete examples of this. This is, as we saw, not surprising given the times we live in. However there were also more sceptical papers. Queipo de Llano argues against the universalism of Human Rights and restates the criticism against liberalism and Dworkin in particular. He argues that their models are based on an unreal because abstract picture of universal features of individuals out of their concrete societal and cultural context. Therefore, their universalism is not morally neutral but the expression of a specific cultural form of life, that of a modern western life-style. Here then we come to the crux of the problem. For though the papers eloquently show the importance of universalism in the form of rights, we also see the need to concentrate on the particular and the specific culture or person. An answer to Queipo de Llano’s problem might come from Penski’s essay. He argues that some laws can be called universally valid even if not recognised in all legal systems. To solve this seeming contradiction, he shows that the most plausible candidate for an universal law, the right to freedom as inherent in human nature, requires rather then forbids particularised legal systems and excludes logically an “uniform world law”. To reach this conclusion, he reconstructs the universal right of freedom to a “claim to recognition of freedom as freedom amongst free individuals”. From this claim alone, no concrete law follows. This requires its realisation in concrete social circumstances by a coordinating authority. A world authority however could not guarantee all freedom laws, e.g. not the right to leave the country or the right of asylum.

Kenneth Campbell, London

The Variety of Rights

The analysis of the concept of rights has advanced greatly this century. In the nineteenth century the only sustained attack on the problem in the Anglo-American tradition was that of John Austin in the lectures he delivered at the University of London in the 1820's and '30's.[1] For the rest of the century most further discussions were highly derivative from his views. Then in the first decades of our century came the fresh analysis of Wesley Newcomb Hohfeld whose approach still exercises considerable influence.[2] In the latter decades of the century there was an explosion of published material on the topic. Not all of this was of great quality, but certain writers stand out. The late H.L.A. Hart greatly extended our understanding of Bentham's largely forgotten work on the topic in the late eighteenth century whilst also offering his own distinctive account.[3] More recently, writers such as Jeremy Waldron and Joseph Raz have added their valuable contributions.[4] However, it is in the nature of these problems that there is often more to be said on aspects of them. I wish to offer some further thoughts on one particular aspect.

Analytical problems about the nature of rights can be roughly divided into two main groups. The first concerns the analysis of rights. For example, the competing merits and demerits of interest-based and choice-based theories; or whether rights are to be seen as reasons for action which outweigh all non-right-based reasons; or whether rights are unanalysable, being as primitive as such other notions as duty, permission and so on, into which they are usually analysed. The second group concerns the variety of rights there are. For example, are there claim-rights and liberty-rights, or are these reducible one to the other, and if so which way? Are there also other varieties, such as power-rights and immunity-rights, and perhaps even more exotic types? Of course, the groups are overlapping in the sense that the answer that one favours with regard to one is very likely to colour one's views with regard to the other.

It is this second group of problems I wish to address here. I take as my starting point Hohfeld's discussion. The position for which I shall argue is that undue proliferation is both unnecessary and misleading but that, on the other hand,

1 *Lectures on Jurisprudence, or the Philosophy of Positive Law*, ed R Campbell, 5th edn, 2 vols, London, 1885.

2 *Fundamental Legal Conceptions as Applied in Judicial Reasoning*, ed WW Cook, New Haven, 1923 (originally published as articles in 1913 and 1917).

3 Bentham on Legal Rights, in AWB Simpson, ed, *Oxford Essays in Jurisprudence*, 2nd Series, Oxford, 1973, 171; reprinted in Hart, *Essays on Bentham: Jurisprudence and Political Theory*, Oxford, 1982, 162; discussing principally Bentham's views in *Of Laws in General* (1780–82), ed Hart, London, 1970.

4 Waldron, A Right to do Wrong, *Ethics* 92 (1981) 21; reprinted in his *Liberal Rights: Collected Papers 1981–1991*, Cambridge, 1993, 63; Raz, On the Nature of Rights, *Mind* 93 (1984) 194; reprinted in his *The Morality of Freedom*, Oxford, 1986, 165; Legal Rights, *Oxford Journal of Legal Studies* 4 (1985) 1; reprinted in his *Ethics in the Public Domain: Essays in the Morality of Law and Politics*, Oxford, 1994, 238.

some contemporary theories which attempt a total reduction to one kind do so at the expense of giving insufficient attention to the subtlety of our ordinary thought on this matter and that at least one distinction in varieties should be maintained in any philosophical analysis.

Hohfeld thought that the term 'a right' is often used to refer to at least four different things: claims, liberties, powers and immunities. He himself thought that, strictly, only claims were rights. However, Hohfeld is not alone in maintaining this general type of view. Others both before and after have argued for a diversity of types, for example Bentham and Hart, though in their case they seem to have thought these were all quite correctly referred to as rights. I shall look initially at Hohfeld's arguments, before passing to more general considerations. It should, however, not be forgotten, as a preliminary, that some have argued that Hohfeld did not go nearly far enough. Albert Kocourek claimed in the later 1920's that there were sixteen different meanings in legal contexts of 'a right'.[5] In an article published in the 1960's the authors maintained that there were twenty six different meanings.[6] I am not going to consider any of these more extravagant views. If Hohfeld's arguments largely fail then so *a fortiori* do the more extreme ones.

Hohfeld's schema is so well-known that I shall do no more than set out its leading features. First, all rights are relations between two, and only two, persons, where this should be taken to include groups of persons who are treated by the law as if they were a single person. This thesis I shall call for convenience the 'atomic thesis'. Secondly, there are four different relations between persons to which the phrase 'X has a right' has been used to refer. Thirdly, each of these relations is *sui generis*, which makes attempts to define them unsatisfactory, if not useless.

The third of these contentions should not be taken too seriously. Hohfeld offers no reasons to support it, and he himself violates its suggestion of impossibility both by defining some of the relations in terms of others, and some in terms of independent concepts such as duty.

The atomic thesis is, however, fundamental to Hohfeld's scheme. All his explanations proceed on that basis. This point has sometimes been misrepresented by commentators, who have written as if considering the relations between two persons were no more than the particular application of a general case. In other words, for any right, one should for clarity consider independently how it affects any two persons. But this is erroneous. On Hohfeld's theory whenever there are more than two legal persons involved there is more than one right.[7] As we shall see, this means that the atomic thesis must be rejected.

The four relations are: claim – duty, privilege – no-claim, power – liability, immunity – disability. (To avoid confusion I use 'claim' to refer to that which Hohfeld calls a 'right in the strictest sense'. Hohfeld himself suggested 'claim' as

5 *Jural Relations*, 2nd edn, Indianapolis, 1928.

6 S & H Kanger, Rights and Parliamentiarism, *Theoria* 32 (1966) 85.

7 Hohfeld believes this is true even of a right *in rem*,which he analyses as a right against a single person but accompanied by a large number of rights of similar content against other persons (*op cit* 72).

a synonym. Similarly I refer to that which Hohfeld called a 'no-right' as a 'no-claim'.)

Let us start with the first of these. Hohfeld explains that "...if X has a claim against Y that he shall stay off the former's land, the correlative (and equivalent) is that Y is under a duty toward X to stay off the place".[8] What kind of equivalence Hohfeld has in mind he does not explain. It might be a relation of identity of meaning or be merely truth-equivalence. Let us assume only the weaker claim.

As an analysis of this type of right it leaves a great deal to be desired. The notion of having a duty towards someone does not appear to be, in itself, any more primitive or perspicuous than that of having a claim against someone. The problem is that one needs an explanation of the force of 'towards' in the *explicans*. Interest- and choice-theories, of course, have their own proposals to make here, but Hohfeld has none. There is simply a gap in the theory. However, we can take it that Hohfeld was asserting that (whatever its ultimate analysis) this was one meaning of a right, a view endorsed by many other writers. It can be argued that in view of his (at least proclaimed) belief that the fundamental relations are indefinable he is trying to show only that we can analyse them sufficiently at least to see that there are four different types of relation involved.

Let us turn then to the second relation. A privilege, explains Hohfeld, is the negation of a duty of the opposite tenor. At first sight it looks as if this amounts to saying that X has a privilege to A if he is under no duty to not-A. However, the correlative of this relation is that Y has a no-claim that X not-A.

This just amounts to saying that Y has no claim that X not-A. So it is clear from this, and would in any case be required by the atomic thesis, that the relation which is being considered is of the form 'with regard to Y, X has a privilege to A'. Here again it is implausible to suggest that the meaning of this phrase is more primitive or obvious than that of its correlate 'Y has no claim that X not-A'.

Does it, however, establish that there is more than one meaning of 'a right'? Certainly the relations are different. But that itself does not prove the point. One relation is of the form 'X has a claim that Y A' and the other is of the form 'Y has no claim that X not-A'. The problem is that it is not clear, *pace* Hohfeld, that we ever do refer to the latter relation as 'a right'. We do not conclude that X has a right to A merely on the basis of the knowledge that there is another person, Y, who has no claim that X not-A. After all, there might be yet another person who has such a claim against X, or X might have a duty to not-A which did not arise from anybody's right. We have little occasion to use phrases of the form 'with regard to Y, X has a right to A' and if we did it is not obvious that we would mean anything other than that X's right was valid against *inter alia* Y. In other words, Hohfeld's explanation of a privilege reveals it as a highly artificial relation which means no more than that someone does not have a claim against one.

Hohfeld supports his contention of a confusion here by pointing to passages in a number of judgments, principally the speech of Lord Lindley in *Quinn v Leathem* [1901] AC 435:

> "The plaintiff had the ordinary rights of the British subject. He was at liberty to earn his living in his own way, provided he did not violate some special law prohibiting him from so doing,

8 Hohfeld, *op cit* 28.

> and provided he did not infringe the rights of other people. This liberty involved the liberty to deal with other persons who were willing to deal with him. This liberty is a right recognised by law; its correlative is the general duty of every one not to prevent the free exercise of this liberty except in so far as his own liberty of action may justify him in so doing. But a person's liberty or right to deal with others is nugatory unless they are at liberty to deal with him if they choose to do so. Any interference with their liberty to deal with him affects him."[99]

Hohfeld's argument is that Lord Lindley starts by talking about a right in the sense of a privilege but slips into talking of the same right as a claim, so that the conclusion rests on a *non-sequitur.* No doubt the passage is open to a number of interpretations, on some of which it may indeed evidence a *non-sequitur*, but there is nothing to suggest that Lord Lindley meant by 'a liberty' that which Hohfeld calls 'a privilege', that is, that there existed a *someone* who did not have a claim that the plaintiff not earn his living in his own way. Indeed, on Hohfeldian analysis, the plaintiff would not have a liberty, but presumably millions of liberties. There is no example cited by Hohfeld which illustrates judicial use of his sense of 'a privilege', and I venture to suggest that none will be found. Whether or not there is a sense of 'X has a right' which is equivalent to 'X has a permission' is a different question, which I shall consider below.

Hohfeld's second pair of relations is that of power – liability, and immunity – disability. A person has a legal power, according to Hohfeld, when his volitional power is paramount in changing a given legal relation. In offering this analysis Hohfeld was following on a fundamental insight of Salmond, namely that legal power must be explained in terms of ability to affect the existence and application of legal rules. This realisation freed legal theory of the erroneous belief that legal power could be explained as a type of physical power.

The correlative of a power is a liability. This means that 'with regard to Y, X has a power' is equivalent to 'with regard to X, Y has a liability'. Hohfeld gives no independent explanation of liability. Its sense is determined by that of power. 'With regard to Y, X has an immunity' is equivalent to 'with regard to X, Y has a disability'. A 'disability' is simply Hohfeld's technical term for an absence of power. So the disability side of this equivalence is 'with regard to X, Y has no power'.

Within this pair of relations the same structure holds as within the previous pair. For here the concept of power is the primitive notion in terms of which both relations are explained. But do we ever refer to these as rights? Again we should need the strongest evidence to convince us that we ever confuse the ideas of having power over a legal relation and someone else not having a legal power over us, and that we refer to both cases as ones of right-possession. Indeed, having a Hohfeldian immunity is even less plausibly a case of having a right than having a Hohfeldian privilege. For consider the implications of Hohfeld's immunity. My next-door neighbour has no power to conscript me into the army, sell my house or exempt me from income tax. To these, and all other, absences of power in anyone else there corresponds a right of mine. But what is the content of my right? There must be something to which I have a right for me to have a right at all. However, on Hohfeld's own scheme any plausible interpretation which can

9 Hohfeld, *op cit* 42.

be given to such a right would place it in one of the other categories. If it were a right that my neighbour not exercise such a power it would be a claim-right against him; if it were a right that he not have such a power it would be a claim-right against a third party, or a number of claim-rights against a number of third parties, that he not be invested with the power, or be divested of it if he already has it; if it were a right to do that which one would be permitted to do if such a power were not exercised it would, presumably, be a privilege. There are no other very plausible candidates for the content of this right. The suspicion must be that while immunities can protect rights, they are not themselves rights, and there is not even a remotely plausible case for them being rights when coupled with the atomic thesis.

The upshot of this is that Hohfeld may be correct that 'a right' is used to refer to a number of different relations, but the ones that he identifies are not very plausible candidates as objects of this confusion, and it is far from obvious that it would better serve our purposes to refer to them instead.

It might, however, well be said that the real problem about Hohfeld's analysis is that it is crippled by the atomic thesis. It is that thesis, it might be claimed, which makes his analyses seem so artificial and lacking in correspondence with ordinary usage. Suppose we drop the atomic thesis. 'Privilege' and 'immunity' would then become closer to ordinary conceptions, and could there then not be a confusion amongst the four primitive concepts such that would lead us to believe that there was this multiple ambiguity in the meaning of 'a right'?

As mentioned, there is much support in the literature for the view that there might be more than one fundamental type of right. By 'fundamental' I mean that although there be may similarities and some connecting threads between rights of all types they are not reducible to one common pattern. Bentham, for example, espoused a version of interest theory according to which all right-holders were beneficiaries, but sometimes the benefit derived from the presence of a duty (on another) and sometimes from the absence of a duty (on oneself). Hart maintained that all right-holders were people who had a legal choice, but sometimes the choice was over other people's duties, sometimes over one's own actions.[10] Both these distinctions correspond very much with Hohfeld's distinction betweeen claims and privileges. It is arguable that Bentham also recognised power-rights as a separate entity. Hart certainly did, and also thought there was much to be said for the separate recognition of immunity rights. I shall work through these four and consider whether the arguments for recognising them as separate types of right are sound.

Take first power and immunity. As Hohfeld rightly noticed, these are related concepts. Power, in the normative context, is the ability to change normative relations, i.e. impose/remove/alter duties, permissions, rights, etc. Immunity is the position of someone who is the beneficiary of an absence of such power in others.

Do powers deserve to be recognised as a separate fundamental type of right? There are two powerful considerations which support the view that they do not. The first is that the difference lies only in the content of the right, that is, in

10 Hart, *op cit.*

that which one has a right to do. I have a liberty-right to pick up my pen. I also have a liberty-right to sign my name with it. When I sign my name in an appropriate context (eg on a cheque) I exercise a legal power which will change legal relations (between me, the bank and the payee). But there is no fundamental difference in the type of right involved here. The difference lies solely in the fact that picking up my pen is a non-normative act and signing my name with it, in some contexts, is a normative one. In other words, in the latter case, exercising a power is that which I have a right to do. It no more follows from this that power-rights are a separate fundamental type of right than the fact that I also have a right to pick up a pencil shows that there is a fundamental difference between pen-rights and pencil-rights.

The second objection to seeing powers as a type of right is that it is not always the case that when one has the power to bring about a certain type of normative change one also has a right to do so. Generally in English law a thief cannot give a valid title to stolen goods, but he can in a 'market overt'. Doing so, however, amounts to the civil wrong of conversion of goods. Similarly, it is sometimes a criminal offence for bankrupts to enter into contracts, but the law may recognise the contracts as valid. Here the law wishes to discourage the relevant normative acts but recognises their validity, if performed, in order to protect the interests of innocent third parties. If one can have a power without a right, then powers are not a species of right.

Immunities, equally, are not rights. My immunity is simply the lack of power of others to change my normative position. Amongst the changes that it may be desirable to protect citizens against is the removal of, or encroachment upon, their rights. So immunities can be important in the protection of rights, but this does not support the conclusion that they are rights themselves.

Turning now to liberty-rights, Bentham and Hohfeld (if we drop the atomic thesis) saw them essentially as permissions. Hart objected that it was not clear that we do refer to a something which is a bare permission, unprotected by a perimeter of claims on others not to interfere, as a right, or that it would be useful if we did. In Hart's view liberty-rights were a combination of permission and the perimeter.

It was perhaps inevitable, however, that some would attempt the ultimate reduction. This step has been taken by Waldron and Raz.[11] Why bother with the normative assessment of the right-holder in liberty-rights? Why not just say that the right consists in the duties on others not to interfere and in nothing more? On this basis, therefore, all rights are traditional claim-rights.

Waldron and Raz have a powerful argument in their favour. The domain of that which one has a right to do cannot simply coincide with that which it is right to do. This would be to give rights little or no independent force. Rights have a significance only when they sometimes countenance the doing of that which is wrong. This argument is sound, but does it support the conclusion that rights consist only of duties on others not to interfere?

The first objection is that this view entails that anything which consists simply of a permission cannot be a right. We have noted Hart's objection to seeing these

11 Waldron, *op cit.* Raz, *Legal Rights*, supra.

as rights, but it might be suggested that there is a confusion here between whether the right is useful and whether it is useful to refer to it as a right. An unprotected right may often not be a very useful one to have. But insofar as it tells us what the right-holder may or may not do within their rights it undoubtedly serves a normative function and is not to be dismissed out of hand as a candidate for right status.

The second objection is related to the first. The oddity of the Waldron/Raz view is that asserting that someone has a right to perform a certain action entails absolutely nothing about the normative assessment of their doing so. The assessment is solely of others, the possible interferers. This, of course, the authors regard as the great advantage of this approach, but it seems to be predicated on the view that permissions have no normative force. That is, one has a permission only if the balance of reasons is not against one performing the action.

This is implausible. The granting of a permission is perfectly consistent with the granter believing that the balance of reasons is against the action. Take a simple domestic example. A teenager asks a parent if they have permission to buy a motorbike. The parent may well believe that the balance of reasons is against this but, out of consideration for the child's increasing entitlement to autonomy, allow them to do so. They are not saying just that they will not interfere, but also that they will act as if they thought the reasons were not against the action; for example, they will not harp on the issue of whether having the bike is advisable or not.

A fortiori with the law. In granting a permission the lawmaker is not necessarily agreeing with the rightness of any possible actions which may fall under the scope of the permission, but is indicating that the courts are to act as if there were no reason against the action.[12] Indeed, it looks as if the Waldron/Raz view overlooks the point that there is often a derivative relationship of justification between the permission and the existence of at least some of the prohibitions on others not to interfere. It may be precisely *because* the legislator has chosen that the action should be viewed in that light that he creates supportive prohibitions on interference. In other words, the very same reasons which support the prohibitions on interference must in consistency also support the weaker normative action of granting the bare permission.

There is a third general consideration which points in the direction of there being a non-reducible distinction between liberty- and claim-rights. It is that, at least in English, right-statements can be used with a different shade of meaning, which reflects this distinction. It is perhaps easier to start with the negative, where the point emerges more clearly.

To say of someone that they have no right to do or have something may mean only that they cannot claim it as a matter of right. However, it may also mean that if they do it or attempt to have it they will be doing something which is positively wrong. Do I have a right to sit at a certain desk in the College library? The denial of such a right may, according to context, mean that I cannot claim that as a

12 Raz himself has actually been an advocate of the view that there are permissions in a stronger sense, which entail more than the action being not merely against the balance of reasons. See his *Practical Reason and Norms*, 2nd edn, London, 1990, 85ff.

matter of right. In other words, if someone is already there that is just my hard luck, but if there were no-one already there I would be doing nothing wrong in sitting there. On the other hand, it may mean that I would be doing something positively wrong in sitting there, for example if it is reserved for the exclusive use of a research student.[13]

Likewise with the positive statement that someone has a right. It may mean that they commit no wrong in attempting to do or have the thing, but no more. However, it may also entail that they are entitled to it as a matter of right, i.e. a wrong is done to them if they are denied it. Take the desk example again. If I have a right in only the weaker, liberty, sense then no wrong is done to me by anyone sitting there before me, but if it is a right in the stronger, claim, sense then a wrong is done to me by anyone preventing my sitting there. It is the kind of distinction that is often disambiguated in English, and particularly by lawyers, by the distinction between being within one's rights in doing/having something and being entitled to do/have it as of right.

Suppose a litigant who has lost his case in the English Court of Appeal asks his counsel if he has a right to appeal to the House of Lords. According to the circumstances, his counsel may say that he is within his rights in doing so, or that he is entitled to an appeal as of right. In the first situation the litigant is legally permitted to ask the House to hear and grant his appeal, but the House is not bound to hear it. In the second situation the House is legally obliged to hear his appeal. Both situations are correctly referred to as being ones of right-holding, but they have different implications which sometimes need to be spelled out.

A fourth argument, which is the converse of the second, is this. If rights consist solely in the duties of non-interference on others it is hard to explain why, to a very considerable extent, the same duties can exist even when there is no right to do something. In going about my lawful business I am protected in person and property by the laws against assault, false imprisonment, theft and so on. But in very large degree these duties apply to others even when what I am doing is unlawful. To be sure, in most legal systems citizens can use reasonable force to prevent crime, but sometimes no degree of force is reasonable. That is probably so if I am committing a minor parking offense. It may not even be an arrestable offence. Granted, my normative position has changed in that I am now liable to be subjected to a penalty of some sort, but that is on the basis that I had no permission to park there. It is the permission which is doing all the work here on the issue of having the right or not.

These arguments have necessarily been compressed ones. However, the general conclusion is that while there seems no need to allow rights to proliferate into some of the many varieties which some have advocated, there is a great deal of sense in the long-standing view that there is a distinction of importance between claim- and liberty-rights, a distinction which has been lost sight of in some of these most recent theories. It does not entail that there is not a more fundamental reason why both are referred to as being rights.

13 Waldron describes this as a deviant use of rights' language; but it is perfectly standard English and has exactly this meaning.

Jan-R. Sieckmann, Kiel

Basic Rights in the Model of Principles

0. Introduction

The central question of my paper is whether there are rights that must necessarily be recognized in legal systems, interpreted as a model of principles, and what these rights are. I will start from the idea of basic rights as conditions of the validity of legal norms (1.) and the idea of a model of principles as a model of justifying definitive norms by weighing principles (2.). A central feature of this model is that definitive norms are established as the result of the weighing of principles, and that the correct result of these weighing procedures is not completely determined by cognitive, intersubjectively valid criteria (3.). But, on the other hand, legal systems claim that their norms are binding. With a lack of cognitive criteria the bindingness of norms can only be justified if the autonomy of the addressees of the respective norms is respected. This leads to the recognition of certain autonomy rights (4.), namely rights to moral autonomy, to personal autonomy and to the participation in a practical discourse. A legal system that claims to be legitimate must aim to realize these pre-legal autonomy rights. Therefore legal systems must necessarily contain certain kinds of basic rights (5.) which are required by those autonomy rights.

1. The Idea of Basic Rights

Basic rights I will call rights that are not simply the result of a legislative procedure but are rights which can be established independently of such a procedure. One may call such rights a priori rights because the existence of these rights can be established before and independently of a legislative procedure <Cf. Nino 1991, 253>. The legal recognition of such rights is necessary because a procedure that denies such rights will not establish a valid norm. The recognition of basic rights thus is a condition of the validity of legal norms <cf. also Habermas 1992, 151ff., 226>. Validity in this context means that a norm is binding on its addressees, that is that it should be applied and followed by them. This is a genuinely normative sense of validity. If a norm is valid in this normative sense one cannot reasonably ask whether one should apply or follow this norm, as it would be possible if one uses a concept of validity that is not genuinely normative.

Basic rights will consequently be understood as rights the legal recognition of which is necessary if the claim of a legal system to the bindingness of its norms shall be justified. Basic rights hence are presuppositions of the bindingness of legal norms. Therefore in order to establish basic rights one must clarify what is necessary to justify the bindingness of norms. This leads to the second basic idea of this paper, the model of principles.

2. The Model of Principles

The model of principles as it is used here is a model of the justification of norms <Cf. Alexy 1985; Sieckmann 1990; 1995>. More precisely it is aimed at the justification of definitive norms. Definitive norms are norms which are valid with that content that they have according to their exact formulation. Definitive norms can be called rules, which are to be applied in an all-or-nothing fashion, in contrast to principles which are to be weighed against each other <cf. Dworkin 1978, 24f.>. On the other hand, principles are used as normative arguments which are reasons for a certain solution of a normative conflict, which however do not require this solution strictly but only to a degree as high as possible, relative to the actual and normative possibilities <cf. Alexy 1985, 75f.>. In this sense principles demand an optimization with respect to all relevant requirements. Principles therefore are to be weighed against other, colliding principles.

For example, A might have information about B which will damage B's reputation if made public. In principle A has the right to free speech. So he should be permitted to make his information public if he wishes to do so. On the other hand, in principle B has a right to personal honour, demanding that her personal reputation should not be damaged. From this it follows that in principle A should not be permitted to make his information public. There is a collision between the right to free speech and the right to personal honour, as they demand incompatible norms (a permission and a prohibition of publication). This collision has to be resolved by a weighing procedure the result of which establishes a definitive norm which decides the case. This norm must determine that, under certain conditions, the publication is permitted, or that it is prohibited <cf. Alexy 1980, 181ff.>.

The model of principles thus is a model of the justification of norms with three kinds of elements, principles, rules, and weighing procedures. Principles can be characterized as optimization requirements, rules as definitive norms. Weighing procedures are processes of deliberation at the end of which a preference relation among the colliding principles is established <cf. Alexy 1985, 78ff.>.

3. Rights and the Problem of Bindingness of Norms

The justification of rights I will suggest is as follows: in the model of principles weighing decisions are not determined by cognitive criteria, that are objective or intersubjectively valid criteria, of what is the correct preference relation among colliding principles, but preference relations are established by individual normative judgments. These judgments claim to be correct, but reasonable persons may differ in their judgments although none of them can be shown to be wrong. This is a central feature of moral autonomy. The bindingness of norms can only be established if this autonomy of the people involved is taken into account. Therefore it is necessary to recognize certain autonomy rights which guarantee the respect for the autonomy of the people involved. This leads to the theses that the bindingness of norms must be established on the basis of the recognition of these autonomy rights.

The argument starts, according to the definition of basic rights, with the question which rights must be recognized in order to carry through a weighing procedure correctly, so that the result of this procedure can be said to be binding. The model of principles by itself does not necessitate the recognition of rights. But in the model of principles outlined so far it is still an open question why the results of weighing procedures should be binding on anyone. Weighing procedures can be done by one person alone, but in order to be binding for anybody else it must be shown that the result of this procedure must reasonably be accepted by the addressees, and hence is intersubjectively binding <cf. Nagel 1991, 3ff.>. One way to justify the bindingness of weighing decisions would be to show that there are cognitive, objective criteria which determine which is the correct weighing decision. If such a criterion existed any reasonable person had to decide accordingly. There would be no necessity to introduce basic rights in the sense defined above. But in the model of principles there is no cognitive criterion for the correct weighing of principles (at least no complete, determinate one) <cf. Peczenik 1989, 84, 95f.>. There are some formal requirements, e.g. of Pareto-optimality and coherence, but no substantial criteria. Weighing problems are essentially characterized by the lack of such criteria.

This lack of objectivity of weighing decisions establishes a link between the bindingness of norms and the recognition of individual rights. As the bindingness of norms cannot be demonstrated objectively there seems to be no other way to establish a norm as binding as by the reasonable consent of the people involved. A consent, however, presupposes that people form individual normative judgments. As the bindingness of a norm depends on the concurrence of individual normative judgments it is necessary to recognize individual rights to form such normative judgments, and to have these judgments taken into account in the decision on the legally binding norms. To establish the bindingness of a norm requires at least the recognition of a right to form one's own individual normative judgment. Furthermore, everybody must have a right not to be subjected to a norm without his or her reasonable consent. These rights shall be called autonomy rights.

To summarize, the argument is that in a model of principles, because of the lack of cognitive criteria for definitive norms, autonomy rights must be recognized in order to make it possible to state norms as valid and hence binding[1]. Legal systems claim the validity and bindingness of their norms for the norm addressees. Hence legal systems must recognize autonomy rights in order to be legitimate.

4. Autonomy Rights

Autonomy rights are, in first instance, the right to form one's own normative judgment and the right not to be subjected to norms one does not consent to or

1 If it is not possible to establish binding norms, or if it is not even tried to justify norms as binding, the argument outlined above does not give a reason to recognize autonomy rights. The general problem of the justification of norms and especially individual rights <cf. Alexy 1995, 127ff.> is not treated by that argument, only the justification of basic rights within a legal system.

at least must reasonably consent to. Other kinds of autonomy rights which must be legally recognized if a legal system can legitimately claim to be binding are rights to personal autonomy, that is to live one's own life according to one's own interests and conception of a good life, and, furthermore, rights to participate in a practical discourse.

The right to personal autonomy can be established starting from the question which principles autonomous persons will reasonably accept, that is what kinds of normative arguments they will introduce in order to establish binding norms. Human beings are beings with own desires, interests, and life plans which more or less integrate individual interests into a coherent scheme <cf. Nagel 1991, 3ff.>. They have an interest in leading their own lives and will reasonably claim that norms should interfere with this interest only as far as this is necessary to solve conflicts with the interests of other people or other valid principles. The development of individual life plans or individual conceptions of a good life may be called personal autonomy, in contrast to moral autonomy as the development of an individual normative conception about what norms should be recognized as valid and hence binding <cf. Raz 1986, 369ff.>. Human beings are capable of personal autonomy, and they realize this capability the more they develop their conception of a good life <cf. also the distinction of the capacity for a conception of the good and the capacity for a sense of justice by Rawls 1995, 164, 167.>. It seems plausible that autonomous persons will claim a right to live their own lives, as far as this is possible with respect to colliding principles. A legal system that does not in principle recognize such a right to personal autonomy cannot claim that it must be reasonably accepted by its citizens. Therefore a right to personal autonomy must in principle be legally recognized in order to justify a claim that legal norms are binding.

From this it follows that each individual interest (whether of moral or of personal autonomy) must be treated as in principle legally relevant. The set of principles that forms the basis of the model of principles therefore is constituted by the interests autonomous persons actually have. This does not mean that all these principles are legal principles. A legal system may use criteria of validity which restrict the set of legally valid principles. But any such restriction must be justified with respect to the set of principles established by the interests of autonomous persons.

A further kind of autonomy rights are rights to take part in a practical discourse, that is rights not only to have one's normative judgments taken into account by others but also to put forward arguments and to decide on any issue in a discourse by oneself. This excludes that an autonomous person is subjected to the decision of anyone else as to what her interests or views "really are".

The recognition of these autonomy rights in the model of principles raises the problem that, in order to justify definitive norms, principles constituted by individual interests, whether of moral or of personal autonomy, have to be weighed against each other. In some cases this will lead to a consensus among reasonable autonomous persons. At least as an ideal one must try to achieve such a consensus in a discursive procedure in which everybody may put forward his normative judgments and may try to convince other people of his views. However, many cases will remain disputed. As a consensus will in many cases not occur by free discussion alone, it seems reasonable to introduce decision procedures which allow for authoritative decisions <cf. Rawls 1995, 148.>. Such procedures are e.g. legislative enactments or court decisions. The norms established by these decisions are binding although they might not be consented to, and it might even be reasonable to dissent. They are valid because it is reasonable to accept these norms as the result of an authoritative decision.

As the introduction of authoritative decision procedures in a legal system limits the autonomy rights of people, the question is under which conditions it is reasonable to accept such authoritative decisions as binding. At least, these decisions must be bound to realize the interest-based principles to a degree as high as possible. That is, the moral and personal autonomy of people must be interfered with as little as possible. Furthermore, the system of decision making must as far as possible let the people themselves decide on the legally valid norms. Decision procedures must not restrict the right to decide on the valid norms by oneself more than is necessary because of other legally valid principles.

5. Substantial Basic Rights

Autonomy rights, as introduced so far, are rights in principle, or ideal rights <for an explanation of the relation between the concept of principles and an ideal ought Alexy 1979, 81f.; Sieckmann 1994>, but not definitive rights. They require legal rights to participate in legal procedures and to the weighing and optimal fulfillment of individual interests by the legal system, and therefore are procedural, not substantial rights. One might question whether these autonomy rights already exhaust the idea of basic rights, or whether also substantial rights can be established as basic rights, that is as conditions of the legal validity of norms, not just as a result of a legislative procedure.

One idea of basic rights is that there are prelegal rights the existence of which does not depend on their legal recognition, and which exist as long as they are not removed by the law. Such rights can be called liberty rights or defence rights (Abwehrrechte) <cf. Alexy 1985, 174ff.>. For example, the right to physical integrity or the right to do what one wants may be said to exist as long as there is no legal regulation to the contrary. But this is not quite the sense in which basic rights have been defined above. Liberty rights can be established independently of legal regulation, but their recognition is not a condition for the validity of a legal regulation. Furthermore, as far as they exist as legal rights, they exist according to the valid legal regulations, as far as they are prelegal, they do not actually exist. Such liberty rights only are subsidiary rights which exist as far as there is no contrary legal regulation.

An argument to establish substantial basic rights can be grounded on the idea of personal autonomy <Raz 1986, 369ff., who however rejects a right to personal autonomy, 247.> or integrity <Williams 1973, 108ff.>. Individuals do not have an overriding interest in correctly justified norms, but also, and primarily, an interest in leading their own life according to their own conception of a good life <cf. Rawls 1995, 169.>. Any decision procedure, be it as rational as it should be, endangers this primary interest. As in this procedure the interests of other people must be respected too, and because it is an open question what these interests will be and how much weight will be put upon them, the result of a decision procedure may be that even fundamental interests of some individuals are sacrificed to the overriding interests of other people. This problem is well known from the right-based critique of utilitarian theories. But the same problem occurs in any procedural theory that is open to a multitude of indeterminate interests and judgments. Therefore, although it is reasonable to accept a rational decision procedure to decide on legally binding norms, it would be unreasonable to do so without reservation. If one subjects oneself to an authoritative decision procedure it seems reasonable to secure in advance that certain fundamental interests will not be violated by the result of this procedure. This is the basis for the introduction of substantial basic rights as a precondition of the bindingness of legal norms.

According to this approach, substantial basic rights are rights which protect individual interests which may be so important for a person that their infringement will make it reasonable for her to reject the bindingness of the law. Such interests are, e.g., those of life and personal integrity, free speech and freedom of conscience and religion. Not every aspect of these interests will be so fundamental that it should be protected by a basic right, but the infringement of these interests may be that great that the person affected cannot be reasonably expected to accept the respective legal regulation. Whether this is the case must be determined by weighing the autonomy interests of the respective person against her reasonable interest in the bindingness of legal norms.

The criteria for this weighing decision need further elaboration <cf. Sieckmann 1995, 180ff.>. It should be mentioned, however, that this decision must be made by organs of the legal system, namely by the courts, not by the individuals affected. This is legitimate because the construction of basic rights suggested here is based on the claim of legal systems to legitimacy, that is the claim that legal norms can correctly be said to be binding. This claim is made by legal organs with their legal decisions. Accordingly, they have to decide whether the conditions for the validity of norms obtain. This includes the weighing of individual autonomy interests and reasonable interests in having binding legal norms. Individuals affected may have a different view on this matter. But this does not raise a problem of legal validity, but a problem of a right to resistance against the law.

To sum up, one can distinguish three kinds of autonomy rights, the right to moral autonomy, that is the right to live according to norms one accepts as valid, the right to personal autonomy, that is the right to live one's own life, and the right to take part in decision procedures on what norms are legally valid. These rights must in principle be legally recognized and fulfilled as far as possible if the claim of a legal system to be binding shall be legitimate. In order to fulfill this demand, legal systems must recognize basic legal rights to the optimal realization of individual interests, and rights to participate in legal procedures, substantial basic rights which guarantee the acceptability of legal regulations.

References

Alexy, Robert: Zum Begriff des Rechtsprinzips. In: *Rechtstheorie* Beiheft 1 (1979), 59–87.
Alexy, Robert: Die logische Analyse juristischer Entscheidungen. In: *ARSP-Beiheft* 14 (1980), 181–212.
Alexy, Robert: *Theorie der Grundrechte*. Baden-Baden 1985.
Alexy, Robert: *Recht, Vernunft, Diskurs*. Frankfurt/M. 1995.
Dworkin, Ronald: *Taking Rights Seriously*. Cambridge/Mass. 1978.
Habermas, Jürgen: *Faktizität und Geltung*. Frankfurt/M. 1992.
Nagel, Thomas: *Equality and Partiality*. New York/Oxford 1991.
Nino, Carlos S.: *The Ethics of Human Rights*. Oxford 1991.
Peczenik, Aleksander: *On Law and Reason*. Dordrecht 1989.
Rawls, John: Reply to Habermas. In: *Journal of Philosophy* 1995, 132-180
Raz, Joseph: *The Morality of Freedom*. Oxford 1986.
Sieckmann, Jan-R.: *Regelmodelle und Prinzipienmodelle des Rechtssystems*. Baden-Baden 1990.
Sieckmann, Jan-R.: Zur Abwägungsfähigkeit von Prinzipien. In: *ARSP-Beiheft* 53 (1994), 205–213.
Sieckmann, Jan-R.: Abwägung von Rechten. In: *ARSP* 81 (1995), 164–184.
Williams, Bernard: A Critique of Utilitarianism. In: J.J.C. Smart/B. Williams (ed.), *Utilitarianism For & Against*. Cambridge et al. 1973.

Ulrich Penski, Siegen

Partikularität des Rechts und Universalisierung von Rechten – Ansätze und Thesen –

I.

Es ist ein unbestreitbarer Befund, daß sich die Rechtswelt in verschiedene partikuläre Rechtsordnungen gliedert. Was als Recht gilt und mit welchem Inhalt es gilt, welche Rechte in diesem Sinne der einzelne hat, bestimmt sich nach diesen Rechtsordnungen als objektivem Recht. Vielleicht kann man bestreiten, daß auf alle diese Ordnungen der Begriff des Rechts anwendbar ist; aber selbst wenn das nicht der Fall ist, bestimmen sie über bestimmte Verhaltensregeln und Ansprüche. Wird bei diesem Sachverhalt von universellen Rechten gesprochen oder wird die Universalisierung von Rechten gefordert, so stellt sich die Frage, was damit angesichts der Partikularität von Rechtsordnungen gemeint sein kann. Sie hat Universalität subjektiver Rechte bei Partikularität objektiven Rechts zum Gegenstand.

Der Annahme universeller Rechte liegt offensichtlich die Auffassung zugrunde, daß es Recht und Rechte unabhängig von partikularen Rechtsordnungen und diese übergreifend gibt. Soll es sich um geltende Rechte handeln, dann kann die Geltung nur in einem Tatbestand gesehen werden, der allen Menschen zukommt, unabhängig von einer Zugehörigkeit zu einer partikularen Rechtsgemeinschaft. Dieser Tatbestand kann nur im Menschsein als solchem liegen. Universelle Rechte müssen allein daran anknüpfen, und insofern wird auch von Menschenrechten als angeborenen gesprochen. Nach Kant ist die Freiheit das „einzige, ursprüngliche, jedem Menschen, kraft seiner Menschheit, zustehende Recht“.1 Wie kann man aber ein solches universell geltendes Recht und – in Spezifikationen – universell geltende Rechte, denken? Und was kann etwa die Forderung nach Universalisierung meinen?

Geht man von universell geltenden Rechten aus, scheint sie ins Leere zu laufen. Sie kann dann nur einen Sinn haben, wenn die angenommene Universalität eben noch nicht insgesamt Wirklichkeit geworden ist, d.h. daß sie noch nicht in allen partikularen Rechtsordnungen gelten. Die angenommene universelle Geltung ist offensichtlich noch keine, die die wirkliche Geltung gewährleistet. Die Forderung nach Universalisierung könnte besagen, daß die bloß universelle Geltung in alle partikularen Ordnungen hineingetragen wird, damit diese Rechte in den partikulären Rechtsordnungen auch wirklich zur Geltung kommen. Universalisierung in diesem Sinne bedeutete eine Um- und Ausgestaltung der partikularen Ordnungen unter Gewährleistung dieser Rechte. In einem weiteren und radikaleren Sinn könnte Universalisierung aber auch meinen, daß die partikularen Ordnungen überwunden werden eben zugunsten einer universalen Rechtsordnung, in der die Rechte allerdings auch einen anderen Geltungscharakter erhielten.

1 Kant, Metaphysik der Sitten, *Werke* (hrsgg. v. Weischedel), Bd. IV, S. 345

Abgesehen von der Frage nach der Geltung universeller Rechte wäre deshalb zu erörtern, ob dieses Ziel vom Begriff der Rechte und des Rechts sinnvoll ist oder ob es nur die Möglichkeit gibt, Rechten in partikularen Ordnungen Geltung zu verschaffen und welche Bedeutung dies für ihre „Universalisierung" hat.

II.

Die Qualifizierung von Freiheit als „angeborenes", jedem einzelnen „kraft seiner Menschheit" zustehendes Recht schließt seine Universalität ein, insofern als es dann zwingend für alle Menschen gilt. Gleichwohl stellt sich die Frage, was mit dieser Qualifizierung eigentlich gemeint ist. Zumindest zwei Deutungen scheinen möglich. Nach einer wäre die Tatsache der Geburt als solche Entstehungsgrund des Rechts; dieses hätte damit ein Naturereignis zu seinem Grund und wäre insofern in der Tat „Naturrecht".[2] Gegen diese Deutung spricht der bekannte Grundsatz, daß aus einem Sein kein Sollen folgen kann. Aus der Tatsache der Geburt könnte danach kein Recht als eine Art von Sollen entstehen. Wird deshalb mit einem Recht ein Sollen ausgedrückt, so kann aus einem Naturereignis kein Recht folgen, auch nicht das Recht der Freiheit.

Insofern müßte Freiheit als angeborenes Recht in einer anderen Weise verstanden werden. Die Tatsache des Geborenseins als Mensch wäre eine Bedingung, und zwar eine natürliche, an die sich Freiheit als Recht anknüpft. Da sie bei allen Menschen gegeben ist, erfüllten diese unterschiedslos die Voraussetzungen von Freiheit als Recht. Dieses kann jedoch nicht von selbst, gleichsam natürlich, entstehen. Seine Entstehung gründet sich vielmehr auf einen *Akt der Anerkennung*, der von anderen jeweils vollzogen wird. Diese Anerkennung setzt ihrerseits voraus, daß sich Menschen als mit Freiheit begabte Wesen verstehen, d.h. ein *Selbstverständnis von Freiheit* haben und aus diesem heraus die Freiheit anderer anerkennen. In ihm liegt die Aufforderung, unabhängig von fremder Bestimmung sich durch eigene Zwecksetzungen und Regeln zu bestimmen. Insofern aber als diese Unabhängigkeit im Verhältnis zu anderen nur erreichbar ist, wenn diesen ebenso Freiheit zugestanden wird, weil sie anders eine solche Unabhängigkeit bestreiten würden, verbindet sich mit jener Aufforderung auch die Forderung nach Anerkennung anderer in ihrer Freiheit. Sie ist keinesfalls schon mit einem argumentativen Sprachgebrauch als unterstellt anzusehen, wie es die Diskurstheorie nahelegt, sondern vermittelt sich durch die skizzierte Reflexion praktischer Vernunft.[3]

2 In Art. 2 der französischen Erklärung der Rechte des Menschen und Bürgers von 1789 wird von „natürlichen und unabdingbaren Menschenrechten" gesprochen. So heißt es auch bei Kant, daß es „jedermann von Natur zukommt", Anm. 1, S. 345.

3 Entsprechend legt Leist, Diesseits der 'Transzendentalprakmatik': Gibt es sprachpragmatische Argumente für Moral?, *Zeitschrift für philosophische Forschung*, Bd. 43, 1989, S. 316, dar, daß Argumentieren gegenüber andern nicht schon ihre Anerkennung als moralische Subjekte einschließt, sondern daß diese Anerkennung unabhängig von argumentativer Einstellung erfolgt.

Ein Recht der Freiheit ohne eine solche Anerkennung bliebe ein bloß gedachter und insofern subjektiver Anspruch. Erst mit der Anerkennung kann Freiheit zu einem geltenden Recht werden. Bei einem Neugeborenen gelangt sie zur Geltung durch Aufnahme in die Familie und eine weitere menschliche Gemeinschaft; im Verhältnis zwischen anfänglichen Feinden durch einen Friedensschluß. Bei diesem Verständnis eines Rechts der Freiheit ist es freilich kein Naturrecht, sondern ein von Anfang an *sozial gestiftetes*, damit aber in diesem Sinne *positives* Recht. Das wäre auch in dem Falle anzunehmen, daß die Anerkennung des Rechts aus religiösen Überzeugungen erfolgt. Auch wenn diese auf ein übernatürliches Wesen zurückgeführt werden, wirken sie gleichwohl als soziale Tatbestände.

III.

Ist das Recht der Freiheit allgemein wie auch besonderer Freiheitsrechte als seine Spezifikationen in dieser Weise zu verstehen, läßt sich freilich eine universelle Geltung des Rechts nicht von vornherein annehmen. Es hat wenig Sinn von solcher Geltung zu sprechen, wenn die Geltung des Rechts von geschichtlichen und sozialen Akten der Anerkennung abhängt. Aus einem Selbstverständnis der Freiheit im dargelegten Sinne läßt sich vielmehr nur ein *Anspruch auf universelle Anerkennung* von Freiheit als Recht herleiten. Abgesehen davon wird die Annahme universeller Geltung fraglich, wenn das Recht auf seinen Gehalt und Umfang hin betrachtet wird. Dies erfordert eine weitere Klärung des Verständnisses von Freiheit.

Zum Begriff der Freiheit gehört wesentlich die Unabhängigkeit von fremder Bestimmung, und insofern ist Freiheit negativ aufgefaßt. Solche Unabhängigkeit kann freilich nicht in der Weise verstanden werden, daß man tun und lassen kann, was man will: also als Willkürfreiheit. Diese führt zu einem Widerspruch nicht nur mit sich selbst, sondern auch mit anderen. Im Verhältnis zu sich selbst gibt es grundsätzlich keinen leitenden Gesichtspunkt für das eigene Tun, so daß sich zufällig auftretende Gesichtspunkte und Interessen durchsetzen und damit gerade keine Unabhängigkeit von fremder Bestimmung gewährleistet wird. Willkürfreiheit im Verhältnis zu anderen setzt sich auch der Willkür dieser aus und macht sich insofern von deren Willkür abhängig.[4] Freiheit kann deshalb nur verstanden werden als Freiheit unter den Bedingungen der Vereinbarkeit von Freiheit anderer und letztlich aller. Sie ist als Unabhängigkeit von fremder Bestimmung in diesem Sinne Freiheit als Selbstbestimmung unter der Bedingung der Vereinbarkeit von Freiheit aller. Damit erhält Freiheit den Sinn von *Autonomie*.

Auch als Recht kann sie nur diesen Gehalt und diesen Umfang haben. Willkürfreiheit kann kein Inhalt eines Rechts der Freiheit sein, weil ein solches Recht – wie oben dargelegt – zu einem Widerspruch mit sich selbst führte, d.h.

4 Entspr. z.B. J. Ebbinghaus, Positivismus – Recht der Menschheit – Naturrecht – Staatsbürgerrecht, in: *Naturrecht oder Rechtspositivismus*, hrsgg. von W. Maihofer, Darmstadt 1962, S. 284

sich selbst aufheben würde. Das Recht der Freiheit wäre demnach eine *allgemeine Befugnis, die Willkür anderer im Hinblick auf Bedingungen der Vereinbarkeit von Freiheit aller einzuschränken.*[5] Dies kann auch nur der Inhalt des Anspruchs auf universelle Anerkennung von Freiheit als Recht sein.

Nun soll dieses konkreten Menschen zustehen, und die Bedingungen der Vereinbarkeit von Freiheit aller sind solche in bezug auf konkrete Menschen in Raum und Zeit, d.h. in geschichtlichen Verhältnissen. Auch wenn man aus diesem Recht solche allgemeinen Ansprüche ableiten kann wie „durch andere nicht zum bloßen Objekt ihres Willens gemacht zu werden", anders: „nicht durch andere verletzt zu werden" – was der allgemeinen Verpflichtung „neminem laedere" entspricht –, „nicht vom Gebrauch von Sachen überhaupt ausgeschlossen zu werden" und „sich Verpflichtungen gegenüber anderen nur aufgrund eigener Zustimmung zu unterwerfen", so werden damit die konkreten Bedingungen der Vereinbarkeit von Freiheit noch nicht bestimmt. Mit der allgemeinen Anerkennung eines Rechts der Freiheit ist deshalb noch nicht viel getan, zu seiner Verwirklichung bedarf es vielmehr der Konkretisierung in der Weise, daß jeweils die Bedingungen der Vereinbarkeit von Freiheit in konkreten sozialen Zusammenhängen bestimmt werden.[6] Dies hat aber zur Folge, daß die Art und Weise der Ausübung von Freiheit entsprechend gegebener geschichtlicher Verhältnisse verschieden ausfällt. Betrachtet man diese Verschiedenheit in den Bedingungen der Vereinbarkeit von Freiheit, so zeigt sich mithin, daß das *Recht der Freiheit mit verschiedenem Gehalt und Umfang verwirklicht wird.* Welche Art von Strafen verhängt werden, welche körperlichen Verletzungen als zulässig, d.h. sozialadäquat, erachtet werden, unter welchen Voraussetzungen Sachen gebraucht und Verpflichtungen eingegangen werden können, bestimmt den konkreten Gehalt und Umfang des Rechts der Freiheit. Insofern als es die Bedingungen der Vereinbarkeit von gemeinsamer Freiheit einschließt, erweisen sich entsprechende Verschiedenheiten als notwendig.

Als universelles Recht kann es deshalb nur im Sinne des oben entwickelten Begriffs aufgefaßt werden. Dieser Begriff stellt zwar das Recht der Freiheit als *Grundsatz und Maßstab* dar, aber aus ihm lassen sich noch nicht die konkreten Bedingungen der Freiheitsausübung und -beschränkung entnehmen, damit auch nicht ein konkretes Recht der Freiheit. Dieses wiederum kann nicht als universelles aufgefaßt werden. Bedarf das Recht der Freiheit notwendigerweise einer Konkretisierung, so stellt sich die Frage, wie diese überhaupt durchgeführt werden kann. Es ist die Frage nach einer konkretisierenden Gewalt und Ordnung.

IV.

Eine Bestimmung durch die jeweils Beteiligten bliebe immer unsicher, da sie nur von den individuellen Interessen her erfolgen kann und für Streitigkeiten keine Schlichtungsinstanz vorhanden wäre. Das Recht der Freiheit wäre also immer

5 Entspr. im Anschluß an Kant J. Ebbinghaus, Anm. 4

6 Allgemeine Normen bedürfen notwendigerweise einer weiteren Konkretisierung, worauf insbes. Kelsen, *Staat und Naturrecht*, 2. Aufl. München 1989, S. 87, hingewiesen hat.

umstritten. Wie schon in der vernunftrechtlichen Tradition – insbesondere auch bei Kant – gesehen wurde, läßt sich eine konkrete Bestimmung der Bedingungen gemeinsamer Freiheit deshalb nicht ohne eine öffentliche und übergeordnete Gewalt vornehmen.[7] Insofern ließe sich sagen, daß zu den Bedingungen gemeinsamer Freiheit eine öffentliche Gewalt gehört, die im übrigen die Bedingungen gemeinsamer Freiheit festlegt.

Die zur Konkretisierung des Rechts der Freiheit aber erforderliche öffentliche Gewalt ist notwendigerweise partikulär. Das gilt nicht nur für die Zeit, solange es keine einheitliche Gewalt über die gesamte Menschenwelt gibt, sondern im Verhältnis zur unabgeschlossenen Zeit der Geschichte überhaupt. Die Überwindung räumlich-partikulärer öffentlicher Gewalten zugunsten einer räumlich-universalen wäre immerhin denkbar; in zeitlicher Hinsicht bliebe allerdings auch eine räumlich-universale Gewalt partikulär.[8] Im übrigen wäre zu fragen, ob sie mit einem Recht der Freiheit überhaupt vereinbar wäre.

Kann das Recht der Freiheit unter Bedingungen gemeinsamer Freiheit nur durch eine öffentliche Gewalt und damit in einem öffentlichen Zustand gesichert werden, so ist aus ihm mit Kant für jeden ein Anspruch an alle anderen, die in „Wechselwirkung" mit ihm stehen, herzuleiten, in einen „gemeinschaftlich-gesetzlichen Zustand zu treten" oder aus seiner „Nachbarschaft zu weichen".[9] Dem Anspruch eines jeden entspricht eine inhaltsgleiche Pflicht eines jeden. Dieser Anspruch bzw. diese Pflicht lassen – wie ersichtlich – dem einzelnen eine Entscheidungsfreiheit offen, insofern als er einem „gemeinschaftlich-gesetzlichen Zustand" mit anderen ausweichen darf, indem er Abstand hält. Mithin sind dieser Anspruch wie diese Pflicht nicht auf einen die ganze Menschheit umfassenden einheitlichen politischen Zustand im Sinne eines Staates ausgerichtet. Sie lassen die Vielheit solcher Zustände und damit auch die *Partikularität von Rechtsordnungen* zu, indem räumliche und rechtliche Abstände gehalten werden. Dies ist jedoch nicht nur zulässig, sondern stellt auch eine Forderung aus dem Recht der Freiheit dar gegenüber Ansprüchen auf einen alle umfassenden einheitlichen politischen Zustand. Dieser Forderung entspricht wohl bei Kant die Ablehnung einer „Universalmonarchie"[10].

Da Freiheit sich insbesondere auch in der Verwirklichung von eigenen Zwecken und Möglichkeiten ausdrückt, muß das Recht der Freiheit gemeinsame Zweckverwirklichung ermöglichen, insofern als der einzelne Mensch als animal sociale seine Zwecke grundsätzlich nur mit anderen verfolgen kann. Damit aber werden vorhandene natürliche Verbindungen und kulturelle Interessen wie geschichtliche Erfahrungen bei der Bildung rechtlich-politischer Einheiten erheblich, die eine notwendige Grundlage gemeinsamer Zweckverwirklichung bilden. Sie stiften als Voraussetzung dafür Gemeinsamkeiten. Das Recht der Freiheit kann sich demnach nicht in der bloßen negativen Abgrenzung zur Freiheit jeweils anderer erschöpfen, es muß sich gleichzeitig auch auf die

7 Kant, Anm. 1, S. 430

8 Entspr. Habermas, *Faktizität und Geltung*, 2. Aufl., Frankfurt 1992, S. 158, wo es heißt: „Denn jedes Gewaltmonopol auf Erden ist, was sogar für eine Weltregierung gelten würde, eine endliche Größe – sie bleibt gegenüber der Zukunft und dem Weltraum provinziell."

9 Kant, Zum ewigen Frieden, *Werke* (hrsgg. v. Weischedel), Bd. VI, S. 203.

10 Kant, Anm. 9, S. 225

Grundlagen gemeinsamer Zweckverfolgung richten. Dies allerdings führt zu besonderen und unterschiedlichen sozialen Verbindungen. Die notwendige Konkretisierung von Bedingungen der Vereinbarkeit gemeinsamer Freiheit ist dabei eher möglich und zu erreichen, wenn sie auf solchen Verbindungen aufbauen kann. Zum Recht der Freiheit unter Bedingungen der Vereinbarkeit von Freiheit aller gehört wesentlich, sich im *Unterschied auch zu anderen zu rechtlich-politischen Einheiten zusammenzuschließen*. In diesem Recht ist nicht zuletzt auch das Selbstbestimmungsrecht der Völker zu sehen.

V.

Vom Selbstverständnis des Menschen als eines mit Freiheit begabten Wesens kommt das Recht der Freiheit allen Menschen zu. Insofern ist es universal. Als solches ist es aber zunächst nur ein *Anspruch* und kann – wie dargelegt – „keinem Menschen irgendein bestimmtes Recht zuteilen oder sichern".[11] Es ist vielmehr auf eine Konkretisierung und Sicherung durch eine bestimmte öffentliche Gewalt angewiesen, die von seinem Begriff her sich als partikular konstituieren muß. Das als universal verstandene Recht der Freiheit sowie seine Spezifikationen können damit nur im Rahmen partikularer Rechtsordnung zu ihrer Geltung kommen. Eine *Universalisierung* läßt sich deshalb *nur vermittelt durch partikulare Ordnungen* denken; sie wäre zugleich auch Partikularisierung, wenn man nicht den Universalstaat befürworten wollte. Dies freilich – wie gezeigt – stünde im Widerspruch zu jenem Recht selbst, führte aber auch zeitlich-geschichtlich nicht zu eigentlicher Universalisierung. Wenn man erkennt, daß das Allgemeine nur bezogen auf Konkretes Allgemeines sein kann, ist diese Partikularisierung kein Widerspruch zu ihrer Universalität.

Unabhängig von seiner Konkretisierung und Sicherung in partikularen Ordnungen hat das *Recht der Freiheit Geltung als ein aus dem Selbstverständnis von Freiheit anerkannter Grundsatz*. Das Recht der Freiheit und Freiheitsrechte als dessen Spezialisierungen beanspruchen Universalität als *Rechtsgrundsätze*.[12] Darunter sollen Normen verstanden werden, die in noch unbestimmter Weise, auch unabhängig von bestimmten Bedingungen, ein Verhalten zur Verwirklichung eines Zieles gebieten oder verbieten.[13] Sie bedürfen deshalb der Konkretisierung. Ihre Universalisierung, die ihre Verwirklichung als universelle bedeutet, können sie deshalb nur als Grundsätze für partikulare Rechtsordnungen erreichen und erhalten. Auch die in den internationalen Pakten anerkannten Rechte sind als solche Grundsätze aufzufassen. Sie sind in der Regel unbestimmt gefaßt und stehen unter Vorbehalten der partikularen öffentlichen Gewalten und Rechtsordnungen.[14] Als entsprechende Grundsätze

11 Ebbinghaus, Anm. 4, S. 300.

12 Hoffmann, Geschichtlichkeit und Universalitätsanspruch des Rechtsstaates, *Universitas* 9/1995, S. 851, spricht von einem „Postulat der individualrechtlich verwurzelten Autonomie".

13 Zu diesem Begriff beziehe ich mich auf meinen Beitrag „Rechtsgrundsätze und Rechtsregeln", *Juristenzeitung* 1989, S. 105 ff.

14 So besteht die Verpflichtung jedes Vertragsstaates nach Teil II, Art. 2 Abs. 2 des Internationalen Paktes über bürgerliche und politische Rechte vom 19.12.1966 „im Einklang

gewährleisten sie mithin nur einen letzten Kernbereich von Freiheitsrechten, eröffnen aber nicht alle weiteren Möglichkeiten. Demgegenüber könnte von einer Universalisierung des Rechts der Freiheit in einer einzigen umfassenden politischen Einheit im Sinne eines Weltstaates wohl nicht gesprochen werden. In einem solchen Staat mit einheitlicher öffentlicher Gewalt würde es ohne anderweitige politische Möglichkeiten konkretisiert und in diesem Sinne totalisiert, d.h. total einer einzigen Konkretisierungsgewalt unterworfen.[15] In einem Weltstaat würde damit nicht eigentlich seine Universalisierung erreicht, vielmehr nur seine *Totalisierung*. Vom strengen Begriff eines solchen Staates wäre u. a. eine Asylgewährung als eine äußerste Sicherung von Freiheit und Leben ausgeschlossen.

VI.

In der Auseinandersetzung um Menschenrechte und ihre Verletzungen wird der Grundsatzcharakter dieser Rechte nicht immer erkannt. Es geht dabei nicht eigentlich um die Verletzung konkret geltenden Rechts, sondern um *behauptete Verstöße gegen entsprechende Grundsätze bei der Gestaltung und Anwendung geltenden Rechts*. Insofern ist aber die Befugnis der jeweils bestehenden öffentlichen Gewalt, d.h. der Staatsgewalt, zu beachten, das Grundsatzrecht der Freiheit unter den gegebenen geschichtlichen und politischen Bedingungen zu konkretisieren. Freilich muß sich diese Gewalt als eine solche ausweisen, die grundsätzlich auf die Bedingungen der Vereinbarkeit von Freiheit ausgerichtet ist. Wann dies der Fall ist, läßt sich nicht leicht feststellen. Als Mindestvoraussetzung wird anzunehmen sein, daß sie eine Friedensordnung gewährleistet und allgemein ein Recht auf Leben, was in der Regel als Grundlage der Anerkennung von Regierungen und Staaten genommen wird. Da das Recht der Freiheit auch grundsätzlich eine Beteiligung an der Festlegung der Bedingungen der Vereinbarkeit von Freiheit einschließt, wird auch ein Mindestmaß an Formen von Öffentlichkeit zu fordern sein. Unter diesen Voraussetzungen bleibt jedoch der betreffenden öffentlichen Gewalt ein Spielraum der Konkretisierung des Rechts der Freiheit. Insofern kann sich die Universalisierung von Rechten nicht den politischen Bedingungen für ihre jeweilige Konkretisierung entziehen. Diese bilden vielmehr ihre *politischen und geschichtlichen Schranken*.

Wenn man von einem universellen Grundsatzrecht der Freiheit ausgeht, kann auch der Maßstab und Gesichtspunkt für die Kritik an der Konkretisierung dieses Rechts durch einzelne partikulare öffentliche Gewalten nicht eine bestimmte Form der Konkretisierung dieses Rechts durch andere partikulare Gewalten sein. Jede Konkretisierung ist Ausdruck besonderer historischer Entwicklungen und politischer Bedingungen und läßt sich als solche nicht ohne weiteres auf andere politische Situationen übertragen, z.B. die Freiheitsgewährleistungen westlicher Verfassungsstaaten auf kulturell und

mit seinem verfassungsmäßigen Verfahren". Auch die Rechte der Europ. Konvention zum Schutze der Menschenrechte und Grundfreiheiten vom 4.11.1950 unterliegen noch weiten Vorbehalten der partikularen Staatsgewalt.

15 Entspr. Habermas, Anm. 8

religiös anders geprägte asiatische Staaten. Daraus kann jedoch kein völliger Relativismus und Verzicht auf Kritik hergeleitet werden. Die Kritik jedoch muß sich am *Grundsatzrecht der Freiheit* als solchem ausrichten und erfaßt insofern zunächst nur seine *Kernbereiche*. In der Form muß sie sich unter Bedingungen der Vereinbarkeit von Freiheit aller stellen, was dann aber bedeutet, daß auf eine bestimmte Konkretisierung des Grundsatzrechtes der Freiheit *im Wege gemeinsamer Verständigung und Vereinbarung* hinzuwirken wäre. Das gilt sowohl für eine Kritik im allgemeinen Raum politischer Öffentlichkeit, insbesondere aber für eine Kritik im Verhältnis der partikulären Gewalten, d.h. Staaten untereinander. Von jenem her erschließt sich keine Befugnis einer partikularen Gewalt, mit Zwang oder Zwangsandrohungen eine bestimmte Konkretisierung dieses Rechts durchzusetzen. Eine solche Gewalt hätte insofern kein *zwangsbewehrtes Einmischungsrecht*. Ein entsprechendes Recht könnte sich nicht auf die vom Grundsatz der Freiheit geforderten Bedingungen der Vereinbarkeit von Freiheit aller stützen, weil einer bestimmten partikulären Gewalt keine hinreichenden Maßstäbe dafür zur Verfügung stehen. Es wäre auch als Recht der Staatengemeinschaft fragwürdig, weil auch die international vereinbarten Freiheitsrechte wegen der weiten Vorbehaltsregelung als Eingriffsgrundlage zu unbestimmt sind. Formen der Zwangsandrohung oder des Zwanges wären nur gerechtfertigt, wenn eine partikulare Konkretisierung des Rechts der Freiheit so unzureichend wäre, daß Freiheit und Freiheitsrechte offensichtlich im Kernbereich verletzt würden wie z.B. bei Massentötungen oder Völkermord oder daß Gewaltausbrüche im Verhältnis zu Nachbarordnungen drohten oder auch Massenfluchten nach dorthin ausgelöst würden.[16] Im übrigen wäre eine Veränderung und Verbesserung konkreter Freiheitsstrukturen eine *Aufgabe verständigungsgerichteter politisch-reformerischer Anstrengungen*, die gleichwohl historisch-kulturelle Eigenheiten zu berücksichtigen hätten.

16 Aufgrund völkerrechtlicher Argumentation entspr. Isensee, Weltpolizei für Menschenrechte, *Juristenzeitung* 1955, S. 426.

Ghita Holmström-Hintikka, University of Helsinki/Boston University

Rights and Responsibilities

In this paper I suggest a distinction be made between instances of rights, such as rights to life, liberty and pursuit of happiness, and instances of responsibilities as for example physician responsibility or parental responsibility. As was pointed out by Bentham, Hohfeld and others a 'right' is a relation between two parties, the beneficiary and the trustee, concerning a condition such that the right of one party correlates with a duty of the other. If a duty is violated this will result in punishment. Some rights, the so-called *no-rights* correspond to no duties. *Privilege* is a case in point.

Like rights, responsibilities are relations between two parties with respect to a condition. But unlike rights, responsibilities have no correlatives. Although the trustee may have a responsibility with respect to a particular condition, this does not create a right for the beneficiary vis-a-vis that same condition. Responsibilities are subject to praise and blame according to some norm system they belong to, moral or legal.

The concept of 'right' is far developed and well documented. We shall therefore not spend much time with further details in this regard. Rather, our interest concerns the basic elements in this complex concept. When we on the other hand turn to the conceptual analyses of 'responsibility' we move onto virgin turf. For understandable reasons, then, we shall have to dwell a somewhat longer time with this matter. Not that it has not been discussed, but the aspect at hand was first developed in Holmström-Hintikka 1994 and is as such a novelty.

As the conceptual problems have been dealt with, I suggest that many an inflamed discussion on fetuses', patients' and animal rights be moved to the sphere of responsibilities and thus be demystified. I also suggest that we should look instead at the responsibility of pregnant women in relation to the fetus with respect to its health conditions, physicians responsibility in relation to their patients with respect to medication and pet owners responsibility in relation to their pets with respect to their well being. By this move from rights talks to talk about responsibility we can hope to gain reason and trust over fanaticism.

1. Rights. Conceptual and Logical Review

As we seek the roots of the concept of 'right' and its derivatives our path undoubtedly goes over Bentham and Hohfeld. Late developments of the theory of right, its logic and systematization leads us from Stig Kanger to Lindahl and Helle Kanger. As this path is well documented and the logical aspects well presented (see Lindahl, 1977 and Helle Kanger, 1981) there is no need to go into these details here. However, as we seek to understand the conceptual divergences between 'right' and 'responsibility' we need a reasonable understanding of both concepts.

Bentham's conceptual views on right are essentially to be found from two sources, *Principles of Morals and Legislation* (Bentham, 1961)[1] and *Of Laws in General* (Bentham, 1970)[2]. The concept of right or power enters the discussion in connection to his observations about offence against trust. He explains that a *trustee* is bound to a certain action when exercising a right to the benefit of the *beneficiary*:

> A party is said to be invested with a trust, when, being invested with a *power*, or with a *right*, there is a certain behaviour which, in the exercise of the power, or of that right, he is bound to maintain for the benefit of some other party. In such case the party first mentioned is styled trustee. (Bentham, 1961, pp. 223–225)

As there is no name for the other party Bentham invents the word *beneficiary* or *the party to be benefited*. A trust is, he also explains, "a species of *condition*" (ibid., p. 226).

In an extensive footnote of the said passage (Bentham, 1961, XVI, sec. XXV) Bentham explains that power and right are disparate but may be employed interchangeably. Power and right "are the results of some manifestation or other of the legislation's will with respect to such and such an act". He continues:

> Now every such manifestation is either a prohibition, a command, or their respective negations; viz. a permission, and the declaration which the legislator makes of his will when on any occasion he leaves an act uncommanded ... the commanding of a positive act may be represented by the prohibition of the negative act which is opposed to it.

The law creates a right by prohibiting that act which would be a violation of that right. For every right which the law confers on one party, whether that party be an individual, a subordinate class of individuals, or the public, it thereby imposes on some other party a *duty* or *obligation*. There may also be laws "which impose duties without any other view than the benefit of the agent: these generate no rights; duties therefore, may be either extra-regarding or self-regarding; *extra-regarding* have rights to correspond to them; *selfregarding*, none". (Cf. pp. 224–225.)

With regard to the two parties, Bentham explains, the trustee is the party who ought to do what he promised or otherwise committed himself to do. A breach of such a legal obligation has a punishment appointed to it. The beneficiary is the "party who ought to receive the benefit, ..." (ibid., p. 226).

Thus Bentham recognizes four deontic positions manifested in the will of the legislation. Actions are either Commanded, Prohibited, Non-commanded, or Permitted. Using a modern terminology we could express these in a semilogical language as follows. An action H is

Commanded	it shall be the case that H
Permitted	it may be the case that H (= it shall not be the case that not-H)
Prohibited	it shall be the case that not-H

1 A preversion of this book, the first part of *An Introduction to the Morals and Legislation* was printed 1780. Though printed, it remained unpublished until 1970. *Principles of Morals and Legislation* was first published 1789. It was reprinted 1948 and 1961.

2 This book was published as late as 1945. A more complete version was published 1970.

Not-commanded it may be the case that not-H (= it shall not be the case that H).

H designates the action condition e.g. that agent X sees to it that r. Bentham's deontic concepts are, as Lindahl points out interdefinable (Lindahl, 1977, p. 9).

At this stage it may be appropriate to add some further observations made by Hohfeld in *Fundamental Legal Conceptions* (Hohfeld, 1919). "One of the greatest hindrances to the clear understanding, the incisive statement, and the true solution of legal problems frequently arises from the expressed or tacit assumptions that all legal relations may be reduced to 'rights' and 'duties' ..." In his way of thinking all the various legal relations may be presented in a schema of "opposites" and "correlatives".

Jural opposites are	right	privilege	power	immunity
	no-right	duty	disability	liability
Jural correlatives are	right	privilege	power	immunity
	duty	no-right	liability	disability

(ibid., p. 36). Right and duty are correlatives means that "if X has a right against Y that he shall stay off the former's land, the correlative (or equivalent) is that Y is under a duty toward X to stay off the place" (ibid., p. 38). Instead of using the word 'right' he suggests the word 'claim'. Thus the legal relations of *duty* and *claim* are correlatives. A *privilege*, however, is the opposite of a duty and a correlative of a no-right. In the previous example, X himself has the *privilege* of entering his own land, or equivalently, X does not have a duty *to stay off.* In relation to Y, X's privilege of entering is the precise negation of a duty *to stay off.* As to correlatives, "the correlative of X's right that Y shall not enter on the land is Y's duty not to enter; but the correlative of X's privilege of entering himself is manifestly Y's no-right that X shall not enter".

Hohfeld's clarifying distinctions about jural opposites and jural correlatives broaden the basis for our discussion about rights; that there is more to it than just rights and duties; that privileges are correlated to no-rights etc.

Bentham clearly recognizes the category of no-rights where the beneficiary has no rights to service, care etc. but where the trustee has an obligation so that he in relation to the beneficiary ought to perform (not-perform) a certain action or else be punished.

Rights are relations between two parties X and Y with respect to a condition S (x, y) between them.

Kanger developed a systematization of what he called simple types of right. In his system he also showed that out of eight simple types twenty-six atomic types of right can be distinguished with respect to two parties and one action. His basic observation is that a right of the type claim can be represented by the statement

> in relation to Y, X has a right of the type claim with respect to S(x,y) if and only if Y shall cause S(x,y). (Cf. Kanger & Kanger, 1966, p. 87f.)

The basic concepts can be identified in the construction of the simple types of right:

(i) it shall be the case that F

and

(ii) p sees to it that F

where p designates a person and F a condition. Using a separate logic for each of these two concepts Kanger's eight simple types of right become

claim	counter-claim
freedom	counter-freedom
power	counter-power
immunity	counter-immunity.

These eight simple types of right are expressed as follows for instance in

1 a. Claim(p,q,F)
 b. It shall be the case that q sees to it that F
 c. q shall see to it that F

2 a. Freedom(p,q,F)
 b. Not: It shall be the case that p sees to it that not F
 c. it is not the case that p shall see to it that not F

(For a complete exposition see Kanger & Kanger, 1966, p. 88.)

The four types *claim*, *freedom*, *power* and *immunity*, and their corresponding counter-types can be given by collecting them together into four pairs of synonyms thus:

{ p has versus q a counter-claim that F
 p has versus q a claim that not-F

{ p has versus q a counter-freedom that F
 p has versus q a freedom that not-F

etc. (see Lindahl, p. 44).

One critical observation that can be made about these explications of Kanger's is that the second agent in the relation, the "beneficiary", has disappeared in the locutions (b) and (c). Another observation is that the governing norm system seems to be tacitly understood. We shall see that these two considerations are attended to in their own way in what follows.

Let me first illustrate the relevance of a discussion about rights and responsibilities by means of an example.

In the State of the Union Address, on January 24, 1995, President Clinton emphasized the new "covenant", that every American should realize his right to life, liberty and the pursuit of happiness but that this should happen through responsibility and opportunity. Referring to what was just said and assuming that claim right is what Mr. Clinton had in mind we can be more specific and say that in this instance Claim(p,q,F) means that "p has in relation to q the right of type claim with respect to F". This in turn is expressed as in 1c, "q shall see to it that p is alive". But, in the President's address, who are these parties? Clearly p is the individual American but the other party was not clear. If the legislator is meant, his message was clear. People should have jobs instead of welfare, the minimum salary should be raised, and it is the duty of the government to do it. If criminality is meant, there were several candidates for the party q. The legislator passes reasonable crime bills, the government sends more police out on the streets, fellow Americans start behaving like fellow beings. All these matters that president Clinton addressed may be fitted in one and the same formula tacitly understood albeit not explicitly spelled out before:

In relation to p, q shall see to it that F according to some norm system S_N.

In this paper I want to enter the grey area of rights and obligations discussed *ad infinitum* in connection to fetus's, patient's and animal rights. I shall not, however, take any standpoint in this discussion whether fetuses *have* rights or not. I realize that many wise things have been said and there is no need to repeat them here.

My focus will be the question whether we should at all bring in the concept of 'right' in this context. Should we perhaps only focus on responsibilities which one party holds in relation to the other party? In other words, I am not asking whether or not patients, animals, fetuses have rights which are or are not violated by certain actions. My suggestion is that we totally delete that word from the discussion and look in the direction of responsibilities instead.

When the legislation tries to protect certain individuals it does so by imposing its will in a specific way. Using Bentham's terminology we could say that the actions of the trustees are regulated by certain laws. This is in fact exactly what many people are looking for, for instance in the animal right discussion. The main point is most of the time to protect the beneficiary, the fetus, animal, patient. But the motivation for proposing laws in that direction has often been by pointing out certain alleged rights that the beneficiary might have. My belief is that we should focus on the trustee instead. The pregnant woman, the physician, the pet owner all have responsibilities. Spelling out what they might be and codifying them in laws is what should be our goal. My next move therefore is to turn to the concept of 'responsibility' in an attempt to present a systematic analysis of this concept.

In different times in the history of philosophy the concept of responsibility has been connected to voluntary actions, free choice or to free will. This was the case with Aristotle and this was the case with the Church Fathers. Aristotle himself had no problems with human freedom. An adult human being is a free agent, he thinks. He is free to make decisions about his actions as long as no physical obstacles come in his way and as long as he is not carried away by fear. Many a philosopher has agreed with Aristotle in his characterization of involuntary actions as being either "done (a) under compulsion or (b) through ignorance; and that (a) an act is compulsory when its origin is from without, being of such a nature that the agent, who is really passive, contributes nothing to it." (*Nicomachean Ethics*, 1109b5–1110a3) The criterion for a morally responsible action is that it can be praised or blamed. A legally responsible action, so it seems, is an action which can be assigned rewards and punishment. (ibid., 1109b30–35) As we will see later, this Aristotelian view still has its followers. For anstance Michael J. Zimmerman, the author of the book *An Essay on Moral Responsibility* proposes a similar idea.

I propose an interpretation of 'responsibility' as a relation between two parties with respect to a condition. I shall follow Aristotle in his view that actions – voluntary actions, he says – are assigned rewards and punishments. In addition the fact that praise and blame, reward and punishment are distributed in accordance to some norm system or other that the agent belongs to shall be discussed.

2. Responsibility, Conceptual Distinctions

As I see it 'responsibility' is a relation, R(x,y,p) between two agents x and y and a condition (state of affairs) p such that

(1) in relation to y, x is responsible for p.

Often, however, it is the case that a person, an agent is responsible only for an *aspect* of the condition in case. For instance, a heart specialist is responsible for the patient's health improvement with respect to her heart functions. He is not responsible for her broken leg. An adjustment of (1) gives us

(2) in relation to y, the agent x is responsible for the *aspect* w of the condition u. Even here a further clarification is needed regarding the grounds that are referred to in ascribing somebody's responsibility. We shall in other words have to say that

(3) In accordance to the norm system S_N the agent x is in relation to the agent y responsible for the *aspect* w of the condition u.

The formulation, as proposed in the statement (3), is in my mind the one which closest explains what is meant with 'responsibility'.

The *agent* or agents are thought of as being individual persons, a robot, God or a collective such as an institution, company, association, etc. The *object* of the responsibility, u, may be an action, the outcome or result of an action, or any other condition of the world such that the agent has to see to it that it occurs or has to prevent it from occurring. The second argument, w, is the particular *aspect* of the object that the agent is responsible for. It also has the same features as has the object, being a condition such as an action, a result of an action etc. For instance

in relation to the heart patients, the cardiologist is responsible for their hearts with respect to its proper function.

There is a distinction to be made between a) having responsibility, b) being responsible, and c) feeling responsible. In this context I am only interested in the concept of '*being responsible*'. Furthermore, I believe that 'having responsibility' and 'feeling responsible' can be expressed in terms of this concept 'being responsible'.

Zimmerman, in his book *Essays on Moral Responsibility* distinguishes a) *prospective* and b) *retrospective* responsibilities. Without otherwise discussing his theory here we shall think of

a) *prospective* responsibility as a forward looking responsibility. The agent shall see to it that a certain condition obtains or occurs.

For instance, the cardiologist shall see to it that the safety precautions have been taken.

b) *Retrospective* responsibility is a backwards looking responsibility. The agent was under an obligation to see to it that a certain condition, obtained or occurred.

For instance, the cardiologist was under the obligation to see to it that the safety precautions had been taken.

Not unexpectedly a retrospective responsibility becomes actual if something has happened, if somebody has broken a rule, a norm, a law etc., if somebody has neglected his duties, in other words, if something goes wrong.

Zimmerman also makes a distinction between *causal* and *personal* responsibility. The lightning was responsible for the fire is an example of the former. Our example with the cardiologist illustrates the latter. I shall concentrate on personal responsibility here.

3. Actions, Conceptual Distinctions

When we look at the concept of responsibility, R(x,y,u/w), i.e., in relation to y, x is responsible for u with respect to w, we should of course ask the question, what kind of entities are those objects u and aspects w?

Most of the time, I think, the conditions that we are responsible for concern a) our *actions* or b) *results* of our actions including neglect, abstention and similar kinds of non-doings. A few words about actions is therefore in order here. (For a complete development see Holmström-Hintikka, 1991)

First, let us think of an agent bringing something about without even knowing or thinking about it. For instance, carrying sand on his shoes. This kind of doing I call *sufficient doing* which is characterized as follows:

(3.1) for x, m suffices to make sure that r; C(x, m, r)

As this kind of activity lacks any kind of purpose it is not thought of as an action. On the contrary, it is a *mere causation*.

Thus, when an agent performs an action, what s/he actually does is one of the following:

(3.2) by means of m, x sees to it that r; E(x, m, r)

This is called *instrumental action*. Sometimes the same thing may be read as "with the help of m x sees to it that r" where m denotes the means or method whereby x sees to it that the result r is realized. The second alternative is that

(3.3) x sees to it that r for the *purpose* that p; A(x, r, p).

This in turn is named *purposive* action. (For logical connections and further details see Homström-Hintikka, 1991.)

When I now say that agent responsibility is connected with actions or results of actions – including negligence, etc. – this distinction between two kinds of actions also gives a deeper perspective to the concept of responsibility. Namely, it is clear that both the *object* and the *aspect* of the agent's responsibility can be either an instrumental action or a purposive action. Sometimes it may be even a mere causation, for instance something the agent should have thought of.

A deep structure at this stage may look as follows:

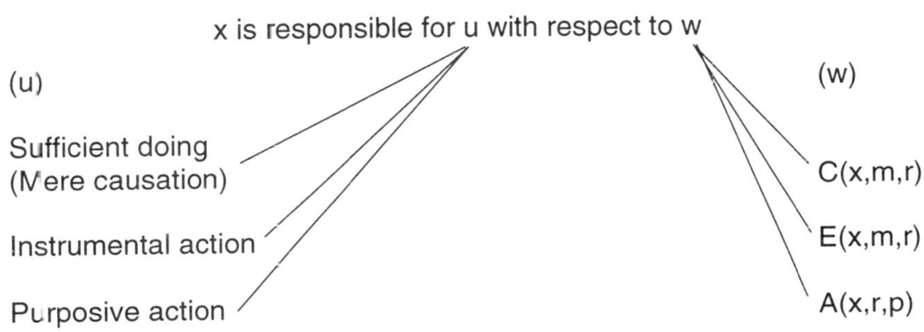

The responsibility of the cardiologist could be explained as follows:

> In relation to the heart patients the chief cardiologist is responsible for the operating team with respect to seeing to it by means of proper hiring that it is competent.

If we were to replace both the object and the aspect with some actions we should say:

> In relation to the heart patients the heart surgeon is responsible for by means of an operation seeing to it that the patients' health is improved with respect to by means of angioplasty (clearing the passages) seeing to it that the arteries are cleaned.

Either of the two conditions, u or w, or both of them can be replaced by an action of any kind (or by a mere causation). The expression then rapidly grows in complexity.

4. Responsibility and Norms

As can be seen from the example,

> the cardiologist is responsible for the operating team with respect to its competence:

What this responsibility boils down to in my representation is that

> the cardiologist shall see to the condition of the operating team with respect to seeing to it that it is competent.

The expression 'shall see to it' suggests that the responsibility relation is always included in some norm system or other. Thus, if S_N is a system in which N is a set of norms $n_1,...,n_k$ then

> (RS_N) R(x, y, u/w) E S_N.

This may be read as

> (RS_N1) according to the norm system S_N, x is in relation to y responsible for u with respect to w.

For instance

> according to the cardiologist's professional code, x shall in relation to y see to it that the operating surgeons have proper training.

The norm systems that usually are involved are either moral, legal, or religious, but one could also allow sets of personal norms, if need be.

The relevant set of moral norms may be a set of deontological rules including one that says that chief cardiologists shall always look after their team. In some legal set of norms there are law paragraphs covering physicians and hospitals and in particular what they shall and shall not do. For instance, the chief cardiologist may be punished in different ways as a consequence of neglect as well as as a consequence of any other action.

The fact that responsibility is connected to a norm system opens up two perspectives. First we can note that the responsibility relation, as we now know it, is in itself related to a set of norms. We can now say that

> according to S_N, x is, in relation to y, responsible for u with respect to w.

Here y may be an individual, an institute etc. and S_N may be thought of as a professional code, a moral or legal norm system. Thus the fact that the cardiologist is responsible for the operating team may be represented as according to the laws governing chief surgeons, x shall in relation to y see to it that the safety precautions are taken care of.

In more general terms

$R(x, y, u/w) \in \cup S_N$

means that, and this is the second perspective

(in relation to y: $\exists m Shall\ E(x, m, u/w)) \varepsilon S_N$ according to S_N x shall in relation to y see to it that u with respect to w.

Assuming that

$Shall_p E(x,m,u/w)$ means that $Shall\ E(x,m,u/w) \varepsilon S_p$

and applying (DfE): $(E(x,r)=\exists m E(x,m,r))$

also assuming that $\exists m Shall\ E(x,m,r) \leftrightarrow Shall \exists m E(x,m,r)$

we can observe that

$R(x, y, u/w)\ \varepsilon\ S_N \leftrightarrow$ (in relation to y: $Shall_n E\ (x,u/w)$)

Let $R_n(x,y,u/w)$ stand for

$R(x,y,u/w) E S_N$

We can now imagine that the fact that x is in relation to y responsible for u/w is something which is included in y's norm system S_y. But since S_N can be seen as the union of all norm systems affecting the agent x, it also has to include S_y at least to the degree that is affecting x.

$$S_N = \bigcup_{i=n_1}^{n_k} S_i$$

If this is agreed upon, $R_n(x,y,u/w)$ actually is reduced to $R_n(x,u/w)$. But $R_n(x,u/w)$ is the same as $\cap \exists m Shall_n E(x,m,u/w)$. Thus, we are now ready to form our thesis

(T*) $R_n(x,u/w) \leftrightarrow \exists m Shall_n E(x,m,u/w)$

it is,

according to S_N, x is responsible for the aspect w of the condition u iff according to S_N, x shall by some means see to it that u with respect to w.

Again, according to the definition (DfE) it follows (and this is the preferred form)

(T) $R_n(x,u/w) \leftrightarrow Shall_n E(x,u/w)$

Being responsible for somebody or something means in other words that one by some means shall see to a certain aspect of one's object of responsibility according to one norm or other, a rule or a law.

For a better understanding of the object of our interest let us make the following observations concerning norms and responsibility. In saying that

in relation to y, x is responsible for u with respect to w

this can mean, and I shall restrict myself to these two kinds

in relation to y

(1) x is morally responsible for u/w

(1.1) x is morally responsible for u/w to occur (*prospective* moral responsibility)

(1.2) x is morally responsible for u/w to have occurred (*retrospective* moral responsibility)

in relation to y

(2) x is legally responsible for u/w

(2.1) x is legally responsible for u/w to occur (*prospective* legal responsibility)
(2.2) x is legally responsible for u/w to have occurred (*retrospective* legal responsibility)

In this sense, what does it mean that an agent is responsible for a certain condition according to a certain set of norms or laws? As I see it, we clearly have to look at responsibility here as a connection between actions and their consequences. A physician who takes good care of his patient deserves praise whereas a negligent physician may be punished if something goes wrong. We are in other words looking at legal consequences of actions performed or not performed by the responsible agent. This is the juncture at which courts of law and punishment may come in, a discussion I shall abstain from here. Note, however, that both prospective and retrospective responsibility are of the strongly conditional form

if according to S_n, x is in relation to y responsible for u/w and if (-u) occurs then the legal consequences set in.

5. Rights and Responsibility. A Summary

From the previous discussion we have learned that rights correlate with duties. We have also learned that there is a vast variety of types of rights, from plain power in early Bentham to Hohfeld's *right, privilege, power* and *immunity* and all the way to Kanger's 26 atomic types of rights. Already Bentham was aware of the fact that duties or obligations can be of different kinds. Both he and Hohfeld emphasize the *no-rights* as a special group that needs to be recognized. Bentham speaks about *extra-regarding* and *self-regarding* duties where the latter have no corresponding rights. In Hohfeld's system *privilege* corresponds to no-rights. The fact that one agent, x, has, in relation to another agent, y, a *claim* with respect to F means according to Kanger that it shall be the case that y causes F.

Responsibilities were also presented as being relations between two parties with respect to a condition. More precisely

(Theses) According to S_N, in relation to y, x is responsible for u/w iff according to S_N, in relation to y, x shall see to it that u/w.

This formula in fact resembles Kanger's explication of claim rights (on y's part).

So, are responsibilities plain correlatives to claim rights after all? Certainly not. Bear in mind that rights, all but privilege, have jural correlates and opposites. But we learned from Bentham that the legislation may create duties where there are no rights. There may be laws "which impose duties without any other view than the benefit of the agent, these generate no rights" (Bentham, 1961, p. 225). Could it be paraphrased that there may be laws "which impose duties without any other view than the benefit of the *beneficiary* and yet generate no rights"? My suggestion is, yes it could and it should. Responsibilities may be considered obligations – or duties – without corresponding rights. The physician is responsible for her patient with respect to providing a particular treatment, the expecting mother is responsible for the well being of the fetus, the pet owner is responsible for the quality of life of his pet. None of these responsibilities correspond to a right for the beneficiary and yet laws may be created to impose such responsibilities, laws which, if broken lead to punishment.

Bibliography

Aristotle, *Nicomachean Ethics*, Loeb Classical Library XIX. Transl. by H. Rackham, Harvard University Press, William Heineman Ltd, Cambridge, Massachusetts, London, MCMLXXXII (1982).

Bentham, Jeremy, 1782, *Of Laws in General.* First published 1945, a more comprehensive edition published 1970, ed. by H.L.A. Hart, London.

Bentham, Jeremy, 1789, *An Introduction to the Principles of Morals and Legislation.* (Publ. later by Hafner Publishing Co, New York; first printing 1948, second printing 1961)

Hohfeld, Wesley Newcomb, 1919, *Fundamental Legal Conceptions*, Yale University Press, New Haven and London. 3rd edition ed by Cook, Walter W. Forword by Corbin, Arthur, L., 1964.

Holmström-Hintikka, Ghita, 1991, *Action, Purpose and Will, A Formal Theory*, Acta Philosophica Fennica, Vol. 50, Helsinki.

Holmström-Hintikka, Ghita, 1994, 'Purpose and Legal Responsibility', forthcoming.

Kanger, Helle, 1981, *Human Rights and their Realization,* Reports of the Research Project 'Models for Justice', Department of Philosophy, University of Uppsala, Uppsala, Sweden.

Kanger, Stig & Kanger, Helle, 1966, "Rights and Parliamentarism", *Theoria*, vol. 32, pp. 85–115.

Lindahl, Lars, 1977, *Position and Change*, D. Reidel Publishing Company, Dordrecht - Holland/ Boston – U.S.A.

Zimmerman, Michael J., 1988, *An Essay on Moral Responsibility,* Rowman & Littlefield, Totowa, U.S.A.

Carol C. Gould, Hoboken, NJ

Group Rights and Social Ontology

Introduction

The increasing globalization and universalization of culture worldwide has paradoxically been matched at the same time by increasing cultural particularism and separatism. These two conflicting trends are reflected in cosmopolitanism or the homogenization of cultures on the one hand and in claims to cultural autonomy or to ethnic and nationalist chauvinisms on the other. At the same time that sixteen year olds all over the world are drinking their cokes while listening to MTV and wearing their Levis (many sizes too large), their parents and siblings are often reviving ancient ethnic feuds, rediscovering their distinctive cultural identities, and attempting to exclude alien others from their midst. Against the background of an increasing awareness of the value of cultural difference, but also in the context of the alternative claims of equal and universal freedom and global interconnectedness, the question of group rights has recently reemerged with particular force and has been developed in newly sophisticated ways in social and political philosophy. What are group rights? Do we need to recognize them as a condition for preserving and enhancing cultural diversity? Are they fundamental rights or do they instead derive from individual rights? And indeed, what do we mean when we speak of a "group" in this connection?

In this paper, I will focus on the question of the rights of cultural minorities and subordinately on the somewhat different question of the rights of oppressed groups within a larger polity, where such groups are identified by discriminatory, exclusionary or exploitative treatment. I will draw upon what I have called social ontology, as a theory of social reality, which I have developed in earlier work.

Groups as constituted entities

In the discussion that has developed on group rights, there has been no little confusion about what the term "group" should be taken to refer to. It is commonly agreed that it is not simply an accidental aggregation of individuals, nor even one where the individuals share some common characteristic. This is far too abstract for a social group of the sort intended. It is also commonly agreed that it is not a reified entity, a collectivity that exists over and above its individual members, on the model of a Platonic class or Durkheimian structure. Instead, a number of theorists have characterized a group as made up of individuals who stand in certain relations to each other, for example, as sharing a common purpose or having a common intentionality, or acting together, or at least having a common interest. I developed a view along these lines in my book *Marx's Social Ontology: Individuality and Community in Marx's Theory of Social Reality* (1978)[1] and

1 Carol Gould, *Marx's Social Ontology* (Cambridge: The MIT Press, 1978), esp. pp. 31–39.

subsequently in *Rethinking Democracy* (1988)[2]. In these works and others[3], I characterized a social group as an entity constituted by "individuals-in-relations," eschewing both the aggregative and holistic readings. Further, I argued that while individuals as agents are ontologically prior to the groups that they constitute, they stand in internal relations to each other such that they become the individuals they are in and through such social relations and may therefore be described as social individuals. I proposed that participation in joint or common activity is one of the main conditions for individual self-development. Groups are defined by such joint activity or common purposes (whether explicitly recognized or not).

Larry May, in his book *The Morality of Groups* (1987), formulated an essentially similar view, speaking of "individuals in relationships" as characterizing a group as the middle position he proposed between a merely aggregative reductive view and a collectivist, structuralist view.[4] DeGeorge had also utilized such a conception in his 1983 paper on social reality and social relations.[5] On my view, in a way that the other views do not articulate, groups are constituted entities, that is, they come into being by virtue of actual relations among their constituent individual members, but are not reducible to the individuals distributively, taken apart from these relations.

How to derive group rights from individual rights

The normative question of whether there are group rights is distinct from though related to the ontological question of what constitutes a group. My view here differs in this respect from that of Buchanan who argues that although there are group rights, the question of ontology is irrelevant. He claims that liberalism is committed to individual moral rights but is not limited to an individualist ontology which would preclude an emphasis on the sociality of individuals. He holds that liberalism's individualism is moral and not ontological.[6] Whatever one thinks of this particular claim about liberalism, I do not accept Buchanan's sharp fact-value or ontological-moral distinction with regard to social facts and would instead suggest that the social ontology of both individuals and groups makes a difference to the normative arguments about group rights.[7] Indeed, I would

2 Carol Gould, *Rethinking Democracy* (Cambridge: Cambridge University Press, 1988), esp. chapter 2.

3 Cf. especially "Beyond Causality in the Social Sciences: Reciprocity as a Model for Non-exploitative Social Relations," in *Epistemology, Methodology and the Social Sciences*: Boston Studies for the Philosophy of Science, ed. by R.S. Cohen and M.W. Wartofsky (Dordrecht: Reidel, 1983), pp. 53–88; and "Ontological Foundations of Democracy," paper presented to the Metaphysical Society of America, 1979, subsequently published in revised form in *Rethinking Democracy*.

4 Larry May, *The Morality of Groups* (Notre Dame: University of Notre Dame Press, 1987), pp. 23–25 and 29–30.

5 Richard DeGeorge, "Social Reality and Social Relations," *Review of Metaphysics*, 37 (Sept., 1983).

6 Allen Buchanan, *Secession* (Boulder: Westview Press, 1991), pp. 8, 79–80.

7 We might observe that Buchanan himself appeals to numerous arguments that are social-ontological in this sense. See, for example, ibid., pp. 39, 77.

suggest that the social ontology itself is already in a way normative, e.g. that the very characterization of individuals as agents or persons with cultural identities supports an argument for certain rights as valid claims of such individuals. Conversely, the values and rights recognized are partly dependent on how one characterizes the existence of individuals, social relations and groups. This does not render such an ontological account "metaphysical," since it remains a regional ontology concerned exclusively with concrete human beings in their social interrelations and practices.

The normative conception that goes along with such a social ontology of individuals-in-relations and constituted social groups centers around a principle of equal positive freedom as the (prima facie) equal right of individuals to the conditions of their self-development or the exercise of their freedom over time. I have argued elsewhere that since participation in common activity is one of the main conditions for such self-development, it follows that individuals as agents have prima facie equally valid claims or rights to such opportunities for participation in joint activity. Among the modes of such activity involving a shared understanding of common interests and a mutual recognition as participants in it are work, political life, culture, and also various forms of voluntary association and face-to-face interactions.

If we focus on culture here it is because it is a pervasive source of social identity, providing a context for thought and action which involves language, values, modes of behavior, education, socialization, practices, traditions, and shared history. Further, a number of very sharp issues concerning the rights of cultural minorities have become the focus of the current discussion on group rights. The other focus of this recent discussion is on the rights of oppressed groups which are not characterizable as (or not simply characterizable as) cultural minorities, e.g., women or African-Americans in the United States context. There is, of course, some overlap, since some oppressed groups are at the same time clearly identifiable as cultural minorities, e.g., Native Americans, and to some degree African-Americans. Moreover, oppressed groups may develop shared modes of understanding and action that may be characterized as cultural. So, for example, some have attempted to talk in this way of "women's culture" or again of "a culture of poverty," but clearly some reification is entailed in attributing such a common culture to all members of these groups. (The same may well be true of more standardly identified cultural groups.) In talking about groups and their rights, then, one has to be sensitive to the degree of diversity even within the framework of a common culture and certainly in those contexts in which the term culture is used by metaphorical extension.

It is evident from the pervasiveness of culture that an individual's participation in some mode of cultural life as a form of common activity is a condition for self-development. It therefore follows that if individuals have equal rights to the conditions of their self-development, they have equal rights to have the opportunity to participate in a culture. We may say that there is an equal right of access to the conditions of cultural self-development. This remains a relatively transparent right, tacitly assumed, as long as there is no special problem concerning access to or participation in one's culture. Thus for dominant cultures what may be at issue is equal educational opportunity or cultural literacy or the availability of cultural resources in a fair distribution, but for minority cultures what is at stake is precisely the question of their continued existence or the denial of the conditions of access to or participation in the life of the culture. This may result from lack of means for learning the language or the history and traditions of a minority culture; or it may mean deliberate discriminatory repression of the minority culture. In such a case, the provision of the equal rights to the conditions of cultural development may justify a claim for group rights.

But what exactly is a group right as against the rights that individual members of a culture have to their own cultural expression and development? And how would such group rights be derived from the cultural rights of individuals? Part of the confusion in talking about group rights is to consciously or unconsciously reify the conception of a group as something independent of or abstractible from its constitution by individuals, in the specific relations that characterize them as members of that group. Such a group as an abstract entity cannot have rights. On the other hand, individual members of a culture, whether majority or minority, cannot develop their cultural activity except with respect to the existence of a culture to which they belong, namely, to a relatively persisting and emergent form of cultural life, which they in turn appropriate in the course of their interaction with others.

Group rights therefore pertain to groups as constituted entities and therefore are rights derived from the rights of the constituent individuals who are members of the group and who have these rights insofar as they are members of the group and not apart from these relations to each other. The group rights that a cultural minority can bear are therefore rights to the cultural conditions for the self-development of its members. Since it is not the group that has the equal right to cultural self- development but the individual members of the culture, these group rights are derivative from and instrumental to the equal rights to self-development of the members. They are not rights of the group sui generis. Yet, group rights are not reducible to or identifiable with the distributive rights of each individual to the conditions for his or her own cultural development, but rather are rights of the constituency of the culture in the literal sense of those who constitute the group collectively. As a necessary condition for the exercise of the individual's rights, the group can make a valid claim against the majority culture to provide the individuals with these conditions. Thus, a minority culture which may be expressed in a language other than a dominant language of the majority would have a group right to provide the means for the perpetuation of that linguistic community through its educational system and other means. This does not entail, however, that the cultural minority could insist that all of its members were required to be educated only in that language, but rather that the choice to be educated in this way would be available to its members.

This addresses a special problem concerning group rights of minority cultures, namely, the preservation of the human rights of members of the culture and their freedom of choice to remain members or to leave the group or indeed to combine their cultural identity in the group with other cultural identities or affiliations. I will have more to say on this later.

Another condition for cultural participation of members of a minority culture could be the freedom to observe certain cultural traditions or practices, whether religious or secular, for example, the celebration of certain festivals or commemorations, or observation of dietary rituals. Here, again, the right of the group would consist in its access to the means to provide for these practices and not to be interfered with in them by the dominant culture or the powers of the state. Yet here too an important constraint will be noted later, namely, that the practices of a minority culture cannot be such as to violate the human rights of its members. In other words, the special group rights must be compatible with the universalistic human rights to which the dominant culture is presumably committed. Where this is not the case and the dominant culture is itself repressive and in violation of the human rights of its members, the minority culture is not thereby absolved from this constraint.

The approach presented here is related in certain respects to the views of such theorists of group rights as Will Kymlicka, Charles Taylor, Michael Hartney, Michael McDonald, Allen Buchanan, Larry May, Vernon Van Dyke and others. In general, though the philosophical discussion is often sophisticated and the concrete examples very rich, it seems to me that there is as yet an insufficient attention to the social ontology of cultural groups and therefore to the relevance of such an ontological analysis for the normative question of rights.

Oppressed groups and group rights

Before proceeding, we might note that there is a parallel construction for the derivation of group rights from rights of individuals in the case of oppressed groups. As I noted earlier, an oppressed group is characterized as a group within a given society which is excluded from the equal rights and benefits of other members of that society or which is subjected to discriminatory or exploitative treatment severely affecting the freedom and/or wellbeing of its members. An oppressed group is excluded in some systematic and effective way from whatever norms of equality may prevail in the society at large. The special rights of an oppressed group would bear on the rectification and compensation for unequal treatment in the past and would aim at providing what has been characterized as a "level playing field" for present members with respect to the rest of society. So in this case, the group rights – whether in the form of affirmative action, compensatory treatment, the removal of special barriers to participation in political and economic life, desegregation, etc. – are justified by reference to the same principle of prima facie equal rights to the conditions of self-development, hence from the rights of individual members of the oppressed groups.

Here, the basis for membership in a group is not a matter of social identification or common purpose or shared understanding, though these elements of solidarity among the oppressed may develop as a common consciousness of their relevantly similar situation. Rather, it is a matter of objective circumstances of being put in a particular situation of oppression not by choice; and of what has been called an ascriptive identity, that is, what members of the group are taken to be by others and in particular by the dominant groups. While such oppressed groups may also be regarded as constituted entities in the sense that the groups do not exist apart from the individuals in relations of oppression, nonetheless such groups are not defined by shared purposes of their choosing or the sort of intentionality often characteristic of cultural groups.

Constraints on group rights for cultural minorities

An interesting and not uncommon problem arises with respect to group rights for some cultural minorities: When the practices of a cultural minority, which are to be supported by group rights, themselves violate the human rights of individual members of the culture, does the autonomy of the cultural group permit the violation of human rights? I would argue that any of the rights of a minority cultural group would have to be compatible with the human rights, for otherwise the justification of the group rights on the basis that they provide conditions for the equal freedom of self-development of the individuals who are members of that group would be undermined. Since the human rights are the fundamental conditions for the exercise of agency and hence are given priority in the application of the principle of equal positive freedom, they cannot be abrogated by group rights applied or interpreted in such a way as to violate them.

This has particularly important bearing for the difficult question of the pervasive oppression of women within many cultural minorities (and majorities as well!). Thus for example, a traditional practice of female genital mutilation is still condoned within certain cultural groups. The claim has been made that the autonomy of a culture demands noninterference or nonintervention even with such practices. Without addressing the difficult issue of intervention here, we may say that cultural group rights would not justify such practices, on the grounds that such practices entail a violation of human rights. Further, insofar as women's equality is formally protected by the human rights, it can be appealed to as a ground for eliminating other cultural practices that oppress women.

Other constraints on cultural group rights that need consideration, though I cannot deal with them here, include the issue of the democratization of decision-making within a cultural minority where autocratic or other antidemocratic practices may prevail. A related issue is that of who is authentically representative of the cultural minority and can speak for it. Another important constraint on the scope of group rights concerns what we may call "minorities within the minority." Especially in territorial situations where a minority culture holds way over a geographical region, there will inevitably be minorities living within this minority cultural framework. Clearly, the rights of these subminorities to their own cultural expression need to be respected and these minorities within the minority should not suffer the same suppression or discrimination that the minority culture had itself suffered. This norm of the protection of minorities within what were previously oppressed cultures or nationalities has been widely and wildly violated in recent history and at present. I would also hazard the suggestion that the issue of such subminorities has not received enough attention from political philosophers.

A practical question emerges from this issue of minorities within a minority. How large must a cultural group be before it is legitimated in its demands for cultural autonomy and recognition of group rights? Will we be led on a slippery slope here to the absurd condition that any group of two or three may call themselves a cultural group and may demand special rights for the preservation and the practice of their "culture"? Clearly, some measure of good judgment is required here, especially in a historical period in which long suppressed minorities of ethnic, religious, or linguistic sorts have emerged to make claims not only for recognition and cultural self- determination, but for secession and national identity.

From Separatism to Multiculturalism

Perhaps the most salient development in the recent period has been a move away from monocultural identity associated with the traditional nation-state to multicultural identities in which there is an interaction and an admixture of two or more cultures. This is to be distinguished from mere assimilationism in which an older or parent culture yields to a dominant culture which essentially replaces it or corrupts it. Especially in large cities and in the context of major waves of immigration, populations have become culturally heterogeneous. Likewise, with the development of the world market and the globalization not only of the economy but of communications and the media, an increasing cosmopolitanism has emerged. There are two aspects to this: the first is a rapidly changing world culture, especially as a youth culture transcending national, ethnic, and geographic barriers; and the second is the interaction among existing cultures and pluralization of cultural identities.

This phenomenon has been identified as multiculturalism, but this is a term which has been used in importantly ambiguous ways, meaning different things to different people. We may distinguish between two uses of the term: In one use multiculturalism designates an aggregate or collection of different and relatively separate cultures together with an awareness within an older dominant culture of these differences and of the contributions of the cultures of oppressed groups – paradigmatically, the recognition of the contributions of African-American, Latino, and other minority cultures in the United States – or an awareness of nonwestern cultures beyond the dominant Eurocentric and male canon. The term multiculturalism has also been used to designate a new interactive model of culture, where cultural identity itself is open to plural definition and where there may be cultural creation through the appropriation of diverse cultural influences. (A noteworthy example of this is American jazz and there have been newer forms of this as well, especially in art and music.) Yet, this does not necessarily entail a homogenization of cultural strains and it is also a continuation of the historically common phenomenon of cultural diffusion. But we may say that this has become a more intensely dynamic phenomenon than it was in the past, due in part at least to the powerful contemporary technologies of global communication.

On the normative side, from the standpoint of a single individual, these developments contribute to the possibilities of cultural choice and change. Customary views of cultural, ethnic, or political identity have most often seen this identity as simply given, as a matter of birth into a culture, or ethnic group, or community; or else have considered this identity to be ascriptive, that is, determined, by what salient or authoritative others take one to be. I would argue that cultural identity and group membership need to be defined in such a way that they are open to choice and to the possibility of multiple cultural identifications. This would add an important element of self- definition and the appropriation of diverse cultures to the more passive traditional characterization of cultures as matters of birth or ascription.

These normative considerations as well as the fact of increasing multiculturalism raise a host of practical and interesting questions concerning cultural group rights. Since determining whether groups have rights and what rights they have also depends on the answer to the question of what makes an individual a member of a group, multiculturalism significantly complicates the identification of a given cultural group as well as the question of which group rights any given individual can lay claim to. This would be especially difficult if we wish to move to a multicultural policy within the public sphere in which there would be public support for cultural groups as a matter of group rights. Questions would arise both in terms of fairness to individuals and in terms of what I have in another paper called cultural justice. But a discussion of these further issues goes beyond the limits of this brief presentation.

Marijan Pavčnik, Ljubljana

Abuse of a Right
A Contribution to Understanding a Right and its Nature

1. Right

1.1. *Right*

The central element of a right is the possibility of a legal subject to conduct himself in a certain manner (*facultas agendi*). This possibility is contained in the abstract and general legal norm (abstract entitlement). Legal subjects have such entitlements (Germ. *Berechtigung*) in order to satisfy their different interests within the legal frame thereof. The possibility of conduct (behaviour), either active or passive, is legally protected.

1.2. *Abstract Right*

The abstract right consists of one or several entitlements (composite right). In a certain sense each right is a composite one because it must necessarily contain at least two entitlements. The basic entitlement enabling the subject to satisfy a certain interest (e.g. an economic one: repayment of a loan) is always accompanied by a legal demand (e.g. claim). The demand (Germ. *Anspruch*) contains the possibility of enforcing a sanction if the obligor (e.g. the debtor) does not act in accordance with his duty. It is an essential element of a right that the basic entitlement is protected. If the basic entitlement is not legally protected, one cannot speak of a right. It may be called a „reflex of a legal norm" (Jhering 1906, 351–352), which in itself is not legally protected.

1.3. *Concrete Right*

The concrete right is based on the abstract one and contains the possibility of conduct in a concrete legal relationship. The possibility of conduct (*facultas agendi*) represents the concretisation of an abstract entitlement with regard to a concrete case. The concrete entitlement arises by a direct application of abstract entitlements (e.g. several basic rights) or by a prior concretisation of the abstract entitlements (e.g. by a credit contract as an individual legal act). In the former as well as in the latter case a concrete entitlement is formed. At first sight it seems that this is only true of the latter case. However, also in the former case the subject must form an idea of the scope of the freedom of his conduct.

The concrete right is connected with will. The subject endowed with consciousness and will has the possibility of a positive or a negative choice. The positive choice means a concretisation and realisation of the abstract entitlement (active right) whereas the negative choice means that the subject remains passive because his interest does not fall together with the „typical content“ and the „typical interest“ expressed by the abstract entitlement (negative right). The positive choice is factually and not only formally greater where the formal legal sources are more flexible as to their contents and allow nuances with regard to „difference in identity“. Also in this case negative choice cannot be avoided – not only because a solely abstract entitlement could not be realised but simply due to individual differences between subjects, which cannot be captured by law: they can only be taken into account by also allowing this kind of choice (negative right).

2. Exercising a Right

Within the proces of exercising a right or in connection therewith three instances can be distinguished. In the first case the subject exercises a right so as to remain within the legally allowed limits without encroaching upon somebody else's right. In the second case the subject infringes a legal duty without being able to refer to a legally protected entitlement which would allow the characterisation of his conduct as a legal one. In the third case, which is a borderline case and possibly the most controversial one, the subject starts out from an abstractly permitted entitlement, yet he exercises it in such a manner that at the same time he encroaches upon somebody else's right.

Though the first example refers to exercising a right and the second one to exercising a duty, this does not mean that no inner connection exists between them. The right and the legal duty are correlative terms. A's right presupposes B's duty and *vice versa*. However, only with reservations can the statement be accepted that only the right appears on one side and only the corresponding duty on the other (and *vice versa*). Without taking into account any terminological misunderstandings, A's right always seems to be connected with his duty and B's duty also with his right. The subject of a right is really entitled to act freely within legally permitted limits, at the same time he is duty-bound not to go beyond these limits. On the other hand, the subject of a duty is bound to behave in a certain manner, at the same time he is also entitled to demand of others not to hinder him in his conduct.

The third case (abuse of a right) takes up the relation between a right and a legal duty. The latter is no element of the right. Though duty is not contained in the right, it is situated next to it since it imposes upon the subject to remain within the limits of legally protected entitlement. If this connection as a constant companion of exercising a right is not given sufficient weight, it might happen that the relativity of the content of a right is at least partly overlooked or its limitability is only considered in the case when the subject acts with intent to damage someone else. From the described relation between the right and the legal duty it follows that at the abuse of a right the legally allowed and the legally forbidden are intertwined. Hence the abuse of a right cannot be considered equal to pure legal violation though the abuse in itself is forbidden. On the other hand it has to be taken into account that the abuse of a right is based on a legally allowed exercising of a right and thus has to be treated separately and to be valued as such.

3. Theories about the Abuse of a Right

The earlier (liberalist) theory denied the possibility that a right could be abused. It was based on the principle *Qui suo iure utitur, neminem laedit* and on the conclusion that the designation of an „abusing exercising of rights“ is logically contradictory: who exercises a right behaves in accordance with the law and his acts are permitted. According to this theory the unlimitable nature of a right corresponds to economic and social competition: whoever achieves superiority in a certain area has the right to damage anyone else. Any damage-causing act originating from this competition is legally allowed. The resulting damage is inevitable and it is not necessary to establish whether it was intended (Planiol 1923, 287 ff.).

The theory of the abuse of a right first found its place within the frame of tortious liability (subjective theory). The standpoint of this theory is that a right is abused by someone who acts with fault and thus damage is caused to someone else. A classic example is the exercising of a right with the exclusive or obvious intent to harm someone else (see e.g. Para 1295/2 of Austrian Civil Code and Para 226 of German Civil Code). A wider scope is covered by objective theories that consider the aim and social function of every right. This final aim is „outside“ the right and „over“ it. The direction of exercising a right is not set by the individual's will but the aim („spirit“) of the right defines the direction of the conduct of the subject. The individual is not only liable when he behaves unlawfully (and does not have a legal basis) but also when he „incorrectly“ exercises a right (Josserand 1935 and 1938, 118–119): if someone deviates from the aim of a right, this means that he abuses it and is liable for his conduct (e.g. unfaithful, untrustworthy, immoral exercising of a right). A similar standpoint is upheld by mixed (objective-subjective) theories, which in addition to objective criteria request that the violator has encroached upon the right of someone else at fault.

With regard to the criteria proposed, the subjective theory ranges from the intentional to any other fault-actions that are damaging to other holders of a right. This makes the subjective theory broader and closer to objective theories which are of a broader character as a rule. The process of broadening proves that the aim of a right plays an important role also in subjective theories. Nevertheless, qualitative differences exist between both theories. The subjective theory puts forward the holder's subjective relation to the exercising of a right and the consequences thereof. It is true that a conduct is forbidden because it is not in accordance with the nature of the right, yet it is forbidden only if the subject can be reproached for fault-conduct.

The objective theory is much more flexible. The criteria it applies are „open“, thus allowing for adaptability in accordance with the changing social conditions (an objective-dynamic manner of interpretation). In this respect it goes much further than the subjective theory because it is not bound to the holder's fault-conduct, the latter being only one of the indexes to the abuse of a right.

The main (basic) criterion is always of objective nature. If the doctrine divides the theories about the abuse of a right into subjective, objective and mixed ones, this division is only valid to the extent as it stresses the direction of different lines of thought. In this connection it should be said that also the objective theory uses supplementary subjective criteria like *animus nocendi*, the reason or lack of justified interest. These criteria point to different forms of abuse and, with the exception of intentional damaging conduct that does not appear by itself, they are formed in such a way as to consider the special features of concrete cases. Apart from *animus nocendi,* they are not of exclusively subjective nature. They are subjective to the extent as they require that the violator's attitude to the exercising of the right has to be established. This subjective attitude is of decisive importance for an abuse when it shows that the subject's conduct deviates from the interest or reason as defined by the aim of the right. It is true that the same qualifying process also applies to the subjective theory, which, however, is much less dynamic since it always considers fault a *condition sine qua non* of the normative state of constituent elements of the abuse of a right.

The dynamics of the objective theory is not supposed to mean that in the case of a dispute the judge will decide at his absolute discretion. In this context the reservation is certainly partly justified that the theory of abuse turns the judge from an applicator into a creator of the law. The extent to which the judge applies the formal legal source (e.g. a statute) and to which he is law-creative depends on the nature of the general legal act on which the individual one is based. The degree of certainty with regard to the object and the aim of law-regulation is different from one field of law to the other. This certainty can never be so incomplete that the individual act would not mean an application of the general legal act at the same time and it can never be so complete that the individual act (e.g. a judicial one) would not mean creation of law at the same time (see Kelsen 1934, 79). In this connection the question arises how and on the basis of which rules (criteria) the responsible government organ (e.g. a judge) will establish the aim and the limits of a right. In addition to this dilemma that should not overlook the principle of legal security, the problem has to be solved whether and to which extent the subjective theory is compatible with the objective one.

4. Constituent Elements of the Abuse of a Right

4.1. *Going Beyond the Limits of the Basic Entitlement*

The normative state of constituent elements (Germ. *Tatbestand*) of the abuse of a right is characterized by three elements. The basic assumption is that the subject starts out from a legally allowed abstract entitlement (Germ. *Berechtigung*) and concretises and materialises it in such a way that his conduct *goes beyond* the limits of entitlement. For instance, the abuse of a right exists when the holder of a tenant's right puts off moving into the new house of his own that can already be lived in and thus makes it impossible for the owner to move into his own apartment. Or, when a party has a cart track on his land and uses it in such a way that the tracks get deeper and the water gathering in them flows to his neighbour's land. Or, if a party uses sanctions due to incomplete fulfilment, yet the incompleteness is so slight that it is not appropriate for the sanction to be realized.

In these and other cases – all cases are stated in Pavčnik 1986, 48ff. – legal and unlawful elements intertwine. The legality of the abuse of a right is sustained by the circumstance that the subject exercises a legally protected entitlement and the unlawfulness thereof is sustained by the realization that the holder's conduct had gone beyond the legally allowed limits. This going beyond the contents of a right must be distinguished from unlawful conduct that is completely illegal.

4.2. *Conflict of Rights*

The second assumption is that a *conflict of two rights* has arisen which do not exclude each other. The conflict arises because two rights face each other and one of them is exercised in such a manner as to make it either partly or completely impossible to activate and realize the other one. One can speak of such a state of facts when the upper water beneficiary takes the water of the lower water beneficiary. Also the above-mentioned cases illustrating the subject's conduct going beyond the scope (limits) of legally protected entitlement belong to this category (especially tangible being the case relating to the tenant's right).

The conflict of rights has to be interpreted in a broad manner. For the normative state of abuse already the element is sufficient that the entitlement (demand) is enforced in a manner damaging to the obligor (Germ. *Verpflichteter*) or simply „making his situation more difficult“ (Sajovic 1975, 439). Also in this case one can speak of a conflict of rights because the subject of a duty at the same time has the right to demand from the other party in the legal relationship to stick to the limits of his rights so as to choose the less burdensome conduct among several possible ones and yet enable the other party to achieve the advantages he is entitled to. Thus a demand to cancel (e.g. to cancel a contract) should not be permitted if an improvement or later fulfilment is possible (Sajovic 1975, 440). Neither can a buyer refuse the receipt of goods if their quality only slightly differs from the contractually agreed one, but he can demand a reduction of price.

Every intrusion into somebody else's sphere cannot be considered an abuse, thus it may be within the limits of serious critique or loyal competition. Also nuisances are permitted if they do not go beyond the extent customary with respect to the nature and aim of the real estate and the local conditions. Thus in court practice the standpoint has been accepted that an interference is permitted when damage has been caused by the shadow falling upon the crops of the neighbouring lot. It is only of secondary importance whether this solution can be generalized and to what extent it can be nuanced. It is only given as an example to point out that the abstract entitlement cannot define with a definite and mathematical certainty how far a concrete right (entitlement) can reach and in what a scope it can legally validly enter the sphere of somebody else, who must accept such an „intrusion“ and limit his own right accordingly. This legally empty (i.e. uncertain) space can only be defined as to its content by relying upon the nature of the legally protected entitlement and upon the prohibition of the abuse of the right, which issues from the nature of the right and keeps returning to it.

4.3. *Prohibition of the Abuse of a Right*

In a conflict of two or more rights it is most difficult to define (the third element) when and why a certain right has been abused (prohibition of the abuse of a right). In modern law the most suitable seems to be a general prohibition based on objective criteria independent of the subject's fault. This is based on the concept that the rights are only limited by the equal rights of others. It follows from this interdependence of rights that in the case of a right being open as to its content, the holder must exercise it in such a manner that his conduct does not go beyond the limit that allows someone else to exercise his right to qualitatively the same extent.

As objective criteria all criteria defining the social function of a right and its fulfilment can be used, e.g. social benefit, normal and social fulfilment, lacking and insufficient appropriate (entitled) interest, aim of the legal relationship, aim of the thing (object) etc. Special weight is given to the criteria determined with regard to the principle of loyalty and good faith, with regard to morals and customs like local and business customs etc.

The enumerated and similar criteria are not valid on the basis of their authority but are legally binding only when advised by the lawgiver. If a criterion is not foreseen in the law, it can be applied in a concrete case only if the appropriate organ (especially the judge) solving the dispute decides so (legal gap). Also in the former instance the content of the criterion is not evident from the text of the statute or of some other general legal act. If the criteria depend on the social concepts of what is positive and what is negative, what is good and what is bad, what is lawful and what is unlawful, the question arises about the extent to which such prohibition of abuse is legally binding. Thus for example, under the pressure of certain economic interests, business morals can come into conflict with the moral concepts of the social community. In this case priority must be given to the morals of the social community because the judge or any other responsible government organ must always establish the content of the business morals and whether this content is in accordance with the principles of the legal order. Thereby the courts (government organs) can consolidate and promote the development of social conceptions that are in accordance with legally protected interests and at the same time reject the ones opposing these interests.

Even more explicitly: the prohibition of the abuse of a right is based on the law that is appropriate (just) in terms of civilisation, which is supposed to define the statute law in more detail as to its contents and to concretise it in a normative manner with regard to the particulars of single cases. The aim of normative concretisation is to bring the contents of conflicting rights in accordance and to introduce therein the principle of legal equality: the cases that correspond to each other in their essential characteristics have to be treated equally and the cases essentially differing from the former have to be treated in an appropriately different manner – but again equally within the latter frame. It is in the nature of this bringing into line as to contents that it has to be based on proportional (Aristotelian) justice: the holder of the more (less) important right should get proportionately more (less) (e.g. in the case when the owners of a farming estate and of a holiday cottage are water beneficiaries) and the holders of two identical rights as to quality and scope should get the same quantity.

4.4. *Coercive Measures (Sanctions)*

The theory of abuse based on objective criteria sets out from the concept of right and its definition as to contents by following the process of the exercising thereof. If, due to the „openness“ of the entitlement, the subject exercises his right in a manner that can be defined as abuse, it is the duty of the responsible government organ to act upon the proposal of the party involved or *ex officio* and to limit the abused right as well as to order reinstatement if it is possible in view of the nature of the intrusion upon somebody else's right. In a conflict of two rights of the same kind (e.g. right of property), this „limitation“ will also be valid for the second holder because he will have to exercise his right so as not to intrude upon the „narrowed“ right, i.e. the right that had earlier prevented him from exercising his entitlement. In addition to these two coercive ones, efficient measures against abuse are also the refusal of the demand for legal protection as well as lack of consideration given to the conduct (behaviour) going beyond the entitlement – either by the government organ (e.g. abuse of procedural rights) or by the subject, who is in legal relationship (e.g. in contract relationship) with the party going beyond his entitlement. If no consent can be achieved in the latter case, official intervention leading to the measure of limitation as to contents will be necessary.

The holder (subject) of a right may also be liable in tort. With respect to the normative state of the abuse of a right, only the liability for the damage caused by negligence is possible. It is self-evident that the violator is also liable for the damage when he acts with the intent to harm the other part or even with the exclusive intent to harm the other party (vexation). In this case the violator's conduct only seemingly lies within the scope of the basic entitlement (which is the central element of the right). In the case of „vexation“ there does not exist a normative state of constituent elements characteristic of the abuse of a right but a conduct that can be characterized as a civil offence (pure legal violation).

5. Instead of a Conclusion: Towards the Nature of a Right

With these measures the theory of abuse returns to its starting point, which is the right and the nature thereof. Its contribution has been to draw attention to the interdependence of the right and of the concrete relationship and to offer criteria and methodological advice enabling the rights (abstract entitlements) to adapt socially with respect to changeable and only partly foreseeable social relationships.

The prohibition of abuse is, of course, merely one of the means leading to the socialisation of law and right. This means can be used only when the rights of different subjects cannot be delimited in an appropriate manner. If a delimitation is possible, it is certainly better that already the lawgiver limits the rights and defines them as much as possible, which considerably reduces the possibility of conflicts. This legislative intervention into a right is also necessary because the prohibition of abuse has the function of mutually bringing rights into line, which only partially changes the nature of a right. If a certain right is not in accordance with the rule of law any more, the prohibition of abuse can only bring it into line with somebody else's right but it cannot abolish it or give it a content that would change it into its opposite. The principle *Qui suo iure utitur, neminem laedit* is thus only true insofar as it is the basis of the demand for legal security as well as of the demand for a legal use of teleological interpretation (cf. Pavcnik 1993, 52-56). Otherwise there is the danger that rights are not taken really „seriously", are unnecessarily narrowed or even uncritically subordinated to „higher" aims and interests.

Literature

Bucher, E. (1965), *Das subjektive Recht als Normsetzungsbefugnis*. Tübingen.

Duguit, L. (1920), *Les transformations générales du droit privé depuis le Code Napoléon*. Paris.

Hohfeld, W.N. (1964), *Fundamental Legal Conceptions*. New Haven-London.

Jellinek, G. (1919), *System der subjektiven öffentlichen Rechte*. Tübingen.

Jhering, R. (1906), *Geist des römischen Rechts*, III/2. Leipzig.

Josserand, L. (1935), Evolucija odgovornosti (Evolution of Liability). In: *Branič*, No. 7–8, 323–336.

–: (1938), *Cours de droit civil positif français*, I. Paris.

Kasper, F. (1967), *Das subjektive Recht – Begriffsbildung und Bedeutungsmehrheit*. Karlsruhe.

Kelsen, H. (1934), *Reine Rechtslehre*. Wien. (Second edition: 1960).

Koller, P. (1992), A Conception of Moral Rights and Its Application to Property and Welfare State. In: *Ratio Iuris*, Vol. 5, No. 2, 153-179.

Lukič, R. (1941), O zloupotrebi prava (About Abuse of Rights). In: *Pravna* misao, No. I–II, 28-43.

Markovitch, M. (1936), *La théorie de l'abus des droits en droit comparé*. Paris.

Mazeaud, H. et L., Tunc, A. (1957), *Traité théorique et pratique de la responsabilité civile*, I. Paris.

Nino, C. (1992, ed.), *Rights*. Aldershot.

Pavčnik M. (1986), *Zloraba pravice* (Abuse of a Right). Ljubljana.

–: (1993), *Juristisches Verstehen und Entscheiden*. Wien-New York.

Planiol, M. (1923), *Traité élémentaire de droit civil*, II. Paris.

Raz, J. (1984), On the Nature of Rights. In: *Mind*, No. 93, 194-214.

Rotondi, M. (1979, ed.), *L'abus de droit*. Padova.

Sajovic, B. (1975), *Načelo vestnosti in poštenja v premoženjskem pravu (Principle of Loyalty and Good Faith in Civil Law)*. Research Study: Ljubljana.

Saleilles R. (1905), *De l'abus de droit. In: Bulletin de la société d'études législatives.*

Wieacker, F. (1967), *Privatrechtsgeschichte der Neuzeit*, sec. ed., Göttingen.

Windscheid, B. (1891), *Lehrbuch des Pandektenrechts*, I. Frankfurt.

Hiroshi Matsuo, Yokohama

Historical and Theoretical Intimacy Between the Concepts of Rights and Property

I. Introduction

As is often pointed out, the concept of rights continues to expand. In addition to the several types of traditional rights, we know of some relatively new types.[1] In such circumstances, it seems that the concept of rights might have a priori a certain connotation, from which some legal conclusions could be deduced. The denotative expansion of this concept, however, appears to be making such a connotation gradually weaker in subject, object and contents. This might be due to the lack of consensus about the concept of rights,[2] and the consensus might be reached by seeking the common ingredients of various existing rights. Still, the fundamental question remains: what should be exactly called "rights" and why do they deserve to be called "rights"? Then it is, I believe, important to ascertain the mechanism, in which rights have been generated and justified. In this context, I especially notice the role of the concept of property. For the concept of property (dominium) has assimilated with the concept of rights (ius), systematised them to form the substantive law, and founded them on the theory of justice (iustitia). In this paper, after tracing the history of the concept of rights, I would like to explore that mechanism in the linkage between property, rights and justice, and to revalue the significance of the concept of property as dominium.

II. Iustitia and Ius in Roman Law

The origin of the concept of rights would be traced back to the multivocal Latin word "ius". In Roman law the term ius was used in different ways: 1) whatever is equitable and good, 2) what is useful to all or to the majority in any state, 3) the place where justice is administered (Paulus, *Digesta* I.i.11; *Lex XII tabularum* I.1, III.2, III.3, VI.5a, 5b; Gaius, *Institutiones* II.31), and 4) incorporeal things such as an inheritance (hereditas), a usufruct (ususfructus), obligations contracted (obligationes contractae), servitudes which belong to urban and rustic estates (iura [servitutes] praediorum urbanorum et rusticorum) (Gaius, *Institutiones* II.14, 31; Gaius, *Digesta* VIII.ii.2; *Institutiones* II.3 pr.–2), a credit (ius crediti)(Callistratus, *Digesta* IV.xiii), a pledge (ius pignoris)(Africanus, *Digesta* XX.iv.9) and an action (ius nominis)(Scaevola, *Digesta* XX.iv.19). It was believed

1 For example, we recognise the right to goodwill, to trademarks and trade names, the right to privacy, the right to receive sunlight, air rights and others. Moreover, other rights are being claimed, such as the right to publicity, the right to residence (habitation), the right to abortion or the right of an unborn baby, the right to development, environmental rights, and even the rights of animals, the rights of nature, etc.

2 Cf. Waldron (1989), p. 503.

possible for a man to have or transfer ius as an incorporeal thing (*Digesta* IV.ii.13, XX.iv.19), but there was also ius attributed to a man as his duty or liability, which should be understood as the objectively just relationship between the parties (Gaius, *Institutiones* II.14).

The most important feature of the Roman ius, however, was that it maintained a direct relationship to the concept of justice (iustitia): ius was defined as the art of good (bonum) and equity (aequum)(Ulpianus, *Digesta* I.i.1 pr., Paulus, *Digesta* I.i.11) and the precepts of ius were to live honestly, to not injure others and to give to everyone his due (suum cuique tribuere)(Ulpianus, *Digesta* I.i.10.1), while the iustitia was defined as the constant and perpetual desire to give to everyone his due (constans et perpetua voluntas ius suum cuique tribuendi)(Ulpianus, *Digesta* I.i.10 pr., *Institutiones* I.1 pr.). However, the meaning of "his due"(suum) appears to have remained obscure in Roman law.

III. Assimilation and Interaction between Ius and Dominium

On the other hand, the Roman concept of "dominium", which implied an actual control over corporeal things, was distinct from the concept of ius: for instance, ius was attributed to a usufructuary (Gaius,*Digesta* XXXIX.ii.19), wheras a "dominus"(proprietor) of a land, where someone had a usufruct, had a "proprietas"(property), but he did not have any "ius" (Ulpianus, *Digesta* VII.vi.5). This fact also implied that dominium was not related to iustitia and that it was not recognized as suum.

Little by little, however, the concepts of ius and dominium fused,[3] in the process of which, I believe, there were two aspects of interaction between dominium and ius: on the one hand, as the notion of ius infiltrated into that of dominium, dominium came to be conceived as a legal relationship between parties; on the other, dominium affected the conception of ius in such a way that also ius had some actual or real effects against others.

The notion of dominium gradually gained legitimacy, and by the Middle Ages it was understood as a kind of ius (Irnerius, c.1055–c.1130) and was included in the classification of "ius in re", a concept newly created by the Glossators. Meanwhile, the concept of ius came to be conceived in an active sense. For example, Azo (c.1150–c.1230) defined ius suum as a claim (meritum) when there happened to be a delict or a breach of contract, and by the late thirteenth century a more active notion of "ius ad rem" was formed, thus enabling a promisee to demand and execute the thing promised from a promisor(Jacques de Révigny, c.1210–1296). Through the medium of dominium which was defined as a power (patestas) of a man (Thomas Aquinas, 1225/26–1274), ius was viewed as a potestas (William of Ockham, c. 1285–1349/50) or, more positively, as a faculty (facultas) of a man, by which means ius came to be distinguished from law (lex) but assimilated with liberty (libertas)(Jean de Gerson, 1363–1429).

3 On this process, which is thought to have begun in the later Roman Empire, see Tuck (1979), pp. 11 ff.

This assimilation was promoted through the extension of the concept of dominium, including the development of a contrast between dominium directum and dominium utile (Accursius, 1182–c.1260). This led to the view that dominium, in a broad sense, contained all iura, including ususfructus and obligatio (Bartolus de Saxoferrato, 1314–1357) or that dominium was equivalent to ius (Conrad Summenhart, 1465–1511)[4]. Nevertheless, the controversy about the relationship between dominium and ius continued until the early seventeenth century. For instance, ususfructus, which was one of iura in re, was not included by Bartolus in dominium utile, but rather by Luis de Molina (1536–1600).[5]

IV. Construction of the Substantive Law as a System of Rights

As long as iura were only classified into ius in re and ius ad rem, which were still dependent on the existence of corresponding legal relief (actio), they could not be described as having been constructed into a system of rights. Hugo Grotius (1583–1645) appears to be the person who first constructed a substantive law as a system of rights around dominium.

Firstly, in order to construct a substantive law as a system of rights independent of a procedural law, it had to be demonstrated that violations of other's rights generated instantly an obligation of the violator to provide restitution, whether or not there preexisted legal procedures, and whether or not the sufferer claimed compensation. Grotius explained this point by using the example of dominium: an obligation was imposed on a possessor without title of another person's property to return that property to its proprietor whether or not the possessor had known that the property was not his property, and whether or not the proprietor claimed a restoration against the possessor. The source of this obligation was explained as a sort of agreement (quasi societas) concluded among proprietors when property had been introduced (Grotius, 1625, II.x.1).[6]

Secondly, there must be a nucleus around which various kinds of rights are consistently integrated to form a system of substantive rights. In this respect, dominium played a significant role: In the theory of Grotius, the legal procedures which stood side by side to preserve the possessive order in Roman law came to be integrated into the system of dominium. For example, 1) the Actio Publiciana in Roman law,[7] which was admitted by Bartolus (n.3 ad *Digesta* XXI.ii.39.1) as "quasi-dominium", was no longer accepted by Grotius. 2) The distinction between usucapation (usucapio), prescriptions of long term (praescriptio longi temporis), prescriptions of the longest term (praescriptio longissimi temporis) and the limitation of the term of an action disappeared.

4 Cf. Coing (1953), pp. 349 ff.; Feenstra (1978), p. 216 ff.

5 Cf. Feenstra (1978), pp. 221 ff.

6 This explanation, however, was based on the practical judgement that if there were no obligation imposed on that possessor, property would be too fragile and the cost of its custody too high (Grotius, 1625, II.x.1).

7 This action enabled a person who acquired a thing from a non-owner but by a proper title to demand a restoration against a possessor who did not have a more proper title than the acquisitor (*Digesta*, VI.ii; Gaius, *Institutiones*, IV.36).

Instead, they were arranged in prescriptions causing a substantive transfer of property to a possessor on the presumption that the proprietor renounced his property (Grotius, 1625, II.iv.3–8; id., 1631, II.vii, III.xlvi.2). 3) Furthermore,the interdicts of possession (interdictum possessionis) in Roman law came to be recognised as a subordinate means for protecting property: on the one hand, a possession of a thing brought about the presumption in favor of a possessor that he had a proper title to that thing; on the other, a moderate degree of self-help was permitted to a true proprietor who did not have possession of the thing (Grotius, 1631, II.ii.6–7, II.iii.3-4). Accordingly the right of possession was no longer regarded as a right in the proper and strict sense (Grotius, 1625, I.i.5).

Thirdly, according to Grotius, real rights other than ownership were conceived to be the lesser part of omnipotent ownership (for example, the right of pledge, which had not been previously identified as dominium, was included in dominium: Grotius, 1625, I.i.5; id., 1631, II), while personal rights also came to be connected to dominium. Personal rights were to be engendered by a promise or by an imbalance. The binding force of a promise, on the one hand, was thought to rest ultimately on the self-evident fact that anyone could transfer dominium. The possibility of transferring one's dominium was logically explained by the fact that a right to transfer one's dominium was included in the concept of dominium. Therefore, one's promise to give something was illustrated as a transfer of the right to transfer dominium of the thing, and a promise to do something was illustrated as a transfer of a part of one's liberty to another on the premise that everyone had a right to one's own actions (liberty) just as to one's things (Grotius, 1625, II.vi.2, II.xi.4.1, II.xi.1.3; id., 1631, III.i.8,12–13). In this way, Grotius annexed the law of contract to the law of property.[8] An imbalance, however, took two forms – the restitution of unjust profits, the grounds, character and contents for which restitution were modeled on a claim in terms of dominium (Grotius, 1631, III.xxx, xlviii, lii), and a delict, where the basis for claiming compensation for damages was explained as a violation of the right in the strict sense on the same principle as applied to the violation of dominium (Grotius, 1625, II.xvii.1–2).

Fourthly, just like real rights, personal rights were also conceded to have an effect on third parties. For example, there could be violations of the personal rights by the third parties, and a sale could not break a previous lease (Grotius, 1631, III.xx.22, III.xix.3,16, III.xv.7). This seems to be the natural consequences of the Grotian theory of rights, where personal rights were related to dominium and were conceived to exist as dominium did.

V. The Linkage of Property, Rights and Justice

We should, then, consider theoretically how the system of rights was formed through the concept of dominium and which element of dominium led to the general concept of rights.

8 Cf. Wieacker (1973), pp. 227 ff.

The notion of personality appears as the key element linking dominium and ius. Grotius refined the concept of dominium and clarified it by stating that the essence of dominium was "proprium" (Grotius, 1604, ch. 12; id., 1631, II.i.60, II.iii.9, II.xxxiii.1), that is, the exclusive appropriation of a thing to someone, which is distinct from the power to exercise one's dominium. This concept of proprium could be used to demonstrate that a person without legal capacity to exercise dominium could nevertheless have dominium (Grotius, 1625, II.iii.6, II.v.2), and that every individual could become the equal subject of dominium. In other words, every individual could have legal personality regardless of one's legitimacy, nationality, earthly and ecclesiastical status, capacity, age, etc., while the father's power over his children, wife and others (ius patriae potestatis in Roman law) was not a constraint on their legal personality but rather the power to care for them and guard their interests (Grotius, 1631, I.iii.8, I.iv.2–5, I.vi.3, I.xii.7–8, I.xiii.2–3, I.xiv.6–7, I.xv.1).

The relationship between property and personality was often illustrated by thinkers like John Locke (1632-1704) or Rudolf von Jhering (1818–1892) in such a way that one's personality could be inscribed on the goods through one's labour, so that the goods became a person's property as an extension of that person's personality.[9] Likewise, G. W. Friedrich Hegel (1770–1831) attempted to prove that a thing became a person's property when the person put his will into it.[10] However, before resorting to such media of labour or will, it is necessary to inquire how a personality itself can be ascertained. In this respect, we could recognise that everyone can ascertain his personality by reflecting on another person's attitudes toward him in the light of his talent, disposition, status, occupation, reputation, property and other things which are recognised to be exclusively assigned to him.[11] In these cicumstances, property could have played an indispensable role in sustaining every person's personality irrespective of his status in the societies.

Meanwhile, the conception of ius also came to be connected to the personality of a person. For instance, Grotius distinguished three meanings of ius: 1) what is not unjust (quod injustum non est), 2) a moral quality of a person (qualitas moralis personae), and 3) a rule of moral actions imposing obligation to do what was right (regula actuum moralium obligans ad id quod rectum est), which has the same force as statute (lex). Among them, the second has a subjective meaning attached to a person. When this moral quality was perfect, it was called faculty (facultas); when not so perfect, it was called aptitude (aptitudo)(Grotius, 1625, I.i.4–9).

According to Grotius, the faculty (called "suum" by jurists) should be called "ius in the proper or strict sense", which included power (potestas), either that exercised over oneself (libertas), or that exercised over others, such as that of the father (patria potestas) and a slave master, dominium and contractual rights. This passage is said to be the proper birthplace of the concept of subjective rights.[12] The faculty was, then, thought to be the object of expletive justice (iustitia

9 Locke (1690), II.ii.6, II.v.26, 44; Jhering (1872).

10 Hegel (1821), §§ 44, 46, pp. 57 ff.; cf. Carter (1989), pp. 89 ff.

11 Attali (1988) says that a person is none other than what he has.

12 Dubischar (1961), pp. 61 f.

expletrix), which was formulated as "justice in the proper and strict sense" (Grotius, 1625, I.i.8.1). Grotius pointed out that this was called contractual justice by Aristotle, with too narrow a use of the term, for though the possessor of another's property should return it, that did not result from a contract; nevertheless the act fell within the purview of expletive justice. Here we can see that expletive justice is modeled on the recovery of property. This type of justice is different from the Aristotelian corrective justice, which was based on the objective equalisation of gain and loss between parties, and also from Thomistic commutative justice (iustitia commutativa), which included not only sanctions to recover the violated property itself but also sanctions against the maliciousness of actors.

Another type of moral quality, aptitude, was described as worthiness (dignitas). Aptitude was associated with the virtues (virtutes) providing others with utility (utilitas), such as a government's generosity (liberalitas), compassion (misericordia) and providence (providentia). Aptitude was connected with attributive justice (iustitia attributrix), which corresponded to Aristotle's distributive justice.[13]

Grotius noted that these two kinds of justice should not be confused (Grotius, 1625, I.i.8.3), and further, he seems to have put more stress on expletive justice than on attributive justice. For instance, expletive justice was described as "justice in the proper and strict sense." Another example is found in the explanation of the right of necessity (ius necessitatis), which, Grotius claimed, was founded not upon the rules of charity (caritas), that is, not upon attributive justice but upon the rule which was immanent in the property of goods, and according to which all goods have been divided among proprietors reserving the right of necessity as the primitive right (ius primitivi)(Grotius, 1625, II.ii.6.4). Thus the right of necessity was not a restriction on property but a natural consequence within the bounds of expletive justice.

What, then, is the criterion for distinguishing between these two types of justice? It seems to me that expletive justice applies to correcting the deviation from appropriation of a thing, whether corporeal or incorporeal, to a person. The point is this correction should be made regardless of a person's character. It is, therefore, irrelevant that the person be rich or poor, talented or incompetent, virtuous or wicked. On the other hand, attributive justice should apply to an attribution of both advantages and disadvantages to a person in accordance with that person's character. In other words, it is relevant that the person be rich or poor, handicapped, talented, virtuous, a hard worker, a ne'er-do-well, a criminal, etc. Both the the correction according to expletive justice and the attribution

13 However, Aristotle's distinction between corrective justice, which applied an arithmetical proportion to private property, and distributive justice, which applied a geometrical proportion to public property, was not identical to the Grotian distinction between expletive justice and attributive justice. For Grotius criticises Aristotle's argument and demonstrates that 1) a partnership agreement was carried out not according to an arithmetical proportion but according to a proportion based on comparison; 2) if only one person could be found fit for a public position, the award would be made to him not according to a geometrical proportion but according to a simple proportion; 3) if a man wished to give a legacy from his property, he should make his bequest in accordance with attributive justice; and 4) when the state repaid from public funds what a citizen had advanced for the public interest, it should be discharged by expletive justice (Grotius, 1625, I.i.8).

according to attributive justice seem to fit with the traditional concept of "suum," which forms the nucleus of the concepts of ius and iustitia.

The next question is the relationship between these two principles. On the one hand, expletive justice, which is modeled on the recovery of property, assures the personality of every individual by treating everyone as an equal subject independently of the status or any other character. However, for that very reason, the characters of each subject must be taken into consideration according to attributive justice so as to maintain the proposition in expletive justice that every individual is an equal subject.

In this context, attributive justice might be regarded as a complementary and subsidiary principle to expletive justice. But on the other hand, attributive justice may affect the realisation of expletive justice. For example, progressive taxation might cause another type of inequality, while, on the contrary, expletive justice may infringe on the field of the attributive justice as in the case when earning differentials necessarily expand as a natural consequence of the free competition. Then, these two principles should be understood to be interrelated, the one playing off against the other. Therefore, in any case, they will make sense only as a significant pair that fits within the respect for every individual's personality, that is, within the individualism.

VI. The Diminishing Linkage between Property, Rights and Justice

However, as the range of alleged rights have expanded, the linkage between property, rights and justice appears to have weakened. In this respect, Locke's theory, by which he changed the concept of property, might prove vital. Locke admitted that "every Man has a 'property' in his own 'person'. This no Body has any Right to but himself"(Locke, 1690, II.v.27), and that "though the things of Nature are given in common, yet Man (by being Master of himself, and 'Proprietor of his own Person', and the Actions or Labour of it) had still in himself 'the great Foundation of Property'"(ibid., II.v.44). The range of property thus extended into one's own person, and this property in one's own person was transformed into the very foundation of property in general. Accordingly, the range of rights in the state of nature extended from "life, health, liberty" to "possession"(ibid., II.ii.6). This concept of property, in a sense, stands in contrast to the Grotian concept of property, in which the right to life, body or liberty (Grotius, 1625, I.ii.1.5) was based on expletive justice that was modeled upon the recovery on the grounds of property of an external thing (Grotius, 1625, II.xvii; id., 1630, III.xxxii–xxxvii).

The concept of property in one's own person seems to have indeed promoted the development of rights which, in association with humanistic thought, have come to be called human rights.[14] But the Lockean concept of property was so comprehensive that in his theory the distinction between the rights based on expletive justice and that based on attributive justice appears

14 On the relationship between the concept of natural rights and the content of human rights, see Jones (1994), pp. 78 ff.

less clear than in Grotian theory. For example, the right to life, health and liberty, which is the most fundamental of the Lockean concept of property, can be understood not only as the right not to be murdered or injured but also as the right to be safeguarded from any injury by government or the right to social security.[15] This ambiguity in the relationship between rights and justice seems to have made the structure of substantive law as a system of rights rather confusing. How are the various kinds of rights related to each other, and what is the most fundamental right among them?

In these circumstances, the significance of property not in one's own person but as the exclusive appropriation of an external thing to a person should be revalued. I do not mean to say that property in an external thing should be placed in a higher rank than property in one's own person. I approve of putting a higher value on the rights to life and liberty of an individual than on property in a thing, as the former are prerequisite to enjoying the latter and accordingly the latter should be more widely restricted in the interest of public welfare than the former. However, it seems improper to view these rights as constituting *a hierarchy*, since they do not exist independently, but instead are intricately interrelated.

It would be meaningless to protect the right to life wholly independent of the property in a thing and vice versa. Therefore, these rights should be understood to constitute an *organised system*. In such a system of rights, the role of property as the exclusive appropriation of an external thing to a person should not be overlooked: in a society where everyone's property in a thing is to be protected promptly without exception against violation, and at the same time, the limits of that property are to be exactly realised by the members of the society, then the right to life and liberty would be naturally much more protected, modelled on that property. On the contrary, where the property is not treated in this way, it is doubtful that the rights to life and liberty can be well guaranteed. In this sense, as long as property in a thing sustains the personality of every equal subject and effectuates the rights to life and liberty, it might deserve of being called *a natural* right.

References

Attali, Jacques (1988), *Au propre et au figuré – Une histoire de la Propriété*, Librairie Arthème Fayard.

Carter, Alan (1989), *The Philosophical Foundations of Property Rights*, Harvester Wheatsheaf.

Coing, Helmut (1959), "Zur Geschichte des Begriffs 'subjektives Recht'", in: *Das subjektive Recht und der Rechtsschutz der Persönlichkeit*, hrsg. von Coing, Helmut et al., Alfred Metzner Verlag.

– (1953), "Zur Eigentumslehre des Bartolus", *Savignys Zeitschrift* (Romanistische Abteilung) 70, pp. 349 ff.

Dabin, Jean (1954), *Droit subjectif*, Paris, Daroz.

Dubishar, Roland (1961), *Über die Grundlagen der schulsystematischen Zweiteilung der Rechte in sogenannte absolute und relative*, Ein dogmengeschichtlicher Beitrag zur Lehre vom subjektiven Privatrecht, Dissertation, Tübingen.

15 Cf. Jones (1994), pp. 83 ff.

Feenstra, Robert (1978), "Der Eigentumsbegriff bei Hugo Grotius im Licht einiger mittelalterlicher und spätscholastischer Quellen", in: *Festschrift für Franz Wieacker zum 70. Geburtstag*, hrsg. von Behrends, O. et al., Vandenhoeck & Ruprecht, pp. 209 ff.

Finnis, John (1980), *Natural Law and Natural Rights*, Oxford University Press.

Grotius, Hugo (1604), *De iure praedae commentarius*. Commentary on the Law of Prize and Booty, the translation by Williams, G. L., 1964.

– (1625), *De iure belli ac pacis libri tres*, ed. by Molhuysen, P. C., 1919.

– (1631), *Inleidinge tot de Hollandsche Rechtsgeleerdheid*.The Jurisprudence of Holland, the translation by Lee, R. W., 1926.

Hegel, Georg Wilhelm Friedrich (1821), *Grundlinien der Philosophie des Rechts*, hrsg. von Hoffmeister, J., 4. Aufl., Felix Meiner, 1955.

Jhering, Rudolf von (1872), *Der Kampf ums Recht*, 7. Aufl., Klostermann, 1989.

Jones, Peter (1994), *Rights*, Macmillan.

Locke, John (1690), *Two Treatises of Government*, ed. by Laslett, P., Cambridge University Press, 1960.

Pufendorf, Samuel (1672), *De jure naturae et gentium libri octo*, Lund, 1688, Amsterdam, ed. by Mascovius, G., Frankfurt und Leipzig, 1759.

Tuck, Richard (1979), *Natural Rights Theories: Their Origin and Development*, Cambridge University Press.

Waldron, Jeremy (1989), "Rights in Conflict", *Ethics* 99, pp. 503 ff.

Wieacker, Franz (1973), "Contractus und Obligatio im Naturrecht zwischen Spätscholastik und Aufklärung", in: Atti, *Per la storia del pensiero guiridico moderno*, I, Milano.

Willoweit, Dietmar (1974), "Dominium und Proprietas", in: *Historisches Jahrbuch* 94, S. 131 ff.

Robert Alexy, Kiel

Discourse Theory and Human Rights*

In present, as well as in past and probably future discussions about human rights as generally in political philosophy one can distinguish four basic positions: with reference to historical models they may be called "Aristotelian", "Hobbesian", "Kantian", and "Nietzschean" (Alexy 1992b, 233 f.). I will attempt here to defend the Kantian conception.

I. The Kantian Position

There are quite a few versions of the Kantian position. What they all share are the principles of universality and autonomy. The principle of the universality of human rights says that all human beings have certain rights. Instead of human beings, one can also refer to all persons, all rational beings or something similar (cf. Nino 1991, 34 ff.). This does not have to be settled here. The principle of autonomy works in two directions. It refers to private as well as to public autonomy. The essence of private autonomy is the individual choice and realization of a personal conception of the good. Public autonomy is defined by a collective choice and realization of a political conception of the right and the good. In public autonomy, human rights and democracy are necessarily connected. To render possible and protect both forms of autonomy is the primary function of the human rights in the Kantian conception. Private as well as public autonomy can be fully unfolded only in a democratic constitutional state, in which human rights have taken on the character of basic rights. If below we should talk about "basic rights" instead of "human rights", it is this connection that is being referred to.[1]

The linking of the ideas of universality and autonomy leads to a liberal political theory. The Kantian conception of human rights is a liberal conception. The liberal conception of human rights is the central political idea of the Enlightenment and the civil revolutions. To this day it is the basis of all constitutions of Western character. Thus it is one of the most successful political ideas so far. Still, there has been dispute about the liberal conception of human rights from the very beginning, and criticism is increasing rather than decreasing.

* The author's thanks are due to Dr. Susanne Gaschke and Kirsten Bock for translating this article into English.

1 One has to distinguish between absolute and relative human rights. Absolute human rights are rights everyone has against everyone else. The right to life is one example. Relative human rights are rights that every member of every legal community has in her respective legal community. The right to vote can be named as an example. Such absolute as well as relative human rights are natural or moral rights. A constitution can only be justified if it contains the absolute and relative human rights as basic rights. If such a constitution is valid as positive law, the human rights have become positive as basic rights. The catalogue of basic rights contained in a constitution can include further basic rights besides the human rights.

The old objections of formalism, emptiness, abstractness, and absence of historical and cultural connections are repeated and sharpened by the communitarian camp. Not only the human rights' contents, also the category of the rights as such are being called into question (MacIntyre 1991, 96 ff.). Criticism turns on the aspect of autonomy as well as on the aspect of universality. Autonomy is claimed to uproot the individual from concrete structures, to destroy naturally grown communities, and to promote the world's final destruction by unleashing greed for pleasure and possession. All is said to become karstic: the souls, the communities, and nature herself. Against the universality of human rights, communitarians argue that these rights in truth are only elements of a certain, the Western, culture, and therefore only have a relative or particular validity. Any claim to universal validity is de-masked as imperialism dressed up as humanity.

The Kantian, and consequently the liberal conception of human rights have to counter these and many other objections. The basis of such a defence must be the substantiation or justification of the Kantian conception itself. I would like to present here the basic features of a certain version of such a justification: those of discourse theory. By employing this justification many objections are removed immediately, others can be invalidated on its basis.

Any justification of human rights must rest on something. Nearly everything possibly relevant has been tried out. One can name eight examples: references to religious revelation, human nature, undeniable evidence, great traditions, existential decisions, individual interests, collective goods and far-reaching factual consensus. The basis for discourse-theoretical justifications is formed by the rules of practical discourse. Any justification is only as good as the premises by which it is supported. The discourse-theoretical justification of human rights consequently has to face two tasks: On the first level it must substantiate the rules of practical discourse in order to justify, on a second level, the human rights on these grounds. I shall begin with the first level.

II. The Justification of Discourse Rules

1. Basic Ideas of Discourse Theory

Discourse theory is a procedural theory of practical correctness. According to it, a norm is correct and therefore valid, if it is or might be the result of a certain procedure, that of rational practical discourse (Alexy 1981, 178). A discourse is a procedure of argumentation. This is what distinguishes discourse theories from procedural theories belonging to the Hobbesian tradition, which refer to procedures of negotiation and decision making (cf. Buchanan 1975, 6 ff., 28 ff.; Gauthier 1986, 113 ff.). A practical discourse is rational to the degree to which conditions of rational practical argumentation are realized in it.

The conditions of rational practical argumentation can be summed up in a system[2] of discourse rules[3]. Some of these rules formulate general demands of

2 A system of 28 discourse rules is to be found in Alexy 1989, 187 ff.

3 The concept of the discourse rule is here understood to include rules as well as principles in the sense of the general theory of norms (cf. Alexy 1992a, 166).

rationality which are also valid independently of discourse theory. They include freedom from contradictions, universalisability in the sense of a consistent use of the predicates employed, linguistic-conceptual clearness, empirical truth, consideration of consequences, and weighing. All those rules are also valid for monologues. We shall only look at specific discourse rules here. Those have a non-monological character. Their aim is the impartiality of the discourse. This aim is to be realized by securing the freedom and equality of the argumentation. The most important rules are:

1. Everyone who can speak may take part in discourse.
2. (a) Everyone may question any assertion.
   (b) Everyone may introduce any assertion into the discourse.
   (c) Everyone may express his or her attitudes, wishes, and needs.
3. No speaker may be prevented from exercising the rights laid down in (1) and (2) by any kind of coercion internal or external to the discourse. (Alexy 1989, 193)

On the level of argumentation these rules express the liberal ideas of universality and autonomy. If they are valid, that is, if everyone can decide freely and equally about what she is willing to accept, the following condition of universal agreement or consent is necessarily valid:

UA: A norm can only find universal agreement in a discourse if the consequences of its general observance for the satisfaction of everyone's interest can be accepted by all.

It is a central assumption of discourse theory that consent in the discourse can firstly depend on arguments and that, secondly, there is a necessary connection between universal consent or agreement under ideal conditions and the concepts of correctness and moral validity (Alexy 1988, 54 ff.; Nino 1991, 57 f.). This connection can be formulated as follows:

Correct and therefore valid are exactly those norms that in an ideal discourse would be judged correct by everyone.

With some softenings, this becomes Habermas' abstract discourse principle:

> "D: Valid are exactly those action norms to which all those possibly affected could agree as participants in rational discourses." (Habermas 1992, 138)

At least in its basic intention this is congruent with Kant's principle of the legislative power:

> "Therefore only the concurring and united will of all, insofar as each decides the same thing for all and all for each, and so only the general united will of the people, can be legislative." (Kant 1991a, 125)

2. An Argument Composed of Three Components

The idea of discourse isn't neutral. It includes universality and the autonomy of argumentation as well as the conception of impartiality which rests upon them.

The idea of discourse is therefore an essentially liberal idea. Therefore, the problems of substantiating a liberal position begin on the level of discourse.

There are authors like Nino who explicitly point out the non-neutrality of moral discourses (Nino 1991, 114) and still regard the justification of its rules as impossible as well as superfluous. A justification or substantiation is claimed to be impossible because morality could not be justified by morality. It is said to be unnecessary, because "an explanation of how moral discourse evolves and why individuals tend to take part in it" was sufficient (Nino 1991, 82). Nino is right in stating that morality cannot be justified by morality, because such a justification would necessarily become circular. He is wrong, however, in declaring evolutionary explanations – as interesting and important as they may be – the only alternative. In doing so, he underestimates the possibilities of transcendental arguments. A contrary view is held by Habermas. He considers a weak transcendental argument both necessary and sufficient. He calls it "weak", because it does not offer an infallible final substantiation but only a "fallible reconstruction of the normative content to be found in factually unavoidable preconditions for argumentation" (Habermas 1991, 195). As a transcendental argument which is weak in this sense he claims it to be strong enough "to substantiate the universal claim to validity obligatory for all subjects able to speak and act, which is raised by a procedurally formulated principle of morality" (Habermas 1991, 194). This is an overestimation of the power transcendental arguments have in practical philosophy.

My thesis is that the universal validity of discourse rules can only be substantiated by one – but at least there is one – argument, which is composed of three widely different parts. The first part consists of a transcendental argument which forms the nucleus of the whole argument and essentially defines its universalist character. This transcendental argument is not only weak, as in Habermas, because of its fallible character, but also because of its limited validity. In order to strengthen that, a second part of the argument referring to the maximization of individual utility or advantage must be added. The Kantian and the Hobbesian line are joined in this way in the justification of discourse rules. In order to make this connection successful, an empirical premise about a general human interest in correctness is necessary as a third part. Only by such a premise can those who are merely interested in maximizing their advantage be bound sufficiently to the result of the transcendental argument with which I shall start now.

a) The Transcendental Basis

What a transcendental argument is, is unclear and contested (cf. Chisholm 1978, 19 ff.; Paulson 1990, 171 ff.). Here, we shall call arguments "transcendental" which consist of at least two premises with the following structure: The first premise identifies the argument's starting point, which consists of things like perceptions, thoughts, or speech acts, and claims that this starting point is necessary in some sense. The second premise then says that some categories or rules are necessary if the matter or issue chosen as starting point is meant to be possible. The final conclusion is that these categories or rules are necessarily valid.

In discourse theory, several versions of transcendental arguments have been suggested (cf., e.g., Apel 1973, 358 ff.; Habermas 1983, 93 ff.). What they all have in common is that the practice of argumentation or single speech acts form the argument's starting point. Therefore, the transcendental argument of discourse theory belongs to a certain category of transcendental arguments: the category of transcendental-pragmatic arguments (cf. Dorschel/Kettner/Kuhlmann/Niquet (eds.) 1983). Transcendental-pragmatic arguments are of language-philosophical or linguistic character, and their aim is to point out the necessary presuppositions of the argumentation or of single speech acts. These presuppositions are said to include freedom and equality of argumentation and consequently the discourse rules mentioned above. If this is correct, it only remains to be shown that, and in which sense, the argumentation or the speech acts which are meant to be the starting point for the justification are necessary. The question is whether such an argument can be successful.

The speech acts of asserting, arguing, and asking are of special importance for the justification of discourse rules. As a starting point for that version of a transcendental-pragmatic argument I intend to suggest here, I choose the speech act of assertion. I shall start with some theses about the necessary preconditions of assertions.

There is hardly any argument about the fact that assertions are only possible if there are any valid rules of asserting at all. This means that assertions necessarily presuppose some kinds of rules. Disagreement focuses on the question which those rules are (cf. Keuth 1983, 334 ff.; Patzig 1986, 213). If the transcendental argument is meant to succeed, these rules must be proved to be necessary preconditions for the possibility of assertions. There must not be any alternatives to them (Albert 1987, 424; Paulson 1990, 174, 176). The problem would be unsolvable if "assertion" could be understood to mean just anything. Then, one could distinguish many concepts of assertion and define each of them by an individual system of rules (cf. Keuth 1983, 334 f.). That this is not possible in an unlimited way can be shown by the fact that assertions are to be distinguished from other speech acts, for example, from expressions of emotional reactions (cf. Patzig 1971, 75) or mere opinions (cf. Keuth 1983, 332). There is a central meaning of the expression "assertion".[4] To this belongs that only such speech acts are assertions, which raise a claim to truth or correctness.[5] My first thesis is therefore:

(1) Anyone who asserts something raises a claim to truth or correctness.

4 This is congruent with Kuhlmann's thesis "that there is a central area of essential rules of argumentation and assertion" (Kuhlmann 1985, 373).

5 Cf. Davidson 1984, 268: "Someone who makes an assertion represents himself as believing what he says, and perhaps as being justified in his belief. And since we want our beliefs to be true, it seems right ... that when someone makes an assertion, he represents himself as intending to say what is true."

6 Fusfield has suggested that the reference to performative contradictions could not really be a justification of discourse rules (Fusfield 1989, 77 ff.). It is correct that the reference to a

This thesis is supported by the circumstance that its denial results in a performative contradiction.[6] A performative contradiction is provoked by someone who, while carrying out a speech act, presupposes, claims, or implies something which contradicts the contents of that same speech act. Take the following assertion:

(1') I assert that it rains, and I emphasize at the same time that this is wrong.

This assertion includes a performative contradiction, because part of what has been said ("I emphasize at the same time that this is wrong") contradicts what is necessarily being presupposed in the actual making of the assertion: a claim to truth or correctness.[7]

My second thesis links the claim to truth or correctness necessarily connected with assertions to the claim to justifiability. It says:

(2) The claim to truth or correctness implies a claim to justifiability.

Who claims that her assertion is true or correct, and at the same time says that there are absolutely no reasons for what she asserts, does perhaps not even make a genuine assertion. At least it is necessarily flawed (Alexy 1989, 127 ff.). This mistake is easily avoided, however, because in order to raise a claim to justifiability one must not refer to good but just to any reasons. Thus, a reference to evidence, revelations, and authorities is sufficient. Decisive is whether reasons make an appearance at all.

That assertions raise a claim to justifiability does not mean that anyone at any time must justify every assertion to everyone. Quite often, the addressee of an assertion already disapproves of the assertion as such and under no circumstances wants to be bothered with reasons for it. On the other hand someone who has made an assertion might have sound reasons for denying a substantiation; he might, for example, just not have time for it. If the addressee of an assertion, however, asks "why?" and demands a justification, and the person who has made the assertion does not have sound reasons for denying it, then the claim to justifiability implies an obligation to justify. My third thesis is therefore:

performative contradiction is no substantiation of a sentence by means of another, independent sentence, because a performative contradiction can only come into existence if the discourse rule in support of which it is mentioned is already valid. Performative contradictions are therefore only a means of *showing* that discourse rules are valid. They serve as an explication of what is considered a common presupposition. As any other explication it can, of course, be inadequate, and the thesis supported by it, wrong.

7 There are contexts in which one might doubt whether (1') actually does include a contradiction and even such contexts in which it certainly does not. There is, for example, certainly no contradiction in (1'), if A, after uttering (1') as an assertion addressed to B (thus committing a performative contradiction) repeats (1') – astonished, startled, or amused – to himself in a way of self-description. But then the "I assert" in (1') is no longer employed for the actual *making* of an assertion. Only this case is of interest here. A contradiction is doubtful, if someone wants to use the term "to assert" in the sense of "to say" and insists that this was the actual meaning of "asserting". Concerning this case we can state that the person in question has either not understood our meaning of "to assert" or intends a change of our language usage. No emphasis is needed that there are contexts in which no one would be accused of the contradiction in (1'). Anyone can utter (1') as a joke, and all could like her the better for it. But as a joke (1') can only be employed because it contains a contradiction.

(3) The claim to justifiability implies a prima facie obligation to justify what one has asserted, if asked to do so.

Insofar, the utterance of an assertion is the entry into the domain of argumentation.

Whoever justifies anything at least pretends to accept the other as an equal partner, at least as far as the justification is concerned. This can be shown by the flaws of an utterance like:

(4.1) Personally, I do not consider the reason R, which I name in support of my assertion, a good reason; but considering your low intelligence you should accept it as such.

This utterance contradicts the postulation of equality in the argumentation. A reason for an assertion is only a good reason if it can be a good reason for everyone. Furthermore, everyone who justifies something does at least pretend neither to employ force nor to rely upon force employed by others – at least as far as the justification is concerned. This can be shown by an example like the sentence:

(4.2) If my reasons do not convince you, you are fired,

which is no substantiation. It contradicts the postulation of freedom from force in the argumentation. Finally, someone who makes an assertion claims to be able to defend it not only against its respective addressee, but against everyone. Therefore, utterances like the following are wrong:

(4.3) If we exclude A, B, and C from our discussion and try to forget their objections, we will be able to convince ourselves that the reason R I have named is a good reason.[8]

Such utterances contradict the postulation of the universality of argumentation. My fourth thesis is therefore:

(4) Whoever gives justifying reasons for something raises claims to equality, freedom from force, and universality, at least as far as the justification is concerned.

To these claims correspond the specific discourse rules mentioned above, which guarantee everyone's right to take part in discourses, as well as grant freedom and equality in discourses. If my argumentation is correct, it has substantiated exactly those discourse rules which express the liberal ideas of autonomy and universality.

One could object that my argument wasn't anything but a definitory trick. The way from the concept of assertion to the specific discourse rules (with stops at the claim to correctness, the claim to justifiability and the prima facie obligation to justify) could be seen as a chain of definitions which did not necessarily have to take on this very form. One might say that I was merely introducing a strong concept of assertion which already implied the discourse rules. It might be regarded as easily possible to employ a weaker concept for which this need not

8 For a similar example cf. Habermas 1983, 101.

be true. One can meet this objection by showing that assertions in the sense explicated here are necessary in some way relevant for the transcendental argument. That is the content of the transcendental argument's first premise.[9]

Assertions, and the arguments connected with them would not be necessary at all if one could do without them at will. According to Apel and Habermas, a consequent refusal of argumentation is supposed to have fatal consequences. With reference to "clinical psychopathology" Apel talks about the loss of "the possibility of self-understanding and self-identification", even about "self-destruction" (Apel 1973, 414), and Habermas about "schizophrenia and suicide" (Habermas 1983, 112). These are empirical assumptions one can argue about (Patzig 1986, 213). Here, a weaker thesis shall be sufficient. It says that it is necessary in the following sense to undertake assertions and justifications:

(5) Who never in his life makes an assertion (in the sense defined in (1) – (3)) and never puts forward an argument (in the sense defined in (4)) does not take part in the most general form of life of human beings.

The transcendental argument is radically weakened in this way. It does not establish an argumentative obligation against everyone. In order to take part in the most general form of life of human beings it is not necessary to make assertions and to give reasons to everyone who demands them; it is sufficient to do this at all in some context and to someone. The stronger one does not have to justify what he wants to burden the weaker one with. He can utter a plain order and enforce it by violence, and still take part in the most general human form of life by exchanging assertions and arguments with members of his own group. Habermas may be right in saying that "to drop out of argumentation and action orientated towards understanding leads into an existential impasse" (Habermas 1983, 112). A justification of discourse rules or of principles of discourse ethics, however, does not follow from this. Extremely particularistic communities can be ways out of such "existential impasses". The acceptance of universal principles is not necessary for this.

In spite of the radical weakening of the transcendental argument, there remains a systematically highly significant residue. Apart from extremely unusual circumstances, such as growing up in total isolation, it is probably factually impossible to opt out of the most general form of life of human beings by never making any assertion at all however trivial, never putting forward any kind of justification, and never asking the question "why?", this counterpart to assertions and justifications. In principle, everyone is able to ask, to assert, to argue, and everyone – leaving aside unusual circumstances – has at least some minimal practice with reference to these faculties.

The thesis about the most general form of life of human beings does not disregard the fact that there are very different concrete forms of life. It says,

9 There is a close relationship between both premises of a transcendental argument. The more normative content is taken up in the second premise (in our case: the stronger the implications connected with the concept of assertion are) the more doubtful becomes the necessity of the starting point (in our case: the necessity of such assertions). Reversely, the normative content of the second premise is lowered if the certainty of the starting point's necessity increases (cf. Watt 1975, 43 ff.).

however, that all human forms of life necessarily include universals of argumentation, which can be expressed by the discourse rules. Those universals may be of ever so little impact in reality due to taboos, tutelage, or terror. They would, however, only vanish totally if the members of a form of life wholly and finally lost their ability to make assertions, to name reasons, and to ask “why?”. The discourse rules therefore do not define any particular form of life, but something that is shared by all human forms of life, notwithstanding the fact that it is of vastly different importance in each of them. To this extent, discourse theory tries to find out potentials of rationality in human reality. In this sense it tries to promote enlightenment about human nature and is insofar, but only insofar, connected with the tradition of natural law.[10]

Nothing much is won so far for the justification of discourse rules. From the fact that someone has the ability to solve conflicts of interests by means of argument, and that he has at least a minimal or rudimentary practice with reference to this ability does not follow that he must make use of this ability in every conflict of interests and against everyone possibly concerned. Whoever is stronger might consider it more to her advantage to employ rituals of domination, orders, and force. This would only be different if one could presuppose an overriding interest in all human beings to solve conflicts of interests correctly, that is justly. Experience tells us that such a presupposition would not be justified.

This finding can be described by distinguishing between real and ideal validity. A rule is really valid if and as far as there is an actually existing motive or interest for obeying it. It is ideally valid if it is valid for all to whom a regulative idea like truth or moral correctness is a positive value. Moral correctness has a positive value for exactly those persons who have an interest in it. The transcendental argument can show those who have an interest in correctness which rules they have to follow. Those rules, furthermore, have categorical validity from the ideal point of view of correctness. But no transcendental argument can generate interests or motivations. Under the aspect of reality or facticity the transcendental argument therefore leads only to a hypothetical validity of the discourse rules: It shows what is valid if there is an interest in moral correctness and if therefore the ideal point of view of correctness is taken up. That is a factually limited validity.

b) Maximization of Utility and the Interest in Correctness

At this point the two further components of my argument in favour of the universal validity of discourse rules come into play, the maximization of individual utility and a thesis about human beings being equipped with an interest in correctness. Consider, for example, an élite that is exclusively interested in exploiting a subjected population. With this population, it could only communicate through

10 Some might take this as an opportunity to come up with the classical objection of the is/ought-fallacy against discourse theory. This objection would overlook the fact, however, that the transcendental argument does not consist of deducing norms from facts, but of the reconstruction of a practice, from the point of view of a participant, in which everyone takes part at least rudimentarily.

orders and the enactment of force. That however would not be optimal. Force is expensive, and an order formed by it is unstable and therefore a risk for the élite. A legitimation is cheaper and in the long run also more secure. This is true at least if one must suppose that there is a sufficient number of persons – both in the élite, especially in its younger generation, and in the subjected population – who have an interest in correctness.[11] It is certainly unfounded anthropological optimism to expect an interest in correctness in every human being, or to judge this interest, if it happens to be there, as strong enough to unfold social effectiveness without being hindered by counter-interests. On the other hand, it is also unfounded anthropological pessimism to expect an interest in correctness in no one or in too few, or to consider this interest, where it can be found, as always or usually so weak that it cannot unfold social effectiveness. Tyrants, dictators, and despots have always known this and have usually attempted legitimations by employing arguments. That those arguments were regularly bad and mere propaganda is not important here. Decisive is the fact that they try to use arguments at all. In this way, the maximization of individual utility leads into argumentation and consequently into the field of discourse rules, because a sufficient interest in correctness has to be taken into account.

One could object that this did not suffice for a justification of the discourse rules. Whoever enters into discourses for mere strategic reasons would only have to pretend to recognize the freedom and equality of others as partners in the discourse. He could act according to a well-known recommendation by Machiavelli:

> "Who has best understood to be a fox has fared best! But one has to learn to hide the fox's nature and be a master of hypocrisy and disguise ... A ruler therefore does not have to own all the good qualities we have mentioned in reality; but he must create the impression that he did." (Machiavelli 1978, 72 f.)

This would however only be an objection if one had to regard the generation of a motivation which in content corresponds to the discourse rules as a necessary part of any substantiation of discourse rules. But that is not the case. In the field of speech, too, one can distinguish between a subjective validity, which rests upon motivations, and an objective validity, which refers to external behaviour.[12] The justification attempted here only aims at the objective validity of discourse rules. Instead of an "objective validity" one could also talk about an "institutional validity". The human rights to be justified here belong to the field of law and therefore to the field of legality. That is why the objective validity of discourse rules can carry at least some of the burden of their justification.

Thus the first part of my argument in favour of human rights is closed. As an interim result we can state that the discourse rules can be justified in a triple sense. First of all, they express a competence belonging to the most general form of life of human beings. Secondly, everyone who has an interest in correctness must make use of this competence. And thirdly, to someone who has no interest in correctness the objective observance of the discourse rules is advantageous under the aspect of the maximization of individual utility.

11 Such an interest in correctness is dangerous for tyrants, especially because it may lead to people taking risks they would avoid if they calculated only their personal advantage.

12 This distinction corresponds to Kant's distinction between morality and legality (Kant 1991a, 46).

III. The Justification of Human Rights

So far, we have been concerned with the discourse rules as rules relating to the realm of speech. Human rights are rules or norms for the realm of action. Human rights can only unfold their full power if they are guaranteed by norms of the positive law, meaning that they are transformed into positive law. That is the case, for example, if they are taken up as binding law into the catalogue of basic rights of a constitution. In justifying human rights one can therefore distinguish between a problem of form and a problem of substance. The problem of substance is concerned with the question which human rights are necessary. The problem of form is concerned with the necessity of transforming this content into positive law. I shall start with the problem of form.

1. The Necessity of Law

The transformation of human rights into positive law is only necessary if it is necessary to have positive law at all. There are three problems which lead to a necessity of the law: the problem of knowledge, the problem of enforcement, and the problem of organization. For discourse theory, the problem of knowledge results from the fact that it does not offer a procedure which always allows for just one right answer by means of a finite number of operations (Alexy 1981, 180 ff.). This leads to the necessity of decisions in a legally organized procedure, for example on the basis of the principle of majority. The problem of enforcement comes into existence because the insight into the correctness or legitimacy of a norm is something different from its observance.[13] Consequently, the unanimous judgement of a norm in a discourse as just and therefore correct does not necessarily occasion its observance by all. But if some are allowed to violate a norm without consequences, its observance can no longer be demanded of anyone. From the fact that discourses can generate insights but not always their corresponding motivations follows the necessity of rules backed by force, and with that the necessity of law.[14] The problem of organization is caused by the fact that many moral demands and desirable aims cannot be met by individual acting and spontaneous cooperation alone. Examples are the support of unemployed people or the help for a suffering country. The necessary organization presupposes law (cf. Habermas 1992, 148 f.). To renounce the regulation of community life by law which is substantiated by the arguments of knowledge, enforcement, and organization would mean anarchy. But in anarchy, human rights would not be guaranteed. The necessity of law can therefore not only be substantiated by considerations of utility but also by human rights.

13 This corresponds to Kant's distinction between the "principium diiudicationis" and the "principium executionis": "If the question is: What is morally good or not, it is the principium of dijudication according to which I judge the worthiness and depravity of actions. But if the question is, what moves me to live according to that law? That is the principium of motivation" (Kant 1974, 274).

14 The problem of knowledge and the problem of enforcement basically correspond to Kant's arguments for the transition from the state of nature to the civil state (cf. Kant 1991a, 123 f.).

The necessity of the law's form is, however, only one side of the matter. The other side is formed by necessary demands to its content and structure. That is the main theme of the discourse-theoretical justification of human rights. As human rights do not only refer to private but also to public autonomy, their justification necessarily includes the justification of democracy. The justification of human rights is therefore the justification of the necessity of a legal system with a certain content and a certain structure.

2. Types of Discourse-Theoretical Justifications of Human Rights

There are two types of discourse-theoretical justifications of human rights: a direct and an indirect one. A direct justification takes place if it can be shown that certain rights are valid independently of actually carrying through real discourses, solely on the basis of discourse theory. Such rights are discursively necessary in the narrower sense. Their non-validity is discursively impossible in the narrower sense.[15] We have a merely indirect justification if the decision about human rights is delegated to a factual political process which, however, has to meet certain discourse-theoretically founded demands.[16] If those demands are met the decisions made about human rights in the political process are legitimate and those rights are therefore discourse-theoretically justified.[17] Indirectly justified rights must never be discursively impossible in the narrower sense, but they do not have to be discursively necessary in this sense. It is sufficient that they are merely discursively possible as far as what concerns the discursive modalities in the narrower sense. Here only those rights shall be of interest which can be directly discourse-theoretically justified, that is, only discursively necessary rights in the narrower sense.

The question is how human rights can be directly justified on the basis of discourse theory. A direct conclusion from the discourse rules to human rights cannot be drawn. The discourse rules are merely rules of speech. To observe them means only to treat the other as an equal partner in the discourse. From this it does not automatically follow that the other as such, hence also in the realm of action, has to be treated as a person. From the language-pragmatical recognition a moral or legal recognition does not necessarily follow (Leist 1989, 303 ff.). In order to get from discourse rules to rules of action further premises are therefore required. Those further premises must belong to discourse theory if one attempts a direct discourse-theoretical justification which leads to discursive necessity in the narrower sense.

15 For the concepts of discursive necessity, impossibility, and possibility cf. Alexy 1989, 207 f. Discursive necessity and impossibility in the narrower sense, which is related to the direct discourse-theoretical justification, are to be discriminated from the discursive necessity and impossibility in a broader sense. The latter are to be classed with indirect justification and therefore are to be relativized to persons and time (cf. Alexy 1981, 181 f.; 1988, 60 f.).

16 The distinction between the direct and the indirect justification is largely congruent with Nino's distinction between a priori and a posteriori rights (cf. Nino 1991, 253).

17 Into the realm of the indirect discourse-theoretical justifications falls everything Habermas leaves to the "self-governing practice of the citizens" as a development or concretisation of his system of rights (cf. Habermas 1992, 160 ff.).

Depending on which further premises are chosen, three kinds of direct discourse-theoretical justifications of human rights can be distinguished: the arguments of autonomy, of consensus, and of democracy. Those three justifications do not compete, but complement and strengthen each other. I shall begin with the argument of autonomy.

3. The Argument of Autonomy

The argument of autonomy says that whoever takes part in discourses seriously presupposes the autonomy of his partners, thus excluding the denial of certain human rights.[18] An interesting version of the argument of autonomy can be found in Nino. According to Nino, anyone who seriously takes part in discourses accepts the following "basic norm of moral discourse":

> "It is desirable that people determine their behaviour only by the free adoption of principles that, after sufficient reflection and deliberation, they judge valid." (Nino 1991, 138)

This norm obviously goes beyond the rules and principles of discourse we have looked at so far. She who accepts it, does not accept only the autonomy of her partner in a discourse, but also his autonomy in the realm of action.

a) The Justification of the Principle of Autonomy

Nino's basic norm of moral discourse shall be called "principle of autonomy" here. If the principle of autonomy was presupposed as necessary in every moral discourse, it would be discursively impossible to deny the other's moral or legal autonomy in discourse. Whoever did this would commit a performative contradiction.[19] With the moral and the legal autonomy one of the two central ideas of the liberal conception of human rights would then be justified or substantiated. The question shall therefore be: Do we really have to presuppose something like Ninc's basic norm if we seriously take part in moral discourses?

The answer to this question depends on what one considers a "serious" participation in a discourse. Two meanings can be distinguished. According to the first one, someone participates seriously in a moral discourse if he is interested in moral truth or correctness and in nothing else. Suppose this to be the case with A. A is uncertain whether the principle P_a he has defended so far, is correct or right and therefore valid or whether this is rather true for the principle P_b, which is defended by B. He engages in a discourse with B. After some time A is convinced that his principle P_a is, after all, the only right one and that no new arguments can be brought forward. He gives up the discourse with B and moves to the realm of action. There, he tries at first to induce B by persuasion and advantageous offers to live her life according to P_a. Then, when this does not help, A employs force. In this constellation, A has treated B as an equal partner

18 If one only makes the definition of the concept of the transcendental argument wide enough, this is another one of this species.

19 Cf. Nino 1991, 140, who talks about a "pragmatic inconsistency".

in discourse for the time his uncertainty, and with it the discourse, lasted. But from the time when A became convinced of the correctness of P_a, with the end of the discourse he has also stopped recognizing B's equality and freedom. The principle of autonomy has not been accepted by A in any phase. This means that there is a way of participating in discourses which can be called "serious" in some sense and does not presuppose the principle of autonomy.

In order to get to the principle of autonomy the concept of serious participation must be understood in a second, stronger sense. According to that someone only participates seriously in moral discourses if he wants to solve social conflicts through discursively generated and controlled consensus. A discursively generated consensus is a consensus that has come into existence on the basis of a discourse. It remains discursively controlled if it can be called into question at any time. If this happens, a new attempt must be made to generate a consensus discursively. The first version of the concept of serious participation allowed A to resort to persuasion and force, as soon as his conviction was firm. This is excluded by the second meaning. Whoever wants to solve social conflicts through discursively generated and controlled consensus accepts her partners' right to orient their behaviour only to principles they judge to be correct, and therefore valid, after sufficient deliberation.[20] This is the recognition of the principle of autonomy. With this recognition, the separation of action and discourse is removed. Thus, the freedom and equality of the discourse are transferred to the realm of action. Discourse and autonomy become two sides of the same thing.[21]

One could come to think that in the second meaning of seriousness, truth and rightness were replaced by consensus and autonomy. But that would be a misconstruction. Even for someone who is only or mainly interested in moral truth or correctness, the second meaning is in the end preferable. Only the permanent possibility of discursive reflection of all norms of action on the basis of autonomy can be a protection against lasting moral errors.[22] Therefore, one can say that a fully developed interest in moral correctness includes an interest in autonomy. Insofar, there is an intrinsic relation between moral correctness or truth and autonomy. Problems can arise, of course, if someone constantly

20 We shall deal with the question whether this right and its corresponding principle of autonomy have a definitive or a prima facie-character below.

21 If one presupposes this concept of serious participation, the problem of the autonomous renunciation of autonomy can easily be solved. Suppose A could convince B in a discourse that it would be the best thing for him to subject himself to A in every respect and only to do what A tells him. The question whether such a conviction can be brought about in a discourse may remain open here. At least it has to remain under discursive control if the presuppositions mentioned above are to be valid. That can only be the case if the non-autonomous state can be called into question at any time, meaning that then a new consensus has to be sought in a new discourse and that any employment of force in order to maintain the status is excluded. So if a non-autonomous, near-slavery state can be founded in discourse at all, it can only be a status which can be removed with arguments at any time (Alexy 1989, 132). Such a status would be something like a free slave status or an autonomous non-autonomous status. Thus, one would not really give up autonomy.

22 This is so not only because of the general possibility of errors, but also because of the dependence of moral correctness on communication (cf. Alexy 1992b, 237 f.).

irrational refuses to agree to a just solution and demands to maintain his autonomy at other people's expense. But that is a problem of limitating the right to autonomy and of the organization of democratic procedures. Both problems shall be treated below.

Whoever takes part in discourses with a fully developed interest in moral correctness can be called a "genuine participant in discourse". Genuine participants in discourse connect the interest in moral correctness and the interest in autonomy. In this way, they necessarily presuppose the principle of autonomy. A likely objection to this is, that one could say all this in this way, but that it did not suffice as a justification, because it was circular. In the end, it was only shown that someone who wanted to solve conflicts by freely recognized principles had a positive attitude to acting according to freely recognized principles. An obligation to take part in discourses in such a serious or genuine way was not founded by it. One could not talk about a necessary validity of the principle of autonomy for all participants in the discourse. The whole justification is claimed to have only hypothetical character: The principle of autonomy was only valid for someone who had decided to respect the autonomy of others. One could, however, take part in discourses without such a decision or such a will. Thus, everything points to the question whether the concept of genuine participation is in any way necessarily connected with the concept of discourse.

At this point, a second view has to be taken at the distinction between the subjective or motivational and the objective or institutional validity. As little as one could justify the subjective validity of discourse rules in a transcendental-pragmatic way, as little implies the participation in discourses the subjective or motivational validity of the principle of autonomy. One can take part in discourses without being the least bit interested in the autonomy of one's partners.[23] There are many people who have neither an interest in moral correctness nor in other people's autonomy, or whose interest is so small that it retreats in each case of collision with the personal advantage, but who will still talk about moral questions. For these persons, the principle of autonomy has no, or no relevant, motivational force and therefore no subjective validity. Still, one can justify or substantiate the principle's objective validity even for them.

We have shown above that an objective or institutional validity of the discourse rules can also be justified for someone who is only interested in the maximization of her individual utility or advantage. Whoever wants to legitimate her social position must at least pretend to observe the discourse rules. This can be extended to the principle of autonomy. Someone who wants to obtain legitimation through a discourse must, in this discourse, at least pretend to accept the autonomy of her discourse partners. She must – in the sense of Machiavelli's recommendation quoted above – at least feign a genuine participation in the discourse. If she does not do this, the interest her partners have in the discourse, and with it her chance of obtaining a legitimation, will tend towards nil. Consider a case in which A knows that B is only interested in maximizing his

23 Cortina rests her attempt at a discourse-theoretical justification of human rights on the thesis that human language was equipped with a telos of understanding (Cortina 1990, 40 f.). If this should refer to subjective validity, the thesis is wrong.

advantage or enforcing his already fixed convictions and has no interest whatsoever in respecting A's autonomy in any way. A could possibly have a certain hope to move B to give up this attitude, and he might also be interested in finding out whether B's already fixed convictions might be right after all. Apart from these rather improbable and weak motives, however, there is no reason for A to argue with B about the just order of their living together. It is not attractive to engage in discourses about justice with someone whose offer of a dialogue has the form of: "Before I force you to live according to my ideas, I will try whether it might not be easier for me to reach this aim by persuasion."

That there are reasons even for persons who do not share the intentions of a genuine participant in discourse to pretend they were genuine participants does not mean that those reasons must always prevail. A tyrant who is tired of talking or considers arguments fruitless can employ brute force. But in the long run that is not to his advantage. Thus starts a discourse-theoretical tyrant-dilemma: On the one hand, terror disguised by arguments is better than naked force, on the other hand, arguing easily leads to a de-masking of the injustice. This dilemma appears already with the discourse rules. The fact that autonomy is hidden in argument makes it even stronger. The tyrant is not only burdened with the risk of argumentation but also with a necessary lie: The autonomy denied in the practice must be pretended in the propaganda.

As an interim result one can state that the principle of autonomy can be substantiated in two ways. First of all everyone who genuinely, that is, seriously in the full sense, takes part in discourses must necessarily presuppose it. Secondly, everyone who is not interested in a genuine participation in discourses must, in discourses, at least pretend to accept this principle if he wants to maximize his personal or individual advantage in the long run.

b) Autonomy and Rights

In order to get from the principle of autonomy to a system of rights many questions still have to be answered. The two decisive steps, however, have been taken. The first was the justification of the necessity to regulate community life by law. The second was the justification of the principle of autonomy. If law as such as well as the protection of the individual's autonomy are necessary, the principle of autonomy corresponds directly to a general right to autonomy, which is the most general human and basic right. This right can be called "general right to freedom".[24] It can be formulated as follows:

Everyone has the right to judge for himself what is right and good, and to act accordingly.

It is obvious at once that this right cannot be valid in an unlimited way. The unlimited autonomy of the one would collide with the unlimited autonomy of the other. The right to autonomy is therefore only a prima facie right. As such it has the character of a principle. It demands the highest possible degree of autonomy

24 The idea of a general right to freedom can also be traced back to Kant (Kant 1991a, 63).

for the individual, relative to moral or legal and to factual possibilities (Alexy 1985, 75 ff.). The right to autonomy can furthermore not only be limited because of other people's autonomy but also in favour of collective goods. The protection of the environment, for example, excludes the full realization of certain plans of life, e.g., the plans made by big-game hunters. Autonomy does, however, have a prima facie priority over collective goods. In discourse this becomes obvious in the form of a burden of argument in favour of individual autonomy and against collective goods (Alexy 1992a, 178 f.). To work out all this is the task of the doctrine of basic and human rights. Here, we shall only take an interest in the structure of the justification of concrete or special rights.

There are two operations which lead from a general right to autonomy to a catalogue of concrete or special basic and human rights. The first one is applied if one tries to show that a certain concrete right is nothing but a special case of the right to autonomy and insofar conceptually contained in it. In this way, the whole catalogue of concrete rights to freedom can be substantiated. The second operation consists in explaining that certain rights are necessary means for acting autonomously. In this way, rights to protection through the state and basic social rights, like the right to the basic means of living, can be justified (Alexy 1985, 454).

Both operations lead to rights which protect and render possible the private as well as the public use of autonomy. The general right to autonomy embraces one and the other. The rights belonging to the second group cover, e.g., the freedom of expression, the freedom of assembly, the freedom of the press, and the right to vote generally, freely, equally, and secretly. In this way, the direct discourse-theoretical justification of the basic and the human rights can be systematically linked with the indirect one. Only this connection leads to a fully developed system of basic rights. A direct discourse-theoretical justification principally[25] allows only for prima facie rights and prima facie priorities. To the directly justified rights belong essentially those which are necessary for delimiting and developing the rights in the process of political opinion and will-formation in a correct and legitimate way. Thus the circle closes.

4. The Argument of Consensus

The argument of autonomy is based on the principle of autonomy and claims that this is a necessary presupposition of genuine participation in discourse. The argument of consensus, on the other hand, is based on assumptions about necessary and impossible results of discourses. These assumptions do not have to be so strong as to already imply or represent a fully developed system of rights. The argument of consensus is interesting already if it leads to some demands concerning the content or the structure of human and basic rights. In this respect, there is a structural parallel to the argument of autonomy.

The argument of consensus is a central element of Habermas' justification of a system of rights. Habermas formulates the aim of his justification as follows:

25 An exception is probably the active right to vote generally, freely, equally, and secretly. Here, only marginal limitations would be possible.

"This system should contain precisely the basic rights that citizens must mutually grant one another if they want to legitimately regulate their living together by means of positive law" (Habermas 1992, 151). The law's legitimacy is thus dependant on the universal consent to it. This corresponds to the principle of discourse mentioned in the beginning, which says that exactly those norms of action are legitimate "to which all those possibly affected could agree as participants in rational discourses" (Habermas 1992, 138). From the connection of this principle with the form of the law result, according to Habermas, the principle of democracy and a system of rights which are said to be two aspects of one and the same thing. Habermas calls this the "logical genesis of rights" (Habermas 1992, 154 f.). In this logical genesis of rights, the thought that the basic rights are not already given when the political process takes place, but have to be generated in this process by making public use of autonomy, which is: the idea of an indirect discourse-theoretical justification is of central importance (Habermas 1992, 160 ff.).

But this is only one side of the matter. The other aspect is that in Habermas one cannot find only the reference to the necessity of concretising the basic rights in a discursively organized democratic process, but also an abstract system of rights which consists of five groups of basic rights. The rights belonging to the first three groups aim at the protection of private autonomy and its "correlates" to which Habermas counts membership in a legal community and legal protection. Political autonomy is the issue of the rights belonging to the fourth group. The rights of the fifth group are designed to secure the social, technical, and ecological preconditions of private and public autonomy. In short: Habermas' system of rights is concerned with the protection and the rendering possible of private and public autonomy, that is, concerned with exactly what has been justified above by the argument of autonomy. The question is whether the argument of consensus is only a second justification of the same matter, or whether it adds something to the argument of autonomy which this alone cannot justify.

My thesis is that the argument of consensus leads to a necessary supplementation of the argument of autonomy. This supplementation consists in the introduction of impartiality, and with it, equality. In this way, the second main element of the liberal conception of human rights is brought into play. The autonomy is supplemented by universality in the form of equality and impartiality.

The discourse-theoretical criterion of impartiality has however one important weakness. It relies on a hypothetical consensus which real persons would reach under ideal conditions (Alexy 1988, 48 ff.). Often one can only speculate about its content. Then, a solution can only be found in a political process which should be organized as discursively as possible, as the next argument, the argument of democracy, will show. But in some elemental cases one can say with sufficient certainty what would be discursively necessary or impossible results. The equality of the human rights belongs to these elemental cases. In a discourse defined by freedom and equality, it is a necessary result.[26] This is at least true under ideal conditions. Unequal human rights cannot be justified in an ideal

26 An instructive example can be found in MacCormick 1991, 228 f.

discourse[27] because under the ruling of freedom, equality, and rationality in argumentation, arguments for an unequal distribution of human rights will not last.[28]

Three objections can be raised against the discourse-theoretical substantiation of the equality of human rights. The first is pointed against the argument of consensus as such, that is against the connection of moral correctness and validity on the one hand and universal consent in an ideal discourse on the other hand. In this way, the adequacy of discourse theory as a procedural theory of practical truth or correctness is denied in principle. This objection cannot be discussed in detail here (cf. Alexy 1988, 48 ff.). One should, however, point out its highly problematical preconditions. The ideal discourse is characterized by the greatest possible unfolding of clarity, knowledge, and impartiality. Whoever denies that a norm recognized as correct under these conditions is correct, either presupposes dubious alternative ways of the recognition of norms, or norms existing independently of human interests and human reason, or he has to deny in general that norms can be correct or legitimate and claim moral validity on that ground. All of this is not acceptable.

The second objection repeats what has already been discussed when dealing with the argument of autonomy: Just like the argument of autonomy, the argument of consensus can only found a subjective or motivational validity for someone who has an interest in correctness. One can meet this objection along the lines of the substantiation of an objective or institutional validity mentioned above.

The third objection one has to take rather more seriously. It is raised by someone who claims that it is possible for a person to observe the discourse rules and to be interested in correctness and still not to agree to the equality of the human rights even under ideal conditions. Thus the possibility of justifying the universality of human rights through the argument of consensus is denied. An example is the racist who claims that members of other races do not have the same human rights simply because of their race. If the racist has an interest in correctness and observes the discourse rules, he must name arguments for his assertion and expose them to criticism. Suppose the racist was a national socialist who considered his racial theory as a scientific theory. He would make the following attempt to defend his assertion:

> "On the basis of strict scientific insight, we know today that man, into the deepest subconscious movements of his psyche, but also into his smallest cerebral convolution, is determined by the reality and unescapability of his people and race. The race forms his spiritual face no less than his outward appearance. It determines his thoughts, feelings, powers, and desires, it is the essence of his being." (Stuckart/ Globke 1936, 10)

27 To this corresponds Habermas' thesis that there can be no legitimate law without the right to "equal subjective freedom of action" (Habermas 1992, 159), his postulation of "equal political basic rights" (Habermas 1992, 161), and his demand that the "use with equal chance" of private and public autonomy be, among other things, secured by social rights (Habermas 1992, 156 f.).

28 An interesting parallel to this is found in Kant 1991b, 99: "As for the principle of equality in relation to the most exalted being I can conceive of, apart from God (e.g. a power such as Aeon), there is no reason, if I and this higher being are both doing our duty in our own stations, why it should be my duty to obey while he should enjoy the right to command."

In this way, he would fail to meet even the most elemental demands of empirical truth and conceptual clarity, that is, the most elemental demands of the discourse rules. The matter becomes serious, however, if the racist rests his theses on religious revelations, on inexaminable metaphysical assertions, or magical insights. Still, the justification of the equality of human rights is not overcome in this way. Discourse theory does not know any conversational restraint[29], but it demands that only arguments examinable by all they concern may be upheld against opponents, if, as with human rights, a solution to a conflict of interests is called for.[30] Accordingly a racist who insists on denying the equality of human rights for religious, metaphysical, or magical reasons is by definition no participant in an ideal discourse. His existence can therefore not devalue the argument of consensus.

The question whether equality of human rights is a necessary result of an ideal discourse has naturally not been fully answered herewith. It could be that in an ideal discourse all come to the conclusion due to arguments that are examinable by all and in this sense rational that an unequal distribution of human rights is the right solution. An opponent of the argument of consensus could argue that this possibility can simply not be excluded because no mortal person has ever participated in an in every respect ideal discourse[31] and no mortal will ever do so. But then, how shall one know which could be its result and which not? Therefore, it can not be excluded that all decide on the reign of an élite which is defined by high intelligence and some other characteristics such as diligence and self-sacrifice. Such a decision for an élite could include the majority's renunciation of rights like the right to vote, the freedom of expression, of religion, and the right to choose occupation or profession. The majority could want this renunciation, e.g., because they expect more wealth and peace and only favour an order of society right that ensures these two values.

Against this attack against the possibility to substantiate the equality of human rights with the help of the argument of consensus three arguments can be stated. All three arguments concede that no human being has ever participated in an in every respect ideal discourse and no one will ever do so. But they advance that simply from this it does not follow that in no case can it be said what would be the result of an ideal discourse.

The first argument runs that there are plausible empirical assumptions which firstly can not be devalued in an ideal discourse and secondly suggest certain results. There are, in order to stay with our example, undoubtedly people who are at the same time very intelligent, diligent and self-sacrificing. Experience teaches us, though, that every renunciation of equal rights in favour of the reign of persons with these or other qualities is more than risky. Participants in an ideal discourse are acquainted with history and know that uncontrolled political power is taken advantage of sooner or later. As long as they do not intend to become victims they will not disclaim their rights.

To this can not be objected that the people can change during an ideal discourse in a way that the fundamental distrust against the holder of the political

29 For the concept of conversational restraint cf. Ackerman 1989, 16 ff.

30 Cf. the rules (6.1) – (6.3) in Alexy 1989, 206.

31 For this concept cf. Alexy 1988, 48.

power is no longer justified. The ideal discourse is a construction related to speech. The temporal unlimitedness is only valid in this construction and in it only in speech. The action to which the result of speech shall refer is action in this world in which the ideal and the real mix.

Against the argument dealt with so far could be argued that it rests on unfounded preconditions. The supposition that participants in an ideal discourse would not leave all rights, especially not all political rights to an élite does not only base on the experience that uncontrolled political power is taken advantage of sooner or later but essentially also on their unwillingness to become victim of that élite. How could one know that after an ideal discourse exactly this or something similar is not the aim of all who do not have the characteristics of the members of the élite? The answer to this question leads to the second and third argument against the possibility that an unequal distribution of human rights can be the result of an ideal discourse. Within both arguments autonomy plays a central role. But it has a different status in each case.

The second argument consists of a connection of the argument of consensus and the argument of autonomy. The argument of autonomy says that someone who takes part in discourses as a genuine participant assumes the autonomy of all participants in the discourse as a positive value. It furthermore says that someone who does not seriously take part in this sense at least has to pretend to accept autonomy as a positive value, if he wants to maximize his advantage in the long run. The latter is of no further importance here because it shall be assumed that the participants of an in every respect ideal discourse are genuine discourse partners. The question of results of an ideal discourse that is pursued here can therefore be based on genuine discourse partners.

The connection of the argument of consensus with the argument of autonomy leads to a considerable relief of the argument of consensus. Autonomy and the connected rights do not have to be substantiated any more within the scope of the argument of consensus. They have already been substantiated by the argument of autonomy due to the structure of discourse, in fact of every and not just of the ideal discourse. Now, the argument of consensus deals only with the equal distribution of the already established good, which is autonomy.

Once autonomy has been substantiated it is only a little step towards equality because there is a close connection between autonomy and equality. One may take political autonomy and from this as an example, the three-class-right to vote. In such an electoral law the members of the lower classes are not only treated unequally, they also have no complete political autonomy. The political decision of each separate member of the lower classes is dominated by the decision of each separate member of the higher classes according to the relationship of the imbalance of votes. This becomes quiet obvious, once the right to vote is completely withheld from certain classes of society. The members of these classes are not only treated unequally; the unequal treatment is at the same time the denial of political autonomy. Whoever values political autonomy positively must value the unequal distribution of political rights negatively. This excludes a positive evaluation of the role of a political victim. The same is true for private autonomy and the corresponding rights. The connection of the argument of consensus and the argument of autonomy therefore leads to the result that principally only an equal distribution of human rights can be the result of an ideal discourse. Something different would only be valid if an unequal distribution of human rights could lead to more autonomy for all. Having all historical experience in mind, this is, besides extreme exceptions, not the case or at least very unlikely.

The third argument differs from the second one in being based on autonomy as subject of elemental human interests and not on the principle of autonomy as a presupposition of discourse. An argument of consensus based on this must work with assumptions about what interests the participants of an ideal discourse would judge as justified under conditions of argumentative impartiality (cf. Alexy 1992b, 246). Such assumptions can, if at all, only be substantiated on the basis of a discourse-theoretical conception of the person. There is much in favour of the possibility to justify a conception of the person with the help of discourse theory in which the interest in autonomy plays a central part. But this shall not be pursued any further at this point. It may only be mentioned that the variant of consensus argument based on the interest in autonomy in the case of its success would not only lead to a supplementation of the argument of autonomy but also to its strengthening. The thesis that the principle of autonomy finds approval by all in an ideal discourse would give a second foundation of this principle and therefore of the general right to freedom as well as of the special rights resulting therefrom.

As an interim result we can state that the argument of consensus leads to the equality of human rights and in this way to the liberal principle of universality. For those who are interested in moral correctness it founds a subjective or motivational, for those who lack this interest, an objective or institutional validity of this principle.

5. The Argument of Democracy

The third discourse-theoretical argument in favour of human rights, the argument of democracy, shall only be roughly sketched here. It consists of three premises. The first says that the principle of discourse can be approximately realized by the institutionalization of democratic procedures of opinion and will-formation, and only by that (Habermas 1992, 161). If an approximation of practical correctness and legitimacy is possible in reality at all, this can only be reached in democracy (cf. Nino 1991, 248 ff.). The second premise takes up from this point and says that a democracy, which approximately realizes the demands of discursive rationality, is only possible if the political basic and human rights are valid and can be exercised with sufficiently equal chances. The third premise says that the exercise of political basic and human rights with sufficiently equal chances presupposes the validity and realization of some non-political basic and human rights. To these belong, e.g., the right to life, to basic means of living, and a certain education. If those three premises are true, the following sentence is valid:

Whoever is interested in correctness and legitimacy must also be interested in democracy; whoever is interested in democracy must also be interested in basic and human rights.

This argument is not so much of interest because it adds a further justification of the basic and human rights to the two mentioned above. Its real significance consists in the fact that it directs the view from the basic and human rights to the democratic procedures and institutions and makes clear that the idea of discourse can only be realized in a democratic constitutional state, in which basic rights and democracy are inseparably connected in spite of all tensions. Discourse theory therefore does not only render possible a justification of basic and human rights, it also emerges as the basic theory of the democratic constitutional state.

References

Ackerman, Bruce A. 1989. Why Dialogue? *The Journal of Philosophy* 86: 5–22.

Albert, Hans. 1987. Die angebliche Paradoxie des konsequenten Fallibilismus und die Ansprüche der Transzendentalpragmatik. *Zeitschrift für philosophische Forschung* 41: 421–28.

Alexy, Robert. 1981. Die Idee einer prozeduralen Theorie der juristischen Argumentation. In *Methodologie und Erkenntnistheorie der juristischen Argumentation.* Ed. Aulis Aarnio, Ilkka Niiniluoto, and Jyrki Uusitalo, 177–88. Berlin: Duncker & Humblot.

– 1985. *Theorie der Grundrechte.* Baden-Baden: Nomos. (Reprint: Frankfurt-on-Main: Suhrkamp, 1986.)

– 1988. Problems of Discourse Theory. *Crítica* 20: 43–65.

– 1989. *A Theory of Legal Argumentation.* Trans. Ruth Adler and Neil MacCormick. Oxford: Clarendon. (1st ed. in German 1978.)

– 1992a. Individual Rights and Collective Goods. In *Rights.* Ed. Carlos Santiago Nino, 163–81. Aldershot/Hong Kong/Singapore/Sydney: Dartmouth.

– 1992b. A Discourse-Theoretical Conception of Practical Reason. *Ratio Juris* 5: 231–51.

Apel, Karl-Otto. 1973. Das Apriori der Kommunikationsgemeinschaft und die Grundlagen der Ethik. In Karl-Otto Apel, *Transformation der Philosophie*, vol. II, 358–435. Frankfurt-on-Main: Suhrkamp.

Buchanan, James M. 1975. *The Limits of Liberty.* Chicago and London: University of Chicago Press.

Chisholm, Roderick. 1978. What is a Transcendental Argument? *Neue Hefte für Philosophie* 14: 19–22.

Cortina, Adela. 1990. Diskursethik und Menschenrechte. *Archiv für Rechts- und Sozialphilosophie* 76: 37–49.

Davidson, Donald. 1984. *Inquiries into Truth and Interpretation.* Oxford: Clarendon.

Dorschel, Andreas, Matthias Kettner, Wolfgang Kuhlmann, and Marcel Niquet, eds. 1983. *Transzendentalpragmatik* Frankfurt-on-Main: Suhrkamp.

Fusfield, William D. 1989. Can Jürgen Habermas' "Begründungsprogramm" Escape Hans Albert's Münchhausen Trilemma? *Jahrbuch Rhetorik* 8: 73–82.

Gauthier, David. 1986. *Morals by Agreement.* Oxford: Clarendon.

Habermas, Jürgen. 1983. Diskursethik – Notizen zu einem Begründungsprogramm. In Jürgen Habermas, *Moralbewußtsein und kommunikatives Handeln*, 53–125. Frankfurt-on-Main: Suhrkamp.

– 1991. Erläuterungen zur Diskursethik. In Jürgen Habermas, *Erläuterungen zur Diskursethik*, 119–226. Frankfurt-on-Main: Suhrkamp.

– 1992. *Faktizität und Geltung.* Frankfurt-on-Main: Suhrkamp.

Kant, Immanuel. 1974. Vorlesungen über Moralphilosophie: Moralphilosophie Collins. In *Kant's gesammelte Schriften,* vol. XXVII, 1. Ed. Akademie der Wissenschaften der DDR and Akademie der Wissenschaften zu Göttingen, 237–473. Berlin: De Gruyter.

– 1991a. *The Metaphysics of Morals.* Trans. Mary Gregor. Cambridge: Cambridge University Press.

– 1991b. Perpetual Peace. A Philosophical Sketch. In *Kant: Political Writings.* 2nd ed. Ed. Hans Reiss. Trans. H.B. Nisbet, 93–130. Cambridge: Cambridge University Press.

Keuth, Herbert. 1983. Fallibilismus versus transzendentalpragmatische Letztbegründung. *Zeitschrift für allgemeine Wissenschaftstheorie* 14: 320–37.

Kuhlmann, Wolfgang. 1985. Reflexive Letztbegründung versus radikaler Fallibilismus. *Zeitschrift für allgemeine Wissenschaftstheorie* 16: 357–74.

Leist, Anton. 1989. Diesseits der 'Transzendentalpragmatik': Gibt es sprachpragmatische Argumente für Moral? *Zeitschrift für philosophische Forschung* 43: 301–17.

MacCormick, Neil. 1991. Moral Disestablishment and Rational Discourse. In *Recht und Moral.* Ed. Heike Jung, Heinz Müller-Dietz, and Ulfrid Neumann, 219–31. Baden-Baden: Nomos.

Machiavelli, Niccolò. 1978. *Der Fürst/Il principe.* 6th ed. Stuttgart: Kröner.

MacIntyre, Alasdair. 1991. Community, Law, and the Idiom and Rhetoric of Rights. *Listenings* 26: 96–110.

Nino, Carlos Santiago. 1991. *The Ethics of Human Rights.* Oxford: Clarendon.

Patzig, Günther. 1971. Relativismus und Objektivität moralischer Normen. In Günther Patzig, *Ethik ohne Metaphysik,* 62–100. Göttingen: Vandenhoeck & Ruprecht.

– 1986. "Principium diiudicationis" und "Principium executionis". In *Handlungstheorie und Transzendentalpragmatik.* Ed. Gerold Prauss, 204–18. Frankfurt-on-Main: Klostermann.

Paulson, Stanley L. 1990. Läßt sich die Reine Rechtslehre transzendental begründen? *Rechtstheorie* 21: 155–79.

Stuckart, Wilhelm, and Hans Globke. 1936. *Kommentare zur deutschen Rassengesetzgebung,* vol. I. Munich and Berlin: Beck.

Watt, A.J. 1975. Transcendental Arguments and Moral Principles. *The Philosophical Quarterly* 25: 40–57.

Gregorio Peces-Barba Martínez, Madrid

Los Derechos Humanos ante Problemas Clásicos de la Filosofía del Derecho

I Introducción: Explicación del punto de vista

El examen de los derechos humanos, vistos desde algunos de los problemas clásicos de reflexión de los filósofos del Derecho, puede ser de gran utilidad para perfilar su concepto. Sometido a varias comparaciones entre los términos respectivos de varias alternativas que incluso pueden ser, en algún caso, dicotomías, su contorno se precisa. Estaríamos haciendo una operación similar a los diversos lavados que se hace en una extracción de mineral de la tierra hasta que ésta se separa de toda ganga y aparece en estado puro.

Este análisis se puede hacer de dos formas. La primera a través de alternativas que surgen de los derechos, del interior del subsistema de derechos fundamentales, como sería el caso de la distinción entre derechos de libertad y derechos de igualdad o la de derechos con garantía y derechos sin garantía. La segunda forma de enfrentarse con el tema es a través de las distintas perspectivas de problemas externos, desde los cuales, se examinan los derechos, y se obtienen resultados para concretar su concepto, y que aunque no surgen de los derechos, son muy influyentes en ellos. Me parece más útil este segundo procedimiento que sirve para marcar las fronteras exteriores de los derechos y su puesto en el conjunto de las relaciones entre moral, poder y Derecho. Un análisis desde las alternativas internas tiene un valor más limitado, y casi se pueden identificar con criterios de clasificación de los derechos. Los problemas externos que vamos a analizar son razón e historia, Etica pública y Etica privada, Moral y Derecho, Iusnaturalismo-positivismo jurídico y universalidad y particularismos ante los derechos. Los problemas que constituyen dicotomías se dividen en dos términos que son "recíprocamente excluyentes y conjuntamente exhaustivos".[1] Las alternativas y las dicotomías que vamos a utilizar van a permitir aclarar muchas de las dudas, disipar muchos simplismos, en definitiva, delimitar un concepto, que al estar en la encrucijada de la moral, de la política y del Derecho, se presenta con perfiles difusos, es manipulado y está sometido a los avatares de todo lenguaje con el uso persuasivo tan propio de las ciencias políticas, jurídicas y sociales. Probablemente, cuando la reflexión se haga frente a dicotomías que vamos a analizar desde el concepto de derechos humanos y para ayudarnos a entenderlo mejor, estaremos en óptimas condiciones para

1 Vid Bobbio "La grande dicotomia" en "Dalla struttura alla funzione" Edizione di comunitá. Milán 1977 p. 145. Bobbio utilizará igualmente esa terminología y ese tipo de conceptos en su reciente trabajo "Destra e sinistra". Donzelli, Roma, 1994. Alexy para fundamentar la tesis según la cual existen conexiones conceptuales y normativas entre Derecho y moral, planteará cinco distinciones que son también cinco dicotomías, (Vid "El Concepto y la validez del Derecho". Gedisa. Estudios alemanes. Barcelona, 1994 pp 29 y sigts). Este tipo de aproximación es muy común y encontraríamos, si esa fuera nuestra pretensión, muchos otros ejemplos en la cultura jurídica.

alcanzar unas conclusiones que se desprenden de exponer ese concepto a una comparación con dos términos contrarios que agotan entre los dos todas las posibilidades[2]. Enfrentados con esos dos términos, los derechos se encuentran ante un dilema que se debe resolver por la oposición de las dos tesis existentes y excluyentes de la dicotomía, y será en la respuesta adecuada a ese dilema donde se irá haciendo luz sobre ese panorama difícil que es el concepto de los derechos humanos[3]. En todo caso, cuando no estemos ante dicotomías sino sólo ante las distintas alternativas que presentan los problemas que nos parecen relevantes para este contraste también, como veremos, se pueden extraer conclusiones que nos ayudarán a avanzar en el perfil identificador de los derechos.

II Problemas relevantes elegidos

De los cinco problemas que me parecen relevantes y significativos para ampliar los conocimientos sobre el concepto de derechos humanos, y para obtener datos identificadores de los mismos, el primero de ellos, razón e historia, proporciona argumentos para entender mejor el fundamento de los derechos, y especialmente con consecuencias en el tiempo. No estamos ante una auténtica dicotomía, porque razón e historia no son dos términos recíprocamente excluyentes, pero sin embargo, como sí que son conjuntamente exhaustivos, pueden contribuir a perfilar el concepto y el fundamento de los derechos. El segundo, ética pública y ética privada, nos servirá para situar correctamente el ámbito de la moralidad de los derechos, para esclarecer su papel en las dimensiones últimas del desarrollo moral de las personas, y para delimitar el puesto de las Iglesias y de las concepciones filosóficas sobre la virtud, el bien, la felicidad etc., en una sociedad política organizada jurídicamente. El tercer problema a partir de la dialéctica entre Moral y Derecho representa la posibilidad de obtener consecuencias y elementos de juicio de las dos caras que tienen los derechos, o si se ve desde el punto de vista externo, de situarlos en el ámbito moral, en el jurídico o en ambos y analizar la relevancia de esas dos posibilidades en el concepto de derechos fundamentales. Algunas de las conclusiones que obtengamos nos sitúan en el cuarto problema, iusnaturalismo-positivismo, que reflejará la respectiva importancia que finalmente se otorgue a la moral y al Derecho. Por último, y también muy vinculada a las posiciones anteriores, universalismo frente a particularismos nos ayudará a perfilar el concepto y el alcance de los derechos humanos en la cultura jurídica actual.

2 En el diccionario filosófico de Ferrater Mora se define la dicotomía como “la división de un concepto en dos contrarios que agotan la extensión del primero”. Vid “Diccionario de Filosofía. A-D”, nueva edición actualizada bajo la dirección de Josep-María Terricabras. Ariel-referencia. Barcelona. Noviembre, 1994 p. 881.

3 Usamos como se ve el concepto de dilema en un sentido muy general y no en el preciso del viejo argumento filosófico del silogismo “con dos filas o “dos cuernos”, el llamado “syllogismus cornutus”. Sobre el concepto de derechos humanos vid. mi libro “Curso de derechos fundamentales. Teoría General”, con la colaboraciós de los profesores Rafael de Asís Roig, Carlos R. Fernández Liesa y Angel Llamas Cascón. Universidad Carlos III de Madrid. Boletín Oficial del Estado. Madrid 1995.

A) Los derechos, la razón y la historia.

Escoger entre razón e historia en la reflexión sobre los derechos supone preferir entre racionalismo e historicismo. Por el primer punto de vista, los derechos son generales, racionales y abstractos, es decir, tienen como destinatarios a todos los hombres, tienen un contenido estable válido para todos los tiempos y para todos los ámbitos, y se pueden justificar racionalmente. Son expresión de la dignidad permanente del hombre y de su condición de libres e iguales desde su nacimiento.[4] Por el segundo, los derechos se sitúan en un tiempo histórico, el de la modernidad, y su configuración es variable, teniendo en cuenta las circunstancias sociales, económicas, políticas y culturales. Sin embargo, si se piensa que no estamos en una auténtica dicotomía, es decir, que razón e historia no son conceptos excluyentes, y se piensa siguiendo a Ortega y Gasset, que toda razón está siempre situada en la historia,[5] se podría construir el concepto de los derechos desde una razón histórica, lo que supondría lo siguiente:

a) Los derechos humanos son un concepto propio del mundo moderno, es decir, aparecen como tales a partir del tránsito a la modernidad en un conjunto de circunstancias políticas, culturales, económicas y sociales dadas. En efecto, no se puede entender su formulación sino en el ámbito de la forma política propia del mundo moderno, en un proceso cultural de secularización, de racionalismo, de individualismo y de naturalismo, y sin una organización económica que supera por un lado el moralismo de la economía medieval, y por otro lado el localismo y los horizontes limitados de los intercambios económicos, con la aparición de los primeros atisbos de la economía capitalista y con el auge social de la burguesía.

b) Su fundamento racional último es la idea de dignidad de la persona humana, que integra la idea del hombre como ser capaz de elegir, de construir conceptos generales, de comunicación y de diálogo, por medio del lenguaje, y finalmente como ser moral, capaz de elegir libremente sus planes de vida, su moralidad privada. Los valores de seguridad, de libertad, de igualdad y de solidaridad, son el fundamento de los derechos para hacer posible en la sociedad política el pleno desarrollo de la dignidad de las personas.

4 En esta línea vid. el artículo del prof. Francisco Laporta "Sobre el concepto de derechos humanos". Doxa, N° 4. Alicante, 1987.

5 Esta idea de la razón histórica vecorre la obra de Ortega y Gasset de prata a cabo. Uno de los textos, iniciales en que trata frontalmente el tema es "El tema de nuestro tiempo" (1923). Obras Completas. Tomo 3. Alianza Editorial. Madrid 1983, pp. 141 y sigts. Allí afirmará que "la vida debe ser culta, pero la cultura tiene que ser vital" (p. 169). Pero el punto de vista de la vida es el histórico, el perspectivista, y esa tesis la confirmará en su trabajo "Historia como sistema" (1935). En efecto, al í divá "... el hombre no tiene naturaleza sino que tiene ... historia. O, lo que es igual: lo que la naturaleza es a las casas, es la historia – como res gestae – al hombre". En edición Obras Completas, citada. Tomo 6, p. 41. Finalmente, como signo de lo permanente de esos planteamientos, los reproduce en unas lecciones que pronuncia en Buenos Aires en 1940, en la Facultad de Filosofía y Letras, con el título de "La razón histórica". Más tarde en Lisboa en 1944, y con el mismo título impartirá otro curso, igualmente de 5 lecciones. Vid Obras Completas, edición citada. Tomo 12, pp 145 y sigts.

c) El desarrollo pleno de la dignidad de las personas supone que cada una se encuentre en condiciones, en la vida social, de elegir, de ejercitar autónomamente su razón, de comunicarse con los demás, y de escoger libremente su moralidad privada. Los derechos humanos son un medio adecuado para obtener esos objetivos, a través de su influencia en el proceso de racionnalización, o de organización racional de la vida social.

d) La toma de conciencia de estas exigencias racionales que fundamentan en el mundo moderno los derechos humanos se ha ido produciendo a lo largo de la historia con aportaciones parciales y plurales, y desde puntos de vista ideológicos distintos, liberales, democráticos y socialistas. Una buena comprensión integradora de todas estas aportaciones permitirá una construcción integral del concepto de derechos humanos que tenga en cuenta los cuatro valores de seguridad, libertad, igualdad y solidaridad.

Razón e historia no son alternativas excluyentes, son dos dimensiones complementarias desde las que se construye el concepto y el fundamento de los derechos.

B) Derechos humanos, ética pública y ética privada

La moralidad de los derechos, con vocación de eficacia a través del Derecho, se sitúa en el ámbito de la ética pública. Llamo ética pública a la que se convierte en moralidad política y luego, en moralidad jurídica. Es sinónimo de la idea de justicia y tiene, como digo, vocación de ser moralidad legalizada o, desde otro punto de vista, Derecho justo. Todo sistema jurídico tiene como trasfondo un sistema de ética pública que lo fundamenta, pero sólo la ética pública de la modernidad dará lugar a la construcción del concepto de derechos humanos.

Una de las grandes causas de las crisis y de la inestabilidad política en las sociedades a partir del tránsito a la modernidad, etapa histórica concernida por los derechos humanos, es la confusión entre ética pública y ética privada, y el uso equivocado de esos dos conceptos en el ámbito político y jurídico. Un uso teórico inadecuado, con reflejos prácticos igualmente inadecuados, será también causa de confusión en el concepto de derechos humanos.

La ética pública de la modernidad, sede de los valores, de los principios y de los derechos relevantes en el ámbito político y jurídico, no es una ética personal, como la ética privada, sino que expresa los criterios de organización de la sociedad que van a permitir la dignidad real de todas las personas a través de las cuatro dimensiones de: capacidad de elección, uso de la razón, comunicación y diálogo intersubjetivo, y opción de moralidad privada. Es una ética procedimental en el sentido de que no establece comportamientos o conductas de moralidad privada, sino criterios de organización de la sociedad y derechos y libertades para que cada persona pueda elegir, esté en condiciones de elegir, su moralidad privada (lo que presupone las tres otras dimensiones de la dignidad humana). Los derechos no pueden ser usados, ni instrumentalizados al servicio de una ética privada, de una concepción del bien, de la virtud, o de la felicidad, sino que están al servicio del pluralismo de esas concepciones,para hacer posible que todas puedan instalarse y ofrecerse libremente a los ciudadanos.

La ética privada por su parte es un proyecto de moral individual que se ofrece por una Iglesia, una escuela, una corriente filosófica, una secta, etc, o que es creada por un individuo y pretende extenderse a todos los sujetos posibles (universalidad) y tiene que ser susceptible de convertirse en ley general, aunque necesita que cada uno preste su consentimiento individualizado (autonomía).[6] Pretende ofrecer un plan de vida, una idea del bien, de la virtud o de la felicidad para cada individuo. Precisamente, la vocación de universalidad de la ética privada, entendida como capacidad de sus propuestas para ser elevadas a ley general, puede llevar a traspasar las fronteras de la ética pública, dificultando el pluralismo, que es un rasgo institucional de esa ética pública de la modernidad.

El entrecruzamiento de los papeles de la ética pública y de la ética privada, y el uso de los derechos humanos con fines desviados (también de los valores y de los principios), que se pueden constatar históricamente, exige sacar consecuencias adecuadas de la reflexión sobre esta dicotomía, puesto que en este caso sí estamos ante una auténtica dicotomía.

La ética pública ha pretendido con las concepciones políticas totalitarias, en el mundo moderno fascismo, nazismo, stalinismo, convertirse en ética privada, pasar de ser ética procedimental a ser ética de conductas. Tengo la impresión de que ese peligro está superado, o al menos permanece dormido a finales del siglo XX. Es el Estado-Iglesia.

La ética privada ha pretendido desde herencias premodernas, permanentemente resucitadas por muchas Iglesias, y en el ámbito cultural europeo y atlántico en los siglos XIX y XX por la Iglesia Católica, convertirse en ética pública, es decir, trasladar las obligaciones de los creyentes a obligaciones de ciudadanos. La ética de conductas se traslada al ámbito público, en detrimento del pluralismo, con la vinculación entre la verdad que esa Iglesia proclama y la libertad de todos. Las encíclicas "Veritatis splendor" y "Evangelium Vitae" de Juan Pablo II, son un signo de ese punto de vista. La idea bobbiana es que uno de los elementos para reconocer una dicotomía es precisamente esa "capacidad potencial, de uno u otro tipo, de asumir el papel de clase universal" y de excluir al otro término de la dicotomía del universo.[7] Es el modelo de la Iglesia-Estado, propia de los fundamentalismos religiosos, sean débiles y aparentemente compatibles con la democracia, sean fuertes y claramente incompatibles con la democracia.

En este segundo movimiento de la ética privada a la ética pública, los derechos fundamentales son los grandes sacrificados, puesto que una de sus funciones es garantizar el pluralismo y evitar convertir a todos los ciudadanos en creyentes. Así, la libertad de expresión, de reunión o de asociación y la libertad religiosa dejan de tener sentido en este modelo. También la soberanía popular o el principio de las mayorías. De ahí que la doctrina pontificia del siglo XIX combata la libertad de conciencia a la que considera pestilente error ("Mirari

6 Al menos estas condiciones se exigen para la ética individual, la que compromete al individuo con su destino último como persona, que escoge su moralidad privada. La segunda dimensión de la ética privada, la ética social, prescribe igualmente comportamientos o conductas referidas a la vida en sociedad (no dañar a los demás, cumplir las promesas, los compromisos y los pactos, etc).

7 Vid "La grande dicotomia" en obra citada p. 147.

Vos", Gregorio XVI), la libertad en general que pone en peligro los sagrados derechos de los príncipes y las libertades modernas ("Mirari Vos", Gregorio XVI, "Inmortale Dei", Leon XIII, "Libertas", Leon XIII).

Los derechos humanos sólo tienen sentido en un correcto entendimiento de la dialéctica entre ética pública, ética privada, situados como moralidad en la ética pública, con vocación de positivación jurídica, y como una de las barreras más importantes para impedir que la ética privada se convierta en ética pública. Desde este punto de vista, se puede decir que un sistema democrático es el que mantiene un correcto equilibrio entre el papel de la ética pública de los ciudadanos y las éticas privadas con sus posibilidades de elección de caminos del bien, de la virtud o de la felicidad para sus respectivos creyentes. De todas formas, las fronteras entre la ética pública y la privada son a veces poco claras y hay parcelas de esta última que realizan incursiones en el ámbito de la pública que pueden verse afectados por algunos principios de la ética pública de la modernidad. Incluso pueden existir materias que en un momento histórico fueron ética privada y que, en un momento dado, se convierten en ética pública. Es el caso de la solidaridad como virtud (amor, caridad, etc) que pasa a convertirse en valor de la ética pública, la solidaridad de los modernos a partir de la progresiva implantación de la económía política influida por Adam Smith y por la idea de que del simple juego de los intereses particulares se deriva el interés general. Normalmente, los aspectos de la ética privada que se convierten en ética pública pertenecen a la ética privada social, y no a la ética privada individual. Sin embargo, cuando hablamos de que a veces la ética privada puede verse interferida o dificultada por planteamientos de la ética pública juridificada o positivizada se está pensando, generalmente, en la ética privada individual, es decir, aquella que conduce directamente a la autonomía moral. La objeción de conciencia es la reacción, desde la ética pública juridificada, frente a las invasiones de la ética privada individual, que puede dificultar dimensiones importantes de la dignidad humana, especialmente el desarrollo de su idea del bien, de la virtud o de la felicidad.

C) Los derechos humanos entre moral y Derecho

Para muchas doctrinas de los derechos humanos, éstos agotan la reflexión sobre el fundamento y el concepto en el plano moral. Es decir, los derechos son en ese sentido, derechos morales, y la dimensión jurídica es un complemento, no me atrevería a decir que un accidente, que no modifica el concepto ni añade nada distinto de lo que está en la perspectiva moral. Más escasa, casi inexistente, es la presencia de un positivismo ideológico en este campo que afirmase que son derechos los que se estableciesen por el legislador positivo. Sólo desde posiciones retóricas, en Estados autoritarios o totalitarios, se llaman derechos a creaciones del legislador, sin nexos ni vínculos con la tradición moral de los derechos en la cultura jurídica y política de la Ilustración y de la modernidad. Aquí la pretensión de convertirse en clase universal y excluyente corresponde a la moral.

Parece pues que el plano moral, ese que hemos identificado con la ética pública, es inseparable del fundamento y del concepto de los derechos. Sólo hay un fundamento posible que es el moral, y el concepto, en parte al menos, incluye una dimensión moral, aunque no aceptemos esa pretensión de excluir el Derecho.

De todas formas, es conveniente señalar que la ética pública es una ética de valores, de principios y de derechos, y no sólo de estos últimos. A veces, las doctrinas de los derechos prescinden de esas dimensiones y eso tiñe sus posiciones de un individualismo y de un subjetivismo inconvenientes para identificar totalmente a la ética pública, que tiene también dimensiones objetivas y de organización. Incluso los derechos realizan una función objetiva como desarrollo de los valores, y como guía de la producción y de la interpretación normativa.

La intuición y la firme convicción de los iusnaturalistas racionalistas como Pufendorf era la insuficiencia de la dimensión moral de los derechos, su condición de derechos naturales, y la necesidad de su positivación para completar su concepto, y para que ampliasen la finalidad y el objetivo que los justifica: favorecer una organización de la sociedad política y un estatuto subjetivo de los ciudadanos que les permita elegir libremente su moralidad privada. Parece que el fundamento es un fundamento moral, pero parece igualmente que el concepto sólo se completa cuando los derechos tienen la doble dimensión moral y jurídica. Un concepto que abarcase exclusivamente su dimensión moral dejaría fuera una parcela enorme, y la más visible, la que realmente modifica la realidad y convierte en efectivos los fines de los derechos. No se debe, por otra parte, producir una escisión tan grande entre el mundo de los filósofos y el mundo de los juristas construyendo un concepto de derechos que careciese de utilidad para los juristas y para los ciudadanos. Aquí los derechos participan, en la formación de su concepto, de elementos morales, de la ética pública, pero con una vocación de jurisdicción que forma parte también del referido concepto.

Sólo restaría señalar que la dimensión jurídica de los derechos no se agota en su validez, es decir, en su incorporación como norma del subsistema de derechos fundamentales, sino que se extiende a su eficacia, es decir, a la capacidad social para que esos derechos sean reales y efectivos. En ese sentido, especialmente en relación con los derechos económicos, sociales y culturales, la escasez será un elemento relevante para la eficacia y debería ser tenida en cuenta en el complejo de elementos que forman el concepto. En efecto, la moralidad de los derechos se realiza a través de las normas del Derecho positivo, en ese proceso que he llamado de juridificación de la ética pública, pero esas dos dimensiones que en algunos derechos, como los individuales, son suficientes para su plenitud, en otros, aquellos que tienen un contenido económico y que dependen de una acción positiva de carácter prestacional de los poderes públicos, de grupos privados o de simples particulares, necesitan asímismo de medios para llevarlos a la práctica. Sin esos medios, es decir, en condiciones de escasez relevante, los derechos no serán operativos, aunque su tenor ético esté muy justificado y su recepción normativa haya sido correcta. De nuevo aparece en este panorama la trilogía justicia, validez y eficacia.

D) Los derechos humanos, el iusnaturalismo y el positivismo jurídico

Iusnaturalismo-positivismo es una de las grandes dicotomías de la cultura jurídica, aunque tiene matices y perspectivas que convierten a ambos términos en claramente excluyentes, y en otros que se orientan hacia una aproximación integradora. Los derechos humanos son un objeto de análisis que sirve de excelente banco de prueba a estos dos tipos de aproximación y también de verificación o falsificacíon de algunas conclusiones sobre la teoría del Derecho acreditadas y consideradas solventes. Vamos a referirnos concretamente a dos tesis:

1) Las teorías positivistas no tienen en cuenta elementos morales en la definición del concepto de Derecho.
2) Las teorías no positivistas tienen en cuenta elementos morales en la definición del concepto de Derecho. Es respectivamente la tesis de la separación y la tesis de la vinculación en la terminología de Alexy.[8]

Parece que el modelo de las teorías positivistas afirmaría la posibilidad de establecer el concepto de Derecho a través de la noción de validez con perspectivas exclusivamente formales. Así, el órgano competente para producir la norma y el procedimiento adecuado de acuerdo con lo que llamo la norma básica de identificación de normas que realiza las funciones de la norma fundamental Kelseniana, aunque para mí es una norma del Ordenamiento que se apoya en el poder, hecho fundante básico, o hecho institucionalizado y referido a valores, primera etapa de la ética pública como ética política, determinarían, la pertenencia al Ordenamiento de una norma, que compondría con esos dos elementos formales su validez.

Sin embargo, un análisis de cualquier sistema jurídico pone de relieve, sin excepción, que todos pretenden una determinada finalidad, un objetivo de justicia, aunque éste sea incorrecto y muy alejado de los parámetros de justicia generalmente aceptados. Las posiciones iusnaturalistas aceptarían que cualquier sistema, incluso los injustos, contienen unas dosis de moralidad, aunque esa ética pública no coincida o no corresponda a la del modelo iusnaturalista. Hemos visto, en mi propio punto de vista, cómo el hecho del poder, que llamo hecho fundante básico, es un hecho institucionalizado, formado por hombres que se agrupan en torno a la fuerza y también al consenso en unos valores de la ética pública, que son, en ese ámbito, ética política con vocación de trasladarse como ética jurídica al Derecho. Todo sistema jurídico pues, pretende realizar una determinada ética pública como ética jurídica mediada por la ética política. Ante esta constatación tendríamos que rechazar como incorrecta la primera tesis de que las teorías positivistas no tienen en cuenta elementos morales en el concepto de Derecho.

Esta conclusión, que se puede establecer con carácter general para cualquier tipo de ordenamiento jurídico, se perfila y se concreta para los ordenamientos que incluyen en su ética pública normas que incorporan derechos humanos, valores y principios, considerados propios de la Ilustración y de la

8 Vid Robert Alexy "El concepto y la validez del Derecho", edición castellana de Jorge Malem Seña. Gedisa, Barcelona, 1994, pp 13 y 14.

modernidad, es decir, propios de una sociedad política democrática. Es la ética pública de la modernidad.

En los Ordenamientos de este tipo, la norma de identificación de normas aparece configurada por dos dimensiones, una formal, órgano y procedimiento de producción de la norma, y otra material, contenido y límites de ética pública, valores, derechos y principios que toda norma del ordenamiento debe contener o, al menos, no debe contradecir.

¿Supone esta conclusión aceptar que sólo son posibles teorías no positivistas para establecer el concepto de Derecho puesto que todas las teorías deben, necesariamente, tener en cuenta elementos morales? ¿Supone también aceptar que toda aproximación a los derechos humanos debe ser iusnaturalista, incluso cuando se tenga en cuenta el elemento jurídico en la formación de su concepto?.

Si la respuesta fuese positiva supondría rechazar definitivamente el tipo de aproximación positivista. Sin embargo, un análisis pormenorizado nos obligará a matizar una conclusión tan unidimensional.

Afirmar que en el concepto de Derecho se tienen en cuenta siempre elementos morales no supone que estemos ante una aproximación iusnaturalista. Dependerá de cómo se tengan en cuenta esos elementos morales. Así, podemos precisar este matiz con la siguiente tesis: Cuando los elementos morales se incorporen directamente al concepto de Derecho, sin pasar por los cauces formales de producción normativa -órgano competente y procedimiento-, estamos ante una aproximación iusnaturalista del tipo de las comprendidas en la tesis 2. Por el contrario, cuando lo hacen a través de los cauces formales de producción normativa de la norma de identificación de normas, seguiríamos estando en la tesis positivista. En efecto, en el primer supuesto estamos ante una moralidad que es al mismo tiempo Derecho, borrándose los perfiles de la distinción entre ambos conceptos. Sin embargo, en el segundo supuesto, la moralidad originaria al positivizarse se convierte en Derecho y de esta forma incluso podríamos aceptar la tesis 1 como tesis positivista, siempre que se interpretase en el sentido de que la moralidad necesaria en todo Derecho, por la vocación de justicia que tiene, no es relevante como moralidad sino como Derecho, por lo que, no se borran los perfiles entre ambos conceptos. Lo que no cabrá es un concepto del Derecho puro, neutro y sólo formal, pero sí cabrá entender que los contenidos materiales de ética pública juridificada, valores de derechos o principios, se toman en consideración como Derecho y no directamente como moral. Así, se entenderá también mejor el papel de los derechos humanos ante la dialéctica moral y Derecho. Los derechos son ética pública y Derecho positivo, como derechos subjetivos, libertades potestades e inmunidades, y se estará ante una posición positivista si la consideración jurídica de esa moralidad se produce por haberse incorporado la moralidad de los derechos por los cauces de producción normativa ordinaria (Derecho legal) (Constitución y ley) y Derecho judicial (especialmente a través de la jurisprudencia del Tribunal Constitucional). Estaremos ante una posición iusnaturalista si la moralidad de los derechos humanos es directamente jurídica sin pasar por los cauces de producción normativa.

E) Los derechos humanos ante universalismo y particularismos

El contraste de los derechos humanos con todos los problemas anteriormente examinados lleva a una paradoja, prima facie, puesto que si la moralidad de los derechos tiene vocación de universalidad, mientras que su juridificación pasa mayoritariamente por el Derecho positivo de los Estados, y sólo todavía de manera secundaria por el Derecho internacional (para simplificar identificaremos ese Derecho internacional con el Derecho cosmopolita, lo que no es totalmente cierto, porque no es el de Derecho internacional un sistema coronado por un poder único), este Derecho estatal no es uniforme, sino plural y variable. El universalismo moral se rompe y se diversifica en particularismos jurídicos.

Incluso en el primer nivel se impugna el universalismo y se sostiene que es una creación europea y occidental que no se puede generalizar a otras culturas particulares. No comparto esta tesis aunque no vaya a entrar aquí en ese problema.

Debemos distinguir entre el universalismo racional, el temporal y el espacial. El universalismo racional de los derechos, en esta primera dimensión moral, supone la generalidad de sus destinatarios y la abstracción de sus contenidos, con independencia de las circunstancias y de las situaciones. El universalismo temporal supondrá la extensión a cualquier tiempo de los derechos y el universalismo espacial a cualquier país y a sus sistemas jurídicos. El universalismo racional es objeto de reflexión por la Filosofía jurídica, el temporal, además, por la historia del Derecho, y el espacial, además, por el Derecho internacional.

El entrecruzamiento con los problemas anteriores descarta ya el universalismo temporal, matizado por el análisis de la relación entre razón e historia. Por su parte, el universalismo espacial conecta el tema con otras dicotomías ya analizadas, la de los derechos entre moral y Derecho, y la de iusnaturalismo y positivismo. Del contraste entre esas dicotomías se desprende que el universalismo espacial debe tener en cuenta la dimensión jurídica de los derechos, puesto que su sentido central consiste en defender la extensión de los derechos a todos los sistemas jurídicos nacionales, y la aplicación del Derecho internacional de los derechos humanos a todos los países del mundo. Si esta dimensión espacial se refiriese sólo al ámbito moral, no sería diferente del universalismo racional, y lo es precisamente por su vocación de extensión territorial efectiva y práctica, en el ámbito del Derecho positivo estatal e internacional.

Aquí pues, el universalismo espacial en la dialéctica moral y Derecho es el camino para superar la aparente paradoja del universalismo racional (propio de la moralidad de los derechos) y la juridificación, que sigue siendo prioritariamente estatal. Podríamos definir el universalismo espacial como el cauce para la superación de la paradoja del paso de una moralidad universal a una legalidad particular, o dicho de otra manera, para la plena positivación de unos derechos con destinatario general y contenido abstracto en todos los sistemas jurídico positivos existentes.

Son relevantes el universalismo racional, esencialmente moral y el universalismo espacial, esencialmente jurídico, mientras es irrelevante el universalismo temporal, que no se corresponde con la realidad. El universalismo racional se encuentra en el punto de partida, mientras que el universalismo espacial es un objetivo a alcanzar y se encuentra en el punto de llegada. Mientras el fin del universalismo espacial no haya concluido, la moralidad de los derechos y el Derecho positivo se encontrarán en situación asimétrica, uno completo y otro "in faciendo". No pretendo una posición determinista, sin que sea inexorable que este ideal se vaya a realizar en cualquier caso.

Esta distinción entre el punto de partida y el punto de llegada es igualmente relevante para analizar el universalismo de los derechos individuales, civiles y políticos, por una parte, y el de los derechos económicos, sociales y culturales por otro. Incluso al identificarse el universalismo de los derechos como a priori, desde el punto de partida, esta conclusión se ha utilizado para negar el carácter de derechos fundamentales de los económicos, sociales y culturales por los partidarios del Estado mínimo. Así, se produce una coincidencia objetiva entre estas posiciones ultraliberales y las posiciones del marxismo-leninismo, al negar ambas la posibilidad de los derechos económicos, sociales y culturales, los primeros por no ser derechos universales, desde el punto de partida, y los segundos por pretender construir la igualdad desde el Estado, sin los derechos.

Efectivamente, la universalidad de los derechos individuales, civiles y políticos es del punto de partida, todos tienen desde el origen los mismos derechos. Es la aplicación del criterio de la igualdad como equiparación, puesto que las condiciones diferentes no son relevantes.

Los derechos económicos, sociales y culturales pretenden ayudar, con la técnica de los derechos, a erradicar diferencias entre personas que sí son relevantes para alcanzar el objetivo genérico y primario de todos los derechos, y crean condiciones sociales para que todos puedan libremente elegir su ética privada. Por eso, el universalismo es un objetivo a alcanzar, y no una condición de salida. Aquí entra en juego la idea de la universalidad como punto de llegada a través de la aplicación a estos derechos del criterio de igualdad como diferenciación, tratando desigualmente a los desiguales. Por esa razón, los derechos económicos, sociales y culturales pretenden satisfacer necesidades básicas de personas que no podrían satisfacerlas por sí mismas, y no de aquellas que pueden hacerlo por sus propias fuerzas. Diferencian y discriminan para alcanzar la igualdad. Así se entiende correctamente, en cuanto a los contenidos y a los destinatarios de los derechos, la universalidad o el universalismo del punto de partida y el del punto de llegada.

Todavía debemos cruzar estas conclusiones con una observación que hemos hecho con anterioridad referida a las dimensiones jurídicas de los derechos humanos, y consistente en considerar no sólo la validez (pertenencia al ordenamiento) sino también la eficacia (aceptación y posibilidad real de implantación) para completar la dimensión jurídica del concepto de derechos humanos. Señalábamos también cómo en la eficacia era muy relevante el concepto de escasez, especialmente debemos añadir en los derechos económicos, sociales y culturales, que exigen en el restablecimiento de la igualdad una acción positiva y normalmente costosa de los poderes públicos con contenido económico. Por esa razón, los derechos económicos, sociales y culturales, como el derecho a la educación, a la protección de la salud, a la seguridad social o a la vivienda, por citar los más relevantes, necesitan inversiones económicas y dependen de la escasez.

La conexión de este punto de vista con la idea de los derechos universales en el punto de llegada y realizables desde la igualdad como diferenciación, contrasta con un gran equívoco que se produce en muchos sistemas de derechos humanos: No existe diferencia con los individuales, civiles y políticos y se plantea su universalidad desde el punto de partida también en los derechos económicos, sociales y culturales. Así, la generalización de la gratuidad de la enseñanza o de la sanidad, especialmente, representan un tratamiento jurídico distinto del que aquí propugnamos. Se considera la universalidad desde el punto de partida y se aplica consiguientemente la igualdad como equiparación y no como diferenciación, dándose el mismo tratamiento al que no puede satisfacer por sí mismo la necesidad básica encuestión, que al que sí puede. El resultado es el beneficio indiscriminado por tanto injusto y un uso inadecuado de medios escasos, con el peligro de la llamada crisis fiscal del Estado y con la imposibilidad de satisfacer las necesidades de quienes son incapaces de hacerlo con su propio esfuerzo. Sólo una reconsideración general del tratamiento de estos derechos, volviendo a la idea de la universalidad del punto de llegada y de la igualdad como diferenciación, permitirá su mantenimiento a medio y largo plazo. Aparece aquí, de nuevo, como muy relevante, el problema de la eficacia que afecta especialmente a este tipo de derechos, que necesitan cuantiosos medios económicos.

Caridad Velarde Queipo de Llano, Navarra

Universalism of Human Rights The Case of Dworkin and his Critics

This paper will attempt to outline some of the problems and contradictions presented by a liberal conception of human rights. It is common to consider Ronald Dworkin's work as paradigmatic of liberal approach. This idea arose from the publication of *Taking Rights Seriously,*[1] but perhaps is emphasized at the moment, because of the current debate with communitarian positions, some of which, as is well known, support a multiculturalism that seems to be on the opposite side of liberal universalism, or tries to complete its abstraction.[2]

From its conception, the discussion on liberalism has affected central topics of moral, political and juridical thought. The subject of this paper is, more specifically, its universalistic conception of the individual, (and consequently of his rights), which liberalism has been maintaining from its enlightened origins. The main criticism that has been made to that position is that universalism implies an abstraction, because it does not work with the human being as something particular or specific but with the notion of individual which is nothing real.[3]

In the origin, not only of the idea of rights, but of liberalism itself, and, ultimately of modernity, is the idea of tolerance. Tolerance arose as a neccessity and in direct connection with religions. Paradoxically, it was born as something that is not a given, but that, on the contrary, has to be learned. That is why every cultural manifestation of humankind, in spite of its social character, has demonstrated the necessity of learning how to live together. One of the questions that this topic leads to is that of the compatibility or incompatibility of a universalistic view of man with the notion of tolerance. It can appear paradoxical because liberal tolerance means the aspiration of a harmonious coexistence of the different conceptions of the good life. Liberalism as a theory does not propose a specific way of living; in practice it does. And what is worse, that conception of the good life is incompatible with other ideas (that is what from the occidental point of view, we tend to call the limits of tolerance). In the same manner, the criticism referring to the abstraction and consequent disconnection with reality that supposes working with an individual not related with a cultural environment, is one of the principal claims of communitarian writers. With all those presumptions, this paper does not intend to be more than an approach to

1 Ronald Dworkin, *Taking Rights Seriously* (Cambridge, Massachusetts 1977).

2 About this discussion, and from a relativistic point of view, see Aulis Aarnio, and Aleksander Peczenik, "On values. Universal or Relative?", *Previous Acts of the 17th IVR World Congress*, Bologna 1995, II, 1–7; see as well Carlos Santiago Nino, "Positivism and Communitarianism: Between Human Rights and Democracy", *Ratio Iuris*, vol. 7, nº 1, March 1994, 14–40.

3 Among the critics of liberal pattern from this point of view, probably one of the sharpest viewpoints is that of Charles Taylor in *The Malaise of Modernity*, (Concorde 1992), especially the first chapter.

problems with difficult solutions, in the least because they deal with concepts that are not univocal at all, and do not belong to schools easy to delimit.

1. The universalistic origin of the idea of human rights

The Enlightenment was essentially a revolution that affected the centre of thought and knowledge, which has presented many different interpretations of it and currents inside it. For example, from the point of view of economic theory, it is possible to distinguish between a continental Enlightenment and an Anglo-Saxon one, keeping in mind the dose of freedom individuals are entitled to; or, better said, according to whether or not individuals should adjust their behaviour to a common goal. The justification can be found in the different view of the relation between human beings and the world that each one proposes. The founding of both has to be looked for in the different currents of knowledge that underlie each of them, rationalistic the first one and evolutive the second.

Conversely, from the point of view of political and juridical thought, it is more important to distinguish between a rationalistic and a historicist Enlightenment. There is the Enlightenment of rationalistic Natural Law, which purports to have found the key building the perfect juridical system; and another one that believes that a perfect law does not exist and that it is important to adjust the normative content to "the spirit of the people". This distinction between rationalism and historicism inside the same Enlightenment is extremely important and has become a recurrent question in the form of debate between liberalism and communitarianism, or better yet, between liberalism and minorities rights claims.

Also, two different versions of iusnaturalism are reflected in the two Declarations of Human Rights. Although both have a iusnaturalistic inspiration, in the French case that inspiration is exclusively rationalistic (we could talk about a iusnaturalism autonomus from any external instance), while the American case supposes a iusnaturalism connected with a moral rule that cannot be separated from the religious fact. In that sense, and because of its pragmatic character of political mechanism, the latter is not as abstract as the French Declaration, because the political matters it deals with have a pragmatic support and goal.

In this last context the study of the polemic between Jellinek and Boutmy about the filiation of the Declaration of Rights of Man and Citizen is an interesing case study. They discuss if this filiation should be attributed to American influence or, on the contrary, to French Enlightenment, especifically to Rousseau.[4] The difference between one and the other conception is vital, because the starting point of the American version of rights is the idea of individual freedom against public power, which, as a consequence, should justify each one of its interferences on the individual behavior. The opposite happened with the

4 Cfr. AAVV, *Orígenes de la Declaración de Derechos del Hombre y del Ciudadano*, ed. Jesús G. Amuchástegui (Madrid 1984).

5 "Richard Schmidt says, opposing to me, that French human rights origins are not Anglo-American, but, the most consequent expression of the Natural Law of Occidental Europe." Jellinek, Ibid., 63.

continental version which is founded in a strong idea of rights, and needs the intervention of the State to achieve and support them.[5]

It could be said that different traditions originate differences in the content of the Declarations too, in the sense that while the American tradition discourses on liberties, the French version discourses on rights with the consequent attribution of different tasks to public authority in each case. On the one hand, the American conception determined the justice of a law keeping in mind its democratic elaboration as a formal requisite, but also the respect and coherence with what is established in the Constitution, and gave to the individuals the capacity of distinguishing between justice and injustice. On the other hand, the French used to consider just every rule that had been democratically elaborated. As such, legislative power is unlimited and absolute and has no rule above it that could limit its competencies, which is the same as saying that it has no external limitation.[6]

Nonetheless, it appears that one of the consequences of Enlightened rationalistic struggle is the attempt to outline the characteristics of human individuals that have to be respected by others. This is summarized in one of the notes of liberalism: its universalistic vocation. Liberalism does not consider itself a cultural result, but the solution of cultural variations, and forgets that it is itself nothing but culture. Liberal theory is abstract and, because of that, unreal, but its fruits are without doubt both cultural and real, and have consequences: among others, that of affecting other cultures.

2. Dworkin and rights in liberal tradition

If liberal origins are complex, the attempt to say what liberalism is nowadays is almost impossible. More difficult even is the attempt to define a liberal idea of rights. Nevertheless, I think that it is legitimate to use as paradigmatic Ronald Dworkin's thesis, not so much because this author has adopted the fight towards rights as a personal task, but because of the innovation of his theory that has raised questions in areas that before him were considered unquestionable.

Nevertheless, it would be an error to consider that the idea of rights Dworkin maintains conforms to a universalistic pattern as that of traditional liberalism. On the contrary, this author repudiates any kind of moral objectivism[7] founding a consideration of rights, and dedicates an extensive part of his work to the development of the possibility of a kind of skepticism sustained over a nucleus of moral values. For example, very interesting is the distinction he makes between internal and external skepticism[8], internal skepticism being grounded in a positive value judgment while the external or Archimedean skepticism remains outside a body of beliefs and judges it from that position.

A first difficulty in approaching Dworkin's theory is the frequency with which in continental thought he is interpreted from parametres that are divorced from the Anglo-Saxon. This has produced not only misunderstanding, but, even

6 Amuchastegui, Ibid. 50

7 On this point, see S. Guest, *Ronald Dworkin,* (Stanford 1991), 132.

8 R. Dworkin, *Law's Empire,* (Cambridge, Massachussetts 1986), 78 y ss.

worse, it has led to erroneous conclusions on his thought. For instance, Dworkin does not enter into the iusnaturalism-iuspositivism dichotomy.[9] On the contrary, his debate is with utilitarianism, which supposes a discussion more on the political field than on the juridical conceptual theory. In this sense, and although sometimes there has been an attempt to make a comparison between his notion of principles and that of general principles of law used in codificated systems as a source of law, it seems very difficult to identify both of them. Only with reservations can Dworkin's idea of principles be useful in the continental system because of the different position and function of the judge and his compromise with law.

Dworkin is not concerned with the way rights were originally enumerated in the American Constitution,[10] but in their current interpretation. His principles are rules of interpretation that determine judicial decision. At this point, the role of the judge is fundamental, not only as an interpreter of American law, but of liberal tradition itself. Making a parallelism with the idea of justification of law in the American Declaration of Rights, Dworkin's thesis is that the judge, when he can justify soundly his decisions, can follow a different way from that marked by the desires of people.

The sum of his thesis is an interpretation of law. The book in which this clearly appears is *Law's Empire*. His strongest thesis is that there is only one interpretation of the law in hard cases and, to defend this, he alleges that the interpreter has to support his asertion in three principles:

> "Hard cases arise, for any judge, when his threshold test does not discriminate between two or more interpretations of some statute or line of cases. Then he must choose between eligible interpretations by asking which shows the community's structure of institutions and decisions – its public standards as a whole – in a better light from the standpoint of political morality. His own moral and political convictions are now directly engaged. But the political judgment he must make is itself complex and will sometimes set one department of his political morality against another (...). Questions of fit arise at this stage of interpretation as well, because even when an interpretation survives the threshold requirement, any infelicities of fit will count against it, in the ways we noticed, in the general balance of political virtues. Different judges will disagree about each of these issues and will accordingly take different views of what the law of their community, properly understood, really is".[11]

From what has been said we could derive the assertion that Dworkin's thesis does not conform to a theory of law,[12] although he himself says he is offering one.[13] His thought should be understood as a differently leveled system in which some parts are supported by the others. An example could be the way in which

9 See R. Dworkin, "Natural Law Revisited", *University of Florida Law Review,* vol. XXXIV, nº 2, winter 1982, 165–186.

10 This affects to the debate between those who want to read the Constitution in a literal way. See Robert H. Bork, *The Tempting of America. The Political Seduction of the Law* (London 1990) and the reaction of Dworkin himself in "Bork's Jurisprudence", *The University of Chicago Law Review*, 57, 1990, 657–677.

11 Dworkin, *Law's Empire*, 255–256.

12 Como una crítica en cuanto a su método cfr. John J.A. Burke, *The Political Foundation of Law and the Need for Theory with Practical Value: The Theories of Ronald Dworkin and Roberto Unger* (San Francisco 1993).

13 Dworkin, "Introduction", *Taking Rights Seriously.*

his understanding of the relations between law and morality are supported in a peculiar way of understanding skepticism, that is itself supported over inmovable logic bases. We have seen that one of the principles on which interpretation has to be based is that of coherence with the system. That is how Dworkin may be considered not only an interpreter of law, but of liberal tradition as well. This is a matter of disagreement among scholars who consider themselves liberals although representing different interpretations of liberalism.[14] That is the case of republican claims of reading literally the letters of rights.

In this sense, we should not forget that the notion of rights is understood in an analytical way. It is not properly something that is possessed, but something which when invoked deprives its justification from the actuation of public power. It is something that destroys the argumentative discourse of justification. In fact, it does not make sense to talk about human rights in Dworkin's case, because not only do his ideas not conform to a metaphysical idea of human nature, but they also cannot be told of every man of every culture. On the contrary, Dworkin believes that he is working only with those rights that are derived from the interpretation of the Anglo-Saxon system.

He is not concerned however, with whether a different culture betrays that which in the American system is considered a right because it is not the object of his study. In the same way, he is not concerned with whether inside the American system cultural specialities are not contemplated because in any case nobody has a duty towards freedom and within the wide framework that liberalism offers, different cultural versions can limit freedom.

3. Critiques to this conception of rights

The critiques against Dworkin's thesis have followed different routes, although the aspect we are interested in now is that of contextualization of the human being. These theories present a critique towards liberalism based on the gap that separates theory from reality. Nevertheless, it is not possible to talk about these theses as a whole.[15] On the contrary, there are various tendencies, from extreme republicanism to a deconstructivism extreme too. It would be useful to classify them in to at least three groups:

One of the tendencies is that which is related with different kinds of nationalism. It has different versions which imply different conclusions as well. One of the claims of some of them is the necessity of dealing with communities inside the state. It affects human rights because it denies a universal conception

14 See Clifford Orwin and James R. Stoner Jr. "Neoconstitutionalism? Rawls, Dworkin and Nozick", *Confronting the Constitution*, Allan Bloom ed. 437–470. See as well Thomas Pangle, "Republicanism and Rights", *The Framers and Fundamental Rights*, (Washington 1991), 102–120.

15 Very interesting is the position of Addis Adeno in, "Individualism, Communitarianism and the Rights of Ethnic Minorities", in *Notre Dame Law Review,* 67, nº 3, 1992, 615–676. He works on the two antagonistic phenomena that appear in today's world: "What one observes is, therefore, a resurgence of ethnic consciousnes and separatism along with developments that seem to recognize the economic and technological imperatives of the late twentieth century: the interdependent nature of the lives of nations and communities", 617.

and claims for its substitution by a cultural one. The state should contemplate minority rights.[16] A part of what is often catalogued as communitarianism would be comprehended here.[17] This is the position of Michael Taylor or Michael MacDonald, both Canadian scholars.[18]

A second version is that which, in spite of being considered communitarian as well, is quite different from the former; it claims a stronger position of the authority inside the community. To some extent, in the North American political debate, it has been identified with the theoretical fundations of the struggle between liberals and republicans[19]. They maintain that liberalism leads necessarily, not to an option about morality, but to a lack of moral sense[20]. Representatives of this tendency are Michael Sandel and Benjamin Barber.

Finally, there is the posmodernist debate. In America it leads to a confrontation between liberals and extreme pragamatists such as Richard Rorty.[21] These theories among others are sustained upon what Dworkin denominates external or Archimedean skepticism.

To these different accusations of lack of context, Dworkin reacted by saying that he had been misunderstood. He does not talk of universalism, but of a concrete and existing reality that is the American juridical system, and in a minor measure, the British one.

> "I began by conceding that integrity would have no distinct role to play in a community that was understood by all its members to be perfectly just and fair. I am defending an interpretation of our own political culture, not an abstract and timeless political morality".[22]

To this we could reply that although it is possible that his proposal is neither universalist nor objectivist, it is indeed abstract because it does not consider the fact that within the American system there are different conceptions of the good life and that liberal tradition proposes itself as another one which can be incompatible with some of them.[23]

16 Jürgen Habermas, has attended lately this debate, cfr. "Human Rights and Popular Sovereignty: the Liberal and Republican Versions", in *Ratio Iuris*, vol 7, nº 1, March 1994, 1-13.

17 Our opinion about communitarianism is the same as of those who consider it as a soft or moderated version of liberalism, in which it is difficult to find an element of identity of its own. That is why most of the authors that, without being liberals, are usually catalogued as communitarians (that is the case of MacIntyre), do not admit that affiliation.

18 Cfr. See C. Taylor, *Multiculturalism and the "Politics of Recognition"*, (Princeton 1992), 56 y ss. Michael MacDonald, "Aboriginal Rights", in *Contemporary Issues in Political Philosophy*, William R. Shea and John King-Farlow eds, (New York 1976). There are other scholars that, from a more moderated point of view, try to recover the aspect of human being as a citizen, see Ronald Beiner, *What's the Matter with Liberalism*, (Berkeley, Oxford 1992), 23 y ss, and "Why Citizenship Constitutes Theoretical Problem in the Last Decade of the Twentieth Century", in *Theorizing Citizenship* (Albany 1995), 1–8.

19 Stephen Gardbaum, "Law, Politics and the Claim of Community", in *Michigan Law Review*, vol 90, February 1992, 749 y ss.

20 On this point see Michael Walzer, *Thick and Thin* (Indiana 1994).

21 See Richard Rorty, "Human Rights, Rationality and Sentimentality", *On Human Rights,* Oxford Amnesty Lectures, Stephen Shute and Susan Hurley eds. (New York 1993), 111–134. Paradoxically, Rorty defines himself as a liberal, see Gardbaum, cit. 707 y ss.

22 Dworkin, *Law's Empire* , 216.

23 As Kymlicka says: "Most contemporary liberals write as if this process of building a common

It is paradoxical that all liberal pretension of being a framework adequate to all the possible cultural positions runs into those positions themselves. This is a manifestation that the supposed neutrality of liberalism is not real at all. Universalism is not compatible with neutrality. And universalism in human rights is just one of the perspectives from which liberal universalism as a whole can be observed, if it wants to be consistent and coherent. But the real problem that affects liberalism is that although it is not real, it creates reality.[24] It talks about a man that is not real (called the individual), about a society that does not exist, about a list of rights that are not real because they are formal or there is no way to claim them. But in spite of all that, when operating with them it generates a new kind of man, society and laws.

References

AAVV, *Orígenes de la declaración de derechos del hombre y del ciudadano,* ed. Jesús, G. Amuchastegui, Editora Nacional (Madrid 1984).

AARNIO, Aulis y PECZENIK, Aleksander, "On Values. Universal or Relative?", *Previous Acts of the 17th IVR World Congress*, II (Bologna 1995), 1–7.

ADENO, Addis, , "Individualism, Communitarianism and the Rights of Ethnic Minorities", in *Notre Dame Law Review,* 67, nº 3, 1992, 615–676.

ARECHEDERRA, Luis, "Revolucíon tecnocracia y demagogia", *Persona y Derecho*, 26, 1992, 29–52.

BEINER, Ronald, *What's the Matter with Liberalism*, University of California Press (Berkeley-Oxford 1992).

– "Why Citizenship Constitutes Theoretical Problem in the Last Decade of the Twentieth Century", in *Theorizing Citizenship* , R. Beiner ed., State University of New York Press (Albany 1995), 1–8.

BORK, Robert H., *The Tempting of America. The Political Seduction of the Law,* Sinclair-Stevenson (London 1990).

BURKE, John J.A., *The Political Foundation of Law and the Need for Theory with Practical Value: The Theories of Ronald Dworkin and Roberto Unger*, Austin & Winfield (San Francisco 1993).

DWORKIN, Ronald, *Taking Rights Seriously*, Duckworth, Harvard University Press (London 1977).

– "Natural Law Revisited", *University of Florida Law Review,* vol. XXXIV, nº 2, winter 1982, 165-186.

– *A Matter of Principle*, Clarendon Press (Oxford 198 –*Law's Empire,* The Belknap Press of Harvard University Press (Cambridge, Masachussetts 1986).

– "Bork's Jurisprudence", *The University of Chicago Law Review,*, 57, 1990, 657–677.

EDGEWORTH, B. "Reading Dworkin Empirically: Principles, Policies and Property" in *Reading Dworkin Critically*, A. Hunt, ed. Berg (Nueva York Oxford 1992), 187–208.

GARDBAUM, Stephen, "Law, Politics and the Claim of Community", in *Michigan Law Review*, vol 90, February 1992, 685–760.

GUEST, Stephen, *Ronald Dworkin*, Stanford University Press (Stanford 1991), 210.

culture extends throughout the entire country, so that there is just one such culture in each country. For example, Dworkin suggests that the United States contains a single 'cultural structure' based on a 'shared language'". Will Kymlicka, *Multicultural Citizenship* (Oxford 1995) 77.

24 See L. Arechederra, "Revolucíon, techocracia y demagogia", *Persona y Derecho*, 26, 1992, 29–52.

HABERMAS, Jürgen, “Human Rights and Popular Sovereignty: the Liberal and Republican Versions”, in *Ratio Iuris*, vol 7, nº 1, March 1994, 1–13.

KYMLICKA, Will, *Multicultural Citizenship*, Clarendon Press (Oxford 1995).

– *Liberalism, Community and Culture*, Oxford University Press (Oxford 1989)

– *Contemporary Political Philosophy*, Oxford University Press (Oxford 1990).

MAC DONALD, Michael, “Aboriginal Rights”, in *Contemporary Issues in Political Philosophy*, William R. Shea and John King-Farlow, eds., Science History Publications (New York 1976).

NINO, Carlos Santiago, “Positivism and Communitarianism: Between Human Rights and Democracy”, *Ratio Iuris*, vol. 7, nº 1, march 1994, 14–40.

ORWIN, Clifford and STONER, James R. Jr., “Neoconstitutionalism? Rawls, Dworkin and Nozick”, *Confronting the Constitution*, Allan Bloom ed. 437–470.

PANGLE, Thomas, “Republicanism and Rights”, *The Framers and Fundamental Rights*, Robert A. Linch Press, AEI Press (Washington 1991), 102–120.

RORTY, Richard, “Human Rights, Rationality and Sentimentality”, *On Human Rights,* Oxford Amnesty Lectures, Stephen Shute and Susan Hurley eds., Basic Books (New York 1993), 111–134.

TAYLOR, Charles, *The Malaise of Modernity*, Anansi (Concord, Ontario 1992).

– *Multiculturalism and the “Politics of Recognition”*, Princeton University Press (Princeton, New Jersey 1992).

WALZER, Michael, *Thick and Thin*, University of Notre Dame Press (Indiana 1994).

Mariachiara Tallacchini, Florence

Human Right to the Environment or Rights of Nature?

1. Law, rights, and the environment

The environment is a fairly recent object for law and rights[1]. The need to place limits on human intervention in the environment has led to the theorization of two opposing rights: the human right to the environment[2], which protects man from man in the exploitation of nature; the rights of nature[3], which protect nature from man. The environment as an object of a human right is the expression of the so-called third generation of human rights – whose reference-value is solidarity, "freedom together"[4] – and aims at defending human beings from environmental degradation produced by industrial development. The configuration of the rights for nature swings between extreme conceptions: a minimal one, which merely exploits the emphasis of the language of rights to refer to human duties; a maximal one, according to which "biorights" are "the rights of unique landscapes to remain untouched"[5]. The first considers subjective rights as a mere persuasive formula, the second leads to the contradictory consequence whereby the complete intactness of nature demands the disappearance of man (and of law). But if the expression "rights of nature" is to have any content at all, the meaning is to be sought by excluding these two definitions.

The elaboration of the defence of nature through two opposing subjective rights suggests several questions and reflections. What conception of the natural environment is subtended at objective law and at subjective rights? Is this conception consistent with the needs of environmental protection? Is the prevalent emphasis on moral or legal aspects in the appeal to rights ? The thesis which I wish to outline is that taking "the path of rights" is a partially inadequate approach to grasping ecological questions[6], since the premises implicit in it conflict with the essential nucleus of ecological thought. If, however, we undertake this path, then the claim for a human right to the environment has even more the meaning of a moral appeal, while the legal needs are better met by the attribution of rights to nature.

1 N. Bobbio, *L'età dei diritti*, Einaudi, Torino 1990, p.XV.

2 W.T. Blackstone, *Ethics and Ecology*, in W.T. Blackstone (ed.), *Philosophy and Environmental Crisis*, University of Georgia Press, Athens 1974, p.32, speaks of "an inalienable right to a decent environment".

3 C.D. Stone, *Should Trees Have Standing ? Toward Legal Rights for Natural Objects*, Tioga Publishing Co., Palo Alto 1988 (Los Altos 1974); R.F. Nash, *The Rights of Nature. A History of Environmental Ethics*, The University of Wisconsin Press, Madison 1989.

4 As described by A.E. Perez-Luno, *Le generazioni dei diritti umani*, in "Nomos", 1989, 3, pp.1–12.

5 T. O'Riordan, *Environmentalism*, Pion, London 1981.

6 See A. Boyle, M.Anderson (eds.), *Human Rights Approaches to Environmental Protection*, Clarendon Press, Oxford 1996.

2. Shallow and Deep Ecology in legal questions

Ecological questions may be treated from two different perspectives[7]: the first, the Shallow Ecology Movement (SEM), environmentalism, consists of believing that environmental themes are only new objects to which to apply "normal" philosophies; the second, the Deep Ecology Movement (DEM), ecologism, instead sees in ecology the source of new philosophical conceptions, a change of cognitive and ethical paradigm.

Shallow Ecologies are bound to a point of view of human usefulness and prudent exploitation of resources. Deep Ecologies, on the contrary, wish to introduce "nature's point of view" into philosophy, an ecosystemic perspective which decentralizes man and authorizes a minimal use of resources. Anthropocentrism, methodological individualism, the instrumental value of nature and resource management are the technical-operational criteria of environmentalism; ecocentrism, methodological holism, intrinsic value and non-interference with nature – because "Nature knows best"[8] – those of ecologism.

This distinction may be applied also to the relationship between law and environment: "legal environmentalism" is the conception in which the environment is for law an object of appropriation or management[9], to which existing normative concepts and legal means are applied; "legal ecologism", on the other hand, refers to a considered source of theoretic changes in legal problems.

We must therefore first consider what is the prevailing attitude of law towards nature.

2.1 Law versus nature: legal anthropocentrism and "the right to destroy"

The connection between law and nature arises within law itself and from philosophical reflection on the idea of normativity. The link between "nomos" and "physis", both as problematization of the relationship between naturalistic normativity and legal normativity, and as relationship between natural law and positive law, has covered a large part of legal-philosophical thought. It is, however, difficult to discern in this reflection a real interest in external nature; the proper domain of law is indicated in the social nature of man – "ubi societas ibi ius" –, and the nature from which natural law has drafted its own directions is not external nature, but human nature[10].

However this may be, the extraneousness of nature to law, far from being translated into neutrality, has been the powerful vehicle of an attitude of dominion and reification[11].

7 See A. Naess, *The Shallow and the Deep, Long-Range Ecology Movement. A Summary*, in "Inquiry" 1973, 16, pp.95–100.

8 Cf. B. Commoner, *The Closing Circle: Nature, Man, and Technology*, Knopf, New York 1972, p.41.

9 Cf. F. Ost, *Le juste milieu*, in P. Gerard, F. Ost, M. van de Kerchove, *Images et usages de la nature en droit*, Publications des Facultés Universitaires Saint-Louis, Bruxelles 1993, pp.13–73; F. Ost, *La nature hors la loi. L'écologie à l'épreuve du droit*, Ed. La Découverte, Paris 1995.

10 Cf. J.Finnis, *Natural Law and Natural Rights*, Clarendon Press, Oxford 1980.

11 In this sense B. Edelman, M.A. Hermitte, *L'homme, la nature et le droit*, Christian Bourgois Ed., Paris 1988.

Natural law and positive law have precise responsibilities concerning environmental degradation: the former because of its strong anthropocentrism, the second for having legitimized a "right to destroy"[12].

If it is possible to recognize in ancient natural law a non-dominating conception of man over nature[13] – a consequence of the pre-technological condition, in which man undergoes nature and cannot transform it – when, with the birth of science, a methodology of dominion is elaborated, nature ceases also for law to represent a regulative principle, and becomes an emancipative principle; subjective natural rights, the expression of freedom and claim[14], shift attention "from duties to rights, from recognition to volition, from life to ownership"[15]. If natural law refers to a defined normative order and to a closed world, natural rights are connected to a logical space of indefinite compatibilities, and to a physical space of unlimited resources.

The lack of attribution of legal worth to environmental goods has strongly contributed to its degradation. The traditional characters of legal objects – quantifiability, scarcity, economic value – were absent in the "res communes omnium" (water, air), removed from any economic relationship and open to the enjoyment of everyone. But what law did not protect, natural selection led to destruction[16].

With the sanctioning of the idea of property in the *Code Napoléon*, possessive individualism found a medium for capillary diffusion. Ownership, the "droit de jouir et disposer des choses de la manière la plus absolue"[17], implies that the owner may use his property or leave it alone, even exercising the fullest form of provision: to destroy it.

The intimately predatory attitude of law concerning nature – an attitude of which even subjective rights bear a reflection, since they have their own paradigm in property – is certainly not a reassuring premise for the defence of the environment: the epistemological assumptions of law seem too compromised with anthropocentrism and the criteria of modern science[18]. But not even the rights of nature are free from criticism. Although the subjective legal standing of nature may appear as "deep" – because recognizing a subjective right means in fact granting the strongest significant means in a legal system – this position remains "shallow". In fact, it only apparently abandons anthropocentrism, since it "merely extends – rather than seriously questions or radically changes – conventional anthropocentric ethics". It is a moral extensionism[19]. The wrong

12 M. Rèmond-Gouilloud, *Du droit de détruire*, P.U.F., Paris 1989.

13 M. Brown, *Natural Law and the Environment*, "Proceedings of the American Catholic Philosophical Association" 1990, LXIII, pp.221–234.

14 For the counterposition between natural law and natural rights see A. Passerin d'Entrèves, *Natural Law. An Introduction to Legal Philosophy*, Hutchinson's University Press, London 1951; for a different position G. Fasso', *Storia della filosofia del diritto*, vol.II, Il Mulino, Bologna 1970, p.111.

15 B. Edelman, M.A. Hermitte, *L'homme, la nature et le droit*, cit., p.4.

16 Cf. G. Hardin, *The Tragedy of the Commons*, "Science" 1968, 162, pp.1243–1248.

17 Art.544 *Code civil.*

18 S. Gutwirth, *Autour du contrat naturel*, in P. Gerard, F. Ost, M. van de Kerchove, *Images et usages de la nature en droit*, cit., p.99-101.

19 J. Rodman, *Four Forms of Ecological Consciousness Reconsidered*, in D. Scherer, T. Attig (eds.), *Ethics and the Environment*, Prentice-Hall Inc., Englewood Cliffs 1983, pp.86–87.

perspective inherent in the two positions depends on the excessive enlargement given to subjective rights: in the case of the rights of nature, the non-qualified growth of the new right-holders; in the hypothesis of the right to the environment, the non-qualified increase of human claims.

Even though there are good reasons to consider the path of environmental rights inadequate, different observations must be made concerning the two rights, distinguishing the moral emphasis from the legal one.

2.2 Environmental rights in morals and law

In the tradition of common law it is usual to distinguish between "moral rights" and "legal rights"[20], expressions which, although not literally translatable in the continental tradition, are very similar to the opposition between natural and positive rights[21].

Moral and legal rights are characterized by different features[22]; those which are relevant here concern the standing requirements for right-holders in the two cases.

As far as moral rights are concerned, many moral philosophers have sought to extend the premises of subjective right to morally relevant non-human beings. The notion of "interest"[23] appears central here, an essential requisite in order to speak rationally of rights. A distinction is made between a subjective interest "interest 1", the capacity to have conative aptitudes, preferences (that which makes it possible to recomprehend many sentient beings), and an objective interest "interest 2", welfare-interest, the tending to a condition of optimality (that which is predicable of every organic or non-organic entity). But if it is acceptable that "interest1" may be the basis for animal rights[24], the possibility of elaborating rights starting from "interest 2" arouses much perplexity[25].

20 Cf. N. Bobbio, *L'età dei diritti*, cit., p.XVII: "in italiano, l'espressione 'diritti legali' o 'giuridici', suona ridondante, l'espressione 'diritti morali' suona contradittoria". ("In italian, the expression 'legal rights' or 'juridical rights' sounds pompous, the expression 'moral rights' sounds contradictory").

21 Although the moral rights/natural rights parallel is not valid concerning animals and environment, since natural rights arise as rights for rational beings: which excludes non-human beings by definition (see J. Rodman, *Animal Justice: The Counter-revolution in Natural Right and Law*, "Inquiry" 1979, 22, pp.3–22).

22 According to T. Regan (ed.), *Earthbound. Introductory Essays in Environmental Ethics*, Waveland Press, Prospect Heights 1990, pp.30-31, "moral rights" are: universal, equal, inalienable. *Contra*, R.Dworkin, *Taking Rights seriously*, Duckworth, London 1977, observes that it is difficult for a serious theory on rights to separate moral rights from legal ones.

23 On interests/rights relation see J. Feinberg, *The Rights of Animals and Unborn Generations*, in W. Blackstone (ed.), *Philosophy and Environmental Crisis*, University of Georgia Press, Athens 1974, pp.43–68; H.J. McCloskey, *Moral Rights and Animals*, "Inquiry" 1979, 22, pp. 23–54.

24 J. Feinberg, *The Nature and Value of Rights*, "The Journal of Value Inquiry" 1970, IV, pp.243–257.

25 See T.Regan, *The case for animal rights*, Routledge & Kegan Paul, London 1983. *Contra*, see E. Sober, *Philosophical Problems for Environmentalism*, in B.G. Norton (ed.), *The Preservation of Species. The Value of Biological Diversity*, Princeton University Press,

As far as legal rights are concerned, on the other hand, law appears less restrictive in the determination of the subjective requisites. It does not seem problematic to give nature legal standing, since law admits the creation of fictitious realities, free from the underlying naturalistic structure. A subjective legal situation may be set up over a natural person with a weak subjectivity (a legal incompetent), and over a legal person, a non-subject (foundation) or a multiple entity (corporation).

But, at the same time, law is more restrictive in order to define the content[26], the legal advantage, to which the legal right refers: this content is still subjected to the features of quantifiability and economic worth.

I want here to emphasize the difference between moral and legal rights with regard to their operational features and to the role these features play in the protection of the environment, so that they may achieve different goals.

2.2.1 The human right to the environment

The theorization of the environment as a human right, as an object of protection, takes on the human need for nature, the essentiality of nature to the humanity of man.

As a general moral claim, it is the unifying precondition for a different hierarchization of freedoms[27] – a new, more concrete and less libertarian qualification of the idea of liberty.

But the right to the environment is no longer only a human aspiration, but has found legislative or jurisprudential recognition in many legal systems. While several constitutional charters state it explicitly[28], in the italian legal order, which has not codified it as "an extension of the sphere of personality"[29] it is considered operational[30] through Article 32 of the Constitution: "The Republic defends health as a fundamental right of the individual and interest of the collectivity" ("La Repubblica tutela la salute come fondamentale diritto dell'individuo e interesse della collettività").

The case of international law is different, where the right to the environment is for the moment an ideal without effective recognition. The *Rio Declaration on*

Princeton 1986, p.184: "species, plants and mountain ranges have needs, but only in the sense that automobiles, garbage dumps, and buildings do too. If everything has needs, the advice to take needs into account in ethical deliberations is empty".

26 On precision and determinacy of legal rights, lacking in moral ones, cf. C. Wellman, *A New Conception of Human Rights*, in J. Feinberg, H. Gross (eds.), *Philosophy of Law*, IV ed., Wadsworth Publ.Co., Belmont Ca. 1991, pp.368–374 (reprinted from E. Kamenka, A.E.S. Tay (eds.), *Human Rights*, E. Arnold, London 1978).

27 Così W.T. W.T. Blackstone, *Ethics and Ecology*, cit.

28 Article 66 of the Portuguese Constitution (2.4.1976) speaks of the "right to human, healthy and ecologically balanced environment"; Article 45 of the Spanish Constitution (31.10.1978) affirms the "right of each person to an adequate environment".

29 S. Rodotà, cit. in S. Salmi *Diritto dell'ambiente. Principi fondamentali di diritto ambientale*, Pirola, Milano 1994, p.22.

30 Cf. S. Patti, *Diritto all'ambiente e tutela della persona*, "Giurisprudenza italiana" 1980, I, pp.859–868; A. Postiglione, *Il diritto all'ambiente*, Jovene, Napoli 1982.

Environment and Development states blandly that "Human beings are at the center of concern" – and do not «have a fundamental right» – "for sustainable development. They are entitled to a healthy and productive life in harmony with nature"[31].

The reasons which testify in favour of a legal human right to the environment may be agreed on. Linking the environment to the value of the person is a guarantee against possible subordinations of it to other interests. In particular, it is said, it would make it possible to overcome the limits of a defence of the environment as an object of ownership and an economic reduction of the legal values[32]: the new rights of personality are a category to set against property rights.

But the legal positivization of the right to the environment arouses some perplexity. The first concerns the conceptual capacity of this right to take up and represent ecological questions. The idea of subjective right, it has been said, is loaded with atomistic premises – the idea of society as a sum of individuals – and individualistic ones – the absolute priority of the individual over society as a whole. Those criticising the right to the environment have a negative view of the parceling of an indivisible, collective good which such right suggests; of the fragmenting an object whose legal importance must be unitary,[33] concerning global changes taking place in society. Moreover, the idea of environment as a subjective revindication gives rise to an untenable logical alternative: either to consider nature as a good which the State must make available to individuals, or indicate as a "right" what in fact is specified in a series of "duties" (not damaging, not polluting...). The first hypothesis takes to an extreme the idea of the Welfare State, neglecting the obvious need for each right to be correlated to a duty; the second emphasizes instead that the theory of rights has reached a paradoxical point, where obligations are called rights.

A further doubt hinges lastly on the concrete characterization which the right to the environment has received in the legal systems which have included it: as a right to a healthy environment.

And it is not by chance, but by necessity, that many legal systems have chosen precisely this kind of right. Healthiness – a systemic idea of health – represents, from an individualistic point of view, the only well-defined, in some way materially-possessed and quantified environmental value – differently from aesthetic, cognitive or existence values[34].

31 *Earth Charter*, 14.6.1992, Principle 1.

32 Against a costs/benefits reduction of environmental problems, see M. Sagoff, *The Economy of the Earth*, Cambridge University Press, Cambridge 1988.

33 C. Salvi, *La tutela civile: diritto individuale o interesse collettivo?*, "Giurisprudenza italiana" 1980, I, p.872.

34 A. Randall, *Human Preferences, Economics, and the Preservation of Species*, in B.G. Norton (ed.), *The Preservation of Species*, Princeton University Press, New Jersey 1986, pp.79–109, has sought to amplify the category of values associated with the preservation of the environment: from use values (exploitation of resources); to option values (if a species is lost, the possibility of use is lost with it); quasi-option value (the growing of knowledge makes new uses possible); existence values (the value related to the mere fact that a species exists, independently from use).

But this hygienistic, medicalized vision of ecological questions is inadequate to deal exhaustively with environmental issues: the right to a healthy environment may give the reason for the problem of pollution, but is silent in front of other ecological themes. It is, for example, not seen how healthiness may be capable of justifying the defence of endangered species, especially those not clearly useful; or the protection of ecosystems with an unhealthy climate (e.g. wet lands, which the *Ramsar Convention* dealt with in 1973); or any other hypothesis in which a functional link with human interests is lacking.

The right to the environment therefore acquires a different meaning, if seen as a moral right or as a legal right. If as a moral claim it appears a unifying principle, as a legal claim, it instead gives rise to the reduction of a general interest to fragmented individual interests, mostly satisfied by an economic compensation, which may also allow the damage to the environment to continue. It has been observed that the "polluter payer" principle[35] easily shifts to a "right to pollute", which is completely compatible with a right to a healthy environment conceived in terms of monetary compensation.

2.2.2 The rights for nature

Taking the moral rights of nature seriously is problematic. Even if we accept that "interest 2" may exceed the subjective limits of the notion of right, the structural feature of the notion of moral right – its individualistic character – however remains: paradigmatic right-holders are individuals, whereas many ecological entities are collective.

Is it therefore possible to speak of the moral rights of species and ecosystems? Species and ecosystems are names for global entities[36], to which the theory of rights is inapplicable. Only by representing the species as a sum of individuals – which however is not possible for an ecosystem – may we speak of the rights of its members[37]. But the notion remains ambiguous.

A rational analogy between collective human rights and species rights is not tenable: while the right of a people to exist does not clash with the right of its members to exist, the interest of a species in perpetuating itself may prove directly contrary to the interests of particular members. It is not at all obvious, in fact, whether it is more in the interest of a species to have a large population or a small, healthy one[38].

We have said that with legal rights the situation is partly different: legal representation and legal personality are means by which law may overcome difficulties related to a lack of natural subjectivity or to the features of superindividual aggregations.

35 Introduced by OCDE (28.5.1972).

36 For the scientific idea of species see A.L. Caplan, *Back to Class: A Note on the Ontology of Species*, "Philosophy of Science" 1981, 48, pp.130–140; for a different opinion see D. Hull, *A Matter of Individuality*, "Philosophy of Science" 1978, pp.335–360.

37 T. Regan, *The case for animal rights*, cit., pp.359–360.

38 B.G. Norton, *Why Preserve Natural Variety ?*, Princeton University Press, New Jersey 1987, p.170.

But this must not be seen to mean that legal rights are free from the substantial reasons which bind moral conditions.

Defending legal rights for natural objects, Stone[39] has argued that the notion of nature having rights makes a significant operational difference: firstly, the thing can institute legal actions at its behest; secondly, in determining the granting of legal relief, the court must take the injury to nature into account; thirdly, relief must run to the benefit of nature. As we saw, in fact, the problem with a human right to the environment is that the right-holder may lack any personal or economic interest in acting upon that right, or that no money he receives goes to the restoration of the damaged ecosystem.

Contrary to what we said concerning the human right to the environment, if the moral rights of nature leave us sceptical, the legal ones appear convincing – though within the epistemological limits of subjective rights. What is meant here is that if within the legal defence of the environment one wishes to operate with the instrument of subjective right, then, in relation to the issues which such a concept may achieve, it is meaningful to speak of the rights of nature and not of the human right to the environment.

2.2.3 Legal "considerateness": the right answer to wrong rights?

There remains the fact that subjective right is based on premises incongruous with the need for a systemic defence of the environment. Applied to the man/nature relationship, rights are "wrong rights"[40]. Environment and rights, Regan has observed, "are like oil and water: they don't mix"[41].

Stone himself, considering the legal personification of nature as anthropomorphistic, has more recently argued that an objective defence is preferable: a legal "considerateness" for nature[42], a situation of objective legal advantage which provides for a strong control over human behaviour[43] and which aims essentially at the prevention of environmental damage or the possible recovery of damaged ecosystems.

39 C.D. Stone, *Should Trees Have Standing ? Toward Legal Rights for Natural Objects*, cit., wrote this paper for the controversial Sierra Club (a well-known association for the protection of the environment) vs. Walt Disney Corp. case for the economic exploitation of the Mineral King Valley in 1972. The U.S. Supreme Court stated that the Sierra Club had no standing to bring the question to the Court, because it was not directly injured: there is not a right to sue "simply because there is no one else willing and able to assert it" (*ibidem*, p.XVII). But writing for the minority opinion, Justice Douglas observed that "(t)he critical question of 'standing' would be simplified (..) if we fashioned a federal rule that allowed environmental issues to be litigated before federal agencies or federal courts in the name of the inanimate objects (..)" (*ib.*, p.73).

40 See E. Wolgast, *Wrong rights*, "Hypatia" 1987, 1, pp.25–43.

41 T. Regan, *The case for animal rights*, cit., p.362.

42 The term "legal considerateness" is introduced by C.D. Stone, *Earth and Other Ethics. The Case for Moral Pluralism*, Harper & Row, New York 1987.

43 Cf. K. Bosselmann, *Eigene Rechte für die Natur?*, "Kritische Justiz"" 1986, pp.1–22.

The path of law is on the other hand the way followed by many systems, although it is not always effective, because the value of nature is not explicitly considered as pre-eminent compared with other interests[44].

This claim does not converge uniformly with the idea of "public interest", because the latter "has so many different shades of meaning as to be quite meaningless on the environmental front"[45]. We need a clear and complete account of the different, competing values involved in environmental questions to establish the rules for the hierarchization of the concrete values in environmental decisions.

The right answer to environmental problems is probably a normative, systemic view of values. The path of rights – shifting from the objective plane to the subjective one – provides only a mistaken surrogate: an inflation of right-holders does not simplify the problem and multiplies conflicts.

44 Only one international document, the *World Charter for Nature* (28.10.1982) has stated in principle that "(e)very form of life is unique, warranting respect regardless of its worth to man..." (Annex, Preamble).

45 *Sierra Club v. Morton*, Justice Douglas, Minority Opinion, cit. in C.D. Stone, *Should Trees Have Standing ?*, cit., p.76.

Donald Galloway, Victoria, B.C.

Constitutions, Civil Rights and Outsiders

The enactment or constitutional entrenchment of a bill of rights is a legal initiative which has recently been adopted in many jurisdictions around the globe. Even where those who promote such a change have not been successful in realizing their aim, they have engendered widespread public discussion about its merits. It appears that this is an idea whose time has now come or is at hand.

In Canada, the decision to enact a Bill of Rights was made originally in 1960. However, it was only in 1982 when the Charter of Rights and Freedoms was entrenched within the Constitution that the meaning and significance of this innovation began to receive close public scrutiny. The proliferation of lengthy and contentious judicial interpretations has deepened public concern and suspicion. The focus of attention has been not so much on the content of these judgements as on deeper questions relating to the very nature of a constitution in a liberal democracy and to the way in which government power is structured. Of particular concern has been the transfer of substantial political power from the legislature to the judiciary. The Canadian experience in this regard has been of interest to other states which are debating the merits of entrenching a similar document. The expansion of judicial power has come to be seen as the basic question around which debates about bills of rights revolve.

From within the judiciary, this issue has been identified, by and large, as a fait accompli rather than as a problem. From the judicial perspective, the deepest structural problem is that of defining those matters which are subject to Charter override. This problem has been reduced to that of distinguishing governmental action, to which the Charter applies, from non-governmental, to which it does not, or, more simply, to that of distinguishing the realm of the public from that of the private.

The fact that these issues have monopolized public and judicial attention has its downside. Some other equally basic questions, which relate to what might be called the architecture of a bill of rights rather than to its substance, have as a consequence been ignored. In this paper, I raise and consider two such fundamental questions which are prompted by the enactment of the Charter: Who are the bearers of constitutional rights? and why should they not be vested in others?

In both Canada and the United States, courts have submitted indefinite responses to the first of these questions and have baulked at offering anything more than a speculative, or ad hoc response to the latter. In both jurisdictions, courts have been hesitant or unwilling to apply constitutional protections to foreigners such as visa applicants who have extra-jurisdictional dealings with the governments of these countries.

Underlying such negative attitudes is a set of unexplored images of a constitution as a document which aims to protect members of the polity but not strangers, or alternatively as a document which applies within a territory but not outside, or even as a curious and chaotic amalgam of these two positions. In no case has the constitution been conceived as a document which binds the government to protect the rights of individuals qua human beings.

One can speculate that courts have been reluctant to explore these images and to settle on a single coherent stance because of a deep-rooted moral uncertainty about the merits of each. Committing oneself to one account of what counts as membership in the polity and of the obligations of government to members and non- members involves the rejection of other incompatible views. The courts, it seems, have found it prudent to hedge their bets.

However, at a time when immigration and citizenship are hot political topics, I suspect that they will be unable to do so for very much longer. When a community is polarized between, on the one hand, those who would relax standards of admission particularly for people in need or people with family or other ties and who would also simplify the criteria of citizenship and, on the other hand, those who would exclude all but those who have highly prized skills, the institution which implements the view of the majority will meet many and different challenges from those in the minority. Given that immigration and citizenship policy is perceived as having a large impact on the character of a society, and given the depth of emotion which nationalism and patriotism can stimulate, those government departments which would toy with these matters as if they were easily controlled and fine-tuned, are regarded with great suspicion as sorceror's apprentices. The legitimacy of a democratically elected legislature, which is subject to the ebb and flow of popular opinion and which is readily seen to be governed more by concern with the next election results than by a vision or programme informed by moral precepts, is probably at its lowest when such fundamental issues are at stake. In a world of moving populations, where communities are composed of both long term residents and strangers in the sense defined by Georg Simmel – "those who come today and stay tomorrow" – a Charter of Rights will come to be used as an important vehicle for defining the very identity of the political community.

The primary significance of the Charter will be found not just in the fact that political power has been transferred to the judiciary, but rather in the fact that we have transferred authority to determine who we are as a collectivity - who is an insider, who is an outsider and the reasons for distinguishing between the two. Questions relating to the grounds of government authority which previously were debated primarily within the confines of academia will be raised within the courtroom. While it seems that academics can live with a never ending debate, litigants demand binding and authoritative answers. In effect, we have legalized the most basic problems of politics.

To discern how deeply into political theory the entrenchment of a Charter has taken us, consider the following four accounts of constitutional rights:

First, if a constitution is regarded as a contractual document which identifies the protections which a self-interested and self-identifying group of individuals has succeeded in extracting from its government through negotiation, then it would make sense to regard all the rights which are listed in the constitution as vesting in members of this entity called "the people". From this perspective both membership and community are defined in a pre-legal way. The law will identify the contractual rights but not the contracting parties. Who has entered the contract is a pre-legal question of fact.

Where a constitution, such as the Canadian Constitution, distinguishes between democratic rights which are vested in citizens, mobility rights which are vested in citizens and permanent residents and fundamental freedoms and equality rights which vest in "everyone", one should regard those who are granted the full range of rights to be "members" and others as being third party beneficiaries to this contract. However, it is difficult to explain why third parties should be protected in this manner in a contract between members and the state. Why should the contracting parties pay heed to anyone else?

In one of the few recent philosophical studies of citizenship, Peter Schuck and Rogers Smith opt for a contractual or consensual account of constitutional membership.[1] They do so for both principled and strategic reasons. They maintain that:

> political membership can result only from free individual choices... [The consensual ideal of citizenship] would be more legitimate in theory, more flexible in meeting practical policy problems and more likely to generate a genuine sense of community among all citizens than the existing scheme, while protecting the established human rights of aliens. (pp.4–5)

Schuck and Smith contrast this ideal of citizenship with an ascriptive account according to which membership is determined by location of birth. Their adoption of the consensual model is premised upon its relative advantages over this ascriptive model rather than upon its objective merits. In fact, they also offer a list of defects which substantially detract from its attractiveness. In particular, they mention the problem of unjust exclusion. They write:

> [C]onsent to membership must be mutual, expressed by the existing community as well as by the individual....But this requirement might imply that a society could deny outsiders opportunities for membership in ways that are harshly restrictive or discriminatory.... [A]dherence to consent may well violate liberalism's other deep commitment to insuring that the basic human rights of all be secured at fully as possible.(37)

Schuck and Smith argue, correctly I believe, that a consensual model of citizenship is not necessarily inconsistent with a liberal immigration policy. However, they also fail to see any contingent inconsistency. They connect consensualism with a spirit of generosity in immigration matters. They state:

> [A]lthough we would not want ... to make it easier for the United States to adopt harshly restrictive immigration policies, this deplorable result need not and should not follow. If contemporary attitudes are perhaps not as generous as they were in the early nineteeth century, neither are they as nativist or restrictive as they were even as recently as the 1950's. (119)

Recent experience seems to belie this optimism that in times of economic decline liberal immigration policies will be maintained.

Schuck and Smith also admit that their ideal may have to be amended so as to embrace a notion of legitimate expectations, such that a community which created the justified expectation that membership would ensue, by, for example, allowing long term residence within the country, may be required to grant it. This seemingly minor exception to their model reveals one of its central flaws.

1 Peter H. Schuck and Rogers M. Smith, *Citizenship Without Consent: Illegal Aliens In the American Polity* (Yale University Press, New Haven, 1985).

Contract will only give rise to rights and obligations if the terms of the agreement are not unjust. The mere fact that a group of individuals has agreed to recognize each other as members in a community and to adopt criteria for others to join is immaterial from a moral point of view if the purpose of the enterprise is unjustifiable or if the criteria of exclusion are unjust. As a moral institution, contract assumes a background set of substantive values which limit its ambit. Without the support of such a set of values, the consensual model falters.

The second model of constitutional rights is a variation of the first. This contractual model of constitutional rights would avoid the troublesome factor of third party beneficiaries by identifying all individuals who have entered the country to have tacitly accepted a contract as a result of which they are accorded the rights allocated to "everyone". According to this account, the very fact of entry signifies an acceptance of a standing offer that in return for obeying laws, constitutional protections will be granted. This variation allows for a wide application of the constitution but it requires qualification. Illegal entrants do not show a willingness to accept and abide by such an agreement; in fact the illegal nature of their act of entry raises the opposite assumption. Only if one were willing to exclude illegal entrants and those who are seeking entry at the border from the protection of the constitution would one accept this variation.

While this model can account for the constitutional recognition of non-citizens and can offer an account of the relevance of being within the country, it suffers from the same problem as the first, namely that it ignores the context which would give the contract moral force. Moreover, it relies on the questionable assumption that one can usually infer consent from the mere act of crossing a border in a legal manner. Such an inference is problematic in the light of the variety of other reasons for visiting a country.

A third model of constitutional rights would attempt to avoid the artifice of regarding neutral actions as signifying tacit acceptance of an agreement by regarding constitutional rights as the benefit which creates a duty of fair play on the part of recipients. From this point of view, the need to ground the obligation to obey the law is the rationale for the recognition of constitutional rights. If one grounds the obligation on the acceptance of benefits, then one may only make the demand of obedience from a particular group by extending the range of fair benefits to it. Governments usually seek to extract obedience only from those within the territory governed, hence the need to extend the Charter to all such individuals. Since foreigners who are outside the country are not regarded as candidates from whom obedience is demanded, there is no requirement that they be accorded constitutional protection, even in their dealings with government, such as when they are applying for a visa.

The move away from viewing a constitution as an agreement is a welcome one. It recognizes that moral and political rights need not originate in voluntary consent, but may have another source. However, as many writers have noted, there are problems with concluding that those who have been accorded legal rights must have "accepted" them in a way that gives rise to obligations. With no option but to take them as given, it is difficult to identify why individuals should be under any reciprocal obligations.

One upshot of this "reciprocity" model is that the rights articulated in a constitution would extend only to those who are subject to the authority of the law or under an obligation to obey it, which in most circumstances would be those who find themselves, legally or illegally, within a country's borders. Furthermore, it would seem to follow that the grant of extra rights to citizens and permanent residents would be explicable only in terms of their additional obligations to the state.

Under a fourth model of constitutional rights, one would trace the obligation to obey the law to the natural duty to support the laws of a just state, with obedience rather than mere non-interference being demanded from those to whom the law applies.

The rights protected in a Charter of Rights are the ingredients of justice, the implication being that a state which recognizes these rights merits obedience. Unlike in the previous model, the rights need not be restricted in application to those from whom obedience is desired. Instead the grant of rights is a grant demanded by justice. There is no inherent restriction in application.

Jeremy Waldron has recently defended a version of the natural duty account of political obligation.[2] I will not rehearse his argument here, but I do want to add a couple of glosses.

Waldron notes that one hurdle which such an account of obligation must overcome is that of explaining why the duty of a state to be just is not global in nature, owed to every individual. Waldron himself solves the problem by noting that we apply range limitations to principles of distributive justice, and can defend this by relying on a Kantian argument. He writes:

> Like other contractarians, Kant thought of the state as an arrangement into which people enter for a resolution of conflict and the establishment of a secure system of property.... Now although Kant acknowledges that in principle all humans share the earth, clearly those with whom I come into conflict will in the first instance be my near neighbors. Since no one can afford to wait until all possible conflicts arise so that all can be definitively settled at once, the Kantian approach implies that I should enter quickly into a form of society with those immediately adjacent to me, those with whose interests my resource use is likely to pose the most frequent and dangerous conflicts.(14)

Waldron reminds us how we use range limiting principles in daily life by reference to a "cute" example. Where a pie is being divided by a father who says "To each an equal amount of pie", we don't expect the neighbour's child who is hanging over the fence to be able to assert a claim. This example can be altered slightly to identify some complexities that arise in contexts where the fences are permeable, as are a country's borders. Where the neighbour's child is visiting, say to watch television, and the pie division is announced, it is much more difficult to justify not allocating an equal slice. Where the child has been invited to dinner, it is even more difficult. These amendments of the example, show that the application of range limitation principles will be a complex matter where the physical barrier between insiders and outsiders is neither hard nor fast.

Thus, while other accounts of constitutional rights may assume that there is a pre-determined and clear division between citizens and others, a model

2 Jeremy Waldron, "Special Ties and Natural Duties" (1993) 22 *Phil. and Pub. Aff.* 3.

founded upon the state's duty to be just may have to inquire into the justice of defining citizenship in a particular way. Where non-citizens are prevented from gaining citizenship unless they are physically present in the country for a lengthy period, or speak a particular language, or are sufficiently knowledgeable about the country's history, we would have to determine the justice of imposing such arduous conditions. The recognition of citizenship as a constitutional status, and the recognition of the constitution as a document which expresses the state's commitment to justice, ensure that the criteria of citizenship will become an issue for the interpreters of the constitution, that is to say, the judiciary, to determine.

A second problem with the model outlined by Waldron, is that it assumes that those who are outside the borders of a country have no claim on the state; that the range limiting principle excludes everyone outside the physical boundary. The justification for defining the limitation of range in this way is open to question on grounds of arbitrariness. At a time when hundreds of thousands of people are each year attempting to enter Canada, when each person's application is submitted to a complex bureacratic examination, it makes little sense to define the range of principles of justice in such a way that these interactions are excluded. Certainly people who are not physically present in a country are unable to disturb the enjoyment of property of those who are within the country, but individual enjoyment of property is not the only issue with which a just government should be concerned. Questions of access are clearly material, especially when those who are seeking access are economically or emotionally dependent on others who are "on the inside". If the obligation to obey the law is contingent upon the just behaviour of the state, one would expect this commitment to justice to be qualified by a range limiting principle which took into account the existing conditions. That a range limiting principle is arbitrary means only that its ambit cannot itself be defended or criticized on grounds of justice. It can however be criticized for its failure to recognize the real extent of government interactions with individuals. To deny constitutional protection to those outside our borders who are entering the immigration process is to deny that they are immediately adjacent to us in the way that Kant identified as significant.

Furthermore, the instrumentalist account of borders and territoriality which explains their existence solely in terms of the need to solve local conflicts first, ignores the fact that membership in a rich cultural community may itself be a benefit which a just state has an obligation to maintain and support and which it has an obligation to supply to those lacking it who come seeking it. To modify Waldron's example again, the child leaning across the fence may first seek to join the family before asserting any claim to pie. Similarly, the refugee who has a well-founded fear of persecution is, in effect, making the claim that she has lost the benefit of community membership within her country of origin and the claim that community membership is something to which she has a right.

Although I believe that the constitutional recognition of democratic rights and fundamental freedoms can best be explained according to a version of the fourth model, I do not intend to suggest that the issues which have been delegated to the judiciary are easily resolved. On the contrary, one of my main points is that these questions are amongst the most difficult that face us as a community. As scholars of nationalism have shown us, our sense of community is in no small way founded upon invented traditions and imagined histories. Yet we demand that immigrants assimilate into our communities. Once the bubble of objective self-definiton has been punctured, it is difficult to justify demanding from those who would become members familiarity with the networks of ideas and practices which are believed to constitute the culture. This seems particularly inappropriate where the culture of a political community is multi-dimensional and fragmented and has a diverse, internationalist flavour rather than a uniform character. Similarly, where people are permitted to immigrate because of their success within a global economy, part of which may be attributable to their willingness to travel continuously, it seems odd to demand (as has been demanded in Canada) that full citizenship should be contingent on physical presence within the country for a lengthy period of time, which would allow the individual to "rub shoulders with others" and thereby get a sense of the culture. To perceive what justice requires in such circumstances is no easy matter.

Juan Ignacio Ugartemendia and Joxerramon Bengoetxea,
San Sebastian/Luxembourg

A Right to Disobey?

I. Introduction

In this paper we wish to discuss certain questions relating to civil disobedience through a particular phenomenon, *insumisión*, which is quite common in our own country. The typical situation is one where a young man refuses to comply with the compulsory military service and with the alternative social service scheme in force in Spain; the police arrest him and he is prosecuted and can be sentenced to up to twenty-eight months and one day imprisonment. The motives behind such defection are not always the same, and perhaps not always noble, just as the official legal responses to this phenomenon are neither uniform nor always noble.[1]

But Basque society at large sees no point in the penalisation of *insumisión*. And those holding major lawjobs – lawyers, prosecutors, judges – often see themselves in a difficult situation where the law goes one way, dictated by *policy reasons*, and their conscience goes another way, dictated by *reasons of principle*. Public prosecution reluctantly takes the necessary steps to prosecute, and when it does so, it follows strict guidelines from the Madrid headquarters; and even then, often calling for the application of the minimum sentences. The panels of judges, which see themselves impelled to impose a sentence, often penalise the *insumiso* with the mildest possible sentence, and in some cases, *insumisos* have been cleared of charges or acquitted altogether. Yet, on other occasions sentences have been severe. Many political parties have openly called for a decriminalisation of *insumisión*.

In our view, insumisión might be a good example upon which a particular conception of civil disobedience as constitutional disobedience can be constructed.

2. A working conception of civil disobedience

When speaking about *disobedience* we refer to a deliberate moral and/or political choice not to obey or not to comply with valid normative provisions enacted by a public authority. It can consist in a positive action infringing some prohibition or in an infringement of or non-compliance with a given duty where such prohibition or such duty are clearly and unambiguously provided for by

1 See Article 2, paragraph 3, of the *Ley Orgánica* 8/1984, (26-12-1984) as amended by *Ley Orgánica* 14/1985 (9–12–1985). The new Criminal Code, passed at the end of 1995, still criminalises insumisión and penalises it with sentences of 8 to 12 years of absolute incapacitation from public service plus a 'fine' of 12 to 24 months.

positive law (in an interpretive sense of law and allowing for the necessary defeasibility conditions).

Disobedience thus defined can operate within a constitutional framework or outside of a constitutional setting or framework. Disobedience can occur in the absence of a constitutional framework, e.g. a resistance to tyranny (pre-constitutional disobedience). On the other hand, disobedience within a constitutional framework can be constitutional or unconstitutional. **Constitutional disobedience** such as right to resistance, unregulated conscientious objection or civil disobedience, presupposes, on the part of the "disobeyer", an acceptance of and, ideally, an appeal to the (democratic) Constitution, and therefore an adoption of an axiologically internal point of view. **Anti-constitutional disobedience** rejects or aims at subverting the Constitution e.g. through terrorism, revolution, military *coup d'Etat*, or even some versions of *insumisión*.

In this paper we are not going to deal with disobedience in a pre-constitutional or non-constitutional society. In our view, the basic contrast is that between a form of disobedience that relies on constitutional values and a form of disobedience that negates or directly rejects those values, even if it takes a non-violent approach.

Civil disobedience as a form of constitutional disobedience has the following features: (1) the actor considers there is a manifest and serious breach of a basic constitutional value, of a fundamental right; (2) the breach originates in a normative or policy-making authority; (3) the disobedient action reacts against this breach; (4) the disobedient action is a sort of *ultima ratio* or last resort because other possible reactions against the breach are considered to be ineffective or because the procedural mechanisms which are available do not react appropriately; (5) the disobedient action is proportionate, and does not breach a greater value or create a greater injustice than that which it purports to correct.

These five features only give us a wide conception of constitutional-civil disobedience, but in order to identify the species "civil disobedience" from the genus "constitutional disobedience", we follow Bedau's narrow working conception of civil disobedience as "a public, nonviolent, conscientious yet political act contrary to law usually done with the aim of bringing about a change in the law or policies of the goverment"[2]. This **narrow** or "orthodox" conception[3] has added several important features (intension) to the **wide** conception: (6) the disobedient action is public, i.e. it is performed in public or with a clear intention to transcend the individuality of the action; (7) the action is non-violent, it does not resort to direct physical coercion or to strong direct psychological coercion and ideally it does not use any form of coercion at all; (8) it is political and not simply moral, i.e. it is a way of publicly engaging in a political claim; and (9) its purpose is to effect a change in the law or in the policies of the government.

Insumisión would be a good example of this narrow conception of civil disobedience. Firstly, it fulfils the criteria of the wide conception: (a) there is an alleged breach of one or more basic constitutional values, freedom of conscience, or the principle of equality and non-discrimination, the right to live in one's

2 H. A. Bedau, "On Civil Disobedience", in 58 *Journal of Philosophy*, 1961, p. 653–61.

language and culture, or the fact that the alternative social service deprives others of the chances to find a job; (b) it reacts, through disobedience, against this manifest, serious and unfair breach; it is a sort of last resort, given that other possible reactions are considered by the *insumiso* to be ineffective, and (c) his action is proportionate, it being very difficult to see which greater value might be breached by *insumisión*.

And moreover it also fulfils the criteria of the narrow conception because (d) it is public, as the *insumiso* does not hide or try to conceal his disobedience; (e) nonviolent, as the insumiso does not resort to coercion; (f) it is not simply moral but also political as it openly breaches the law on conscientious objection and on alternative social service, and is thus criminalised and finally (g), it aims to change the law and the policy of the Spanish State, on the basis of constitutional values.

We do not hereby wish to imply that there cannot be some version of *insumisión* which only fulfils the wider criteria. Indeed one such form is rather close to conscientious objection: this special *insumiso* objects to the military service or its social service alternative (as legally regulated) on moral grounds, without thereby trying to engage in a public political act or in policy or legal discussions leading to a change in the law; he is not necessarily concerned with his peers' obligations, all he wants is to be exempted from a legal duty.

3. Constitution and civil disobedience

The formation of this narrow conception of civil disobedience and its political justification within a constitutional framework mark an important turning point in the very concept of law. In working out a narrow conception of civil disobedience we have assumed a given idea of Constitution, and at the same time paved the way for this idea. Law is thus critically reconstructed in terms of Constitution, and civil disobedience is embedded in the idea of democratic Constitution. Even more dramatically, in adopting a committed attitude to constitutional values, civil disobedience becomes a fundamental incentive and support for constitutional discourse: it enhances a dynamic, discursive, critical or open idea of Constitution.

By Constitution we do not have any specific "constitution" in mind. It might be that a great many elements or dogmas go into one specific constitution of one state, but our notion of Constitution would consider many of them as irrelevant. What is crucial is the recognition, guarantee and development of fundamental rights and freedoms, the principle of democracy and the respect for the *Rechtsstaat* or the rule of law. Fidelity or loyalty to law is understood as fidelity to this constitutional core.

The recognition of Human Rights must ultimately include the acceptance of a supra-state jurisdiction supervising State norms and conduct on the grounds of Human Rights standards recognised by that State. Democracy implies, as the

3 G.G. James, "The Orthodox Theory of Civil Disobedience", (in 2 *Social Theory and Practice*, 1973, p. 475–98). H. A. Bedau, op. cit. and J. Rawls (*A Theory of Justice*, Cambridge, Mass, 1971, p. 364) are the classical examples of this orthodox theory.

minimum, the sovereignty of the people, the division of public power and the separation of powers, and ideally, direct participation of the citizens in the running of their society. Rule of law is extended from its classical conception to include the principle that no sphere of state action escapes the control of the law (rule of law as contrary to *raison d'Etat*), and the principle of transparency.

In a society governed by such a constitution, resistance or disobedience cannot be targetted against the democratic, constitutional order since such order is based on "communal"[4] consensus, on a democratic contract, whereby power resides in the people and the constitution is seen and interpreted as the will of the people. Besides, the respect for Human Rights and the setting up of procedural and other mechanisms to guarantee such rights to all citizens, and to control public action in the light of such rights and on the basis of the rule of law, is the source of legitimacy. Any moral or political justification of disobedience or resistance which aims at undermining or transforming the legal-political foundations of a given society assumes that such society is not organised around a democratic constitution.

In a democratic society the existence of the constitutional core thus defined entails the unjustifiability of any disobedience or resistance which might aim at the undermining of Democracy, Human Rights and the Rule of Law. Any form of civil disobedience will thus rely on the basic constitutional core of the given society. This approach obviously adopts an internal point of view.

A democratic constitution requires a system of rights guarantees and it is to be interpreted in such a way that the rights recognised become fully effective. Indeed, different and divergent interpretations of the same constitution are possible, and civil disobedience will then be the result of a fundamental disagreement toward a particular interpretation of the constitution carried out by the ruling power in a specific subject matter (take the obvious example where the government requires the payment of a given tax in order to enjoy the right to vote). In that case civil disobedience, by relying on a different reading of the constitution, enacts constitutional debate between the official reading and an alternative reading. The fact that a final legal decision is to be made adjudicating between rival, or at least different interpretations does not, in our view, automatically make this decision a "right" one on the moral or political levels, not even the only right legal answer; it only makes it the *institutional* answer.

4. What is the normative status of civil disobedience?

Each normative system – personal morality, group morality, positive morality, political theories and groups, or law – might give a different response to this question, but we are primarily interested in the law and in how other normative systems – morals or politics – find their way into legal discourse by way of justification.

4 Communal as opposed to numerical. See Dworkin's plenary lecture to the Bologna 1995 World Congress of the IVR.

It seems to us that the civilly disobedient actor appeals to, at least, her or his own personal morality and sense of justice, but also to the shared moral and political views of society, as embedded in the constitutional core, and therefore also to law, or to a given interpretation of law as inspired by what she or he thinks is the correct interpretation of the constitutional core. Those claims might be contested, and debated, again, from different normative levels, and more prominently from the common moral and political views and from the law.

Whereas the purely moral and political debate has no dramatic personal consequences for the civil or constitutional dissident, the debate in law might entail dramatic consequences since organised society reacts to a breach of the law by means of coercive sanctions. That is why we are primarily interested in the legal debate on civil disobedience and, ultimately, in how other normative discourses make their way into the legal debate[5]. By appealing to shared constitutional values as justification for her or his action the civilly disobedient actor places herself or himself on an interpretive constitutional debate, i.e. on a debate as to whether civil disobedience is best interpreted as a right (a justified claim), or a justification for a breach of a duty or otherwise, in the defence of constitutional values.

Given that any disobedience implies a breach of a formally valid law (or legal obligation), the short answer from the normative legal discourse is that any disobedience will be unlawful, and cannot therefore be a right. It would be contradictory to put forward the claim that the law recognises the right to disobey the obligations following from that law because it would amount to the law negating itself.

The legal treatment of civil disobedience will then delve into the question whether there might be any *defeasibility* conditions under which either the legal obligation was, after all, invalid in the instant case and therefore never existed, or else the legal obligation existed and was always (constitutionally) valid and it was certainly breached in the instant case but there were additional circumstances impeding or mitigating the application of the legal consequence or the sanction. The first is a question which can be solved in legal discourse by way of a final judicial decision (of a Constitutional Court) which will either confirm the validity (or constitutionality) of the obligation or else will declare its inexistence in law and therefore the lawfulness of the action which, at first sight, was conceptualised as civilly disobedient and illegal. The second is the classical criminal law question of justifications, defences and excuses in law that impede or mitigate the application of the legal consequence or sanction that would normally follow from the breach.

In the case of *insumisión* one can look at the valid legal texts regulating this phenomenon (a classical legal positivist approach), and then the answer might go in one direction: the criminalisation and penalisation of *insumisión* clearly indicate that it is not a right in the Spanish legal system.

But one can take a further step and also look at the political theory behind those and other texts (a constructive interpretive approach[6]) and then the

5 See Ralf Dreier, "Derecho y Moral", in Ernesto Garzón Valdes (ed) *Derecho y Filosofía*, Barcelona 1985, p. 74.

6 Of course, we are here inspired by Ronald Dworkin's *Law's Empire*, London 1986.

answer might go in a different direction: *insumisión* could be seen as an extension of the right to consciencious objection, the freedom of conscience, the right to dissent, the right to live in one's language, which might be constitutionally protected, although few would argue that any such right exists with such a wide extension. In any case we are again placed on the constitutional debate.

Or one can even look at institutional practice (in a legal realist mood) and then many more tones will be added to the picture: some *insumisos* have been acquitted on different grounds by the Courts allowing the *insumisos*' moral convictions to stand.

The legal positivist might at best accept that there is a clash between different norms – e.g. the duty to obey and the freedom of conscience – in certain circumstances and that the right to follow one's conscience will only exist if it has some basis in a source of law. However the herculean interpreter might venture to argue that the political theory behind the Constitution and behind the binding supranational and international Human Rights instruments require that the freedom of conscience be taken seriously in the instant case, and the realist might very well suggest that pragmatic considerations be taken into account when dealing with such conflicts in instant cases. The constitutional debate, in any case, cannot be avoided.

It is very likely that all three approaches will give us a negative answer: no, there is no such thing as a **legal** right to disobey the law (claim-right, privilege, power or immunity in Hohfeldian terms); that would almost be a contradiction in terms. Even if not explicitly stated anywhere in the law, the statement that "one must obey the law" or that "the law is to be obeyed" is inherent to the concept of law as an action-guiding and action-justifying system.

There is therefore no legal right to disobey, but rather a duty to obey and if such is the case, then perhaps one must take a completely different approach and look at the defeasibility conditions or the limits of the duty to obey and at the conditions in which such a duty cannot be imposed or rather the conditions in which failure to observe that duty can find some justification in the law.

This approach has two advantages: the inherent claim to obedience (linked to the claim to validity) is respected while at the same time the debate turns around the question of the possible justifications for the breach of that duty, which calls for the interpretive and pragmatic approaches to be considered. In other words, although there is no **legal** right to disobey there can still be a **moral or even a political** right to follow one's conscience in certain circumstances even if that means breaching a legal duty of obedience, and if these extra-legal rights gain sufficient popular support, then they can somehow make their way into the law, normally at the stage of the judicial application of the law, but possibly also at the stage of norm-making when considering possible justifications, defenses, excuses or even mitigating factors for breach of a given legal duty.

We are then facing a classical situation where the law (legal discourse and the legal process) is the subject of interferences from other normative systems. These interferences can be detected in several judicial decisions of Spanish courts[7]. Those decisions start from the postulation of a conflict of values which

7 See for instance, Resolución de sobreseimiento de diligencias previas 2314/94 del 20 de

originate a "state of necessity" and require a choice of the greater value (the freedom of the person) as against the duty to comply with the military service or the alternative social service. The main elements selected by the judges in order to justify the insumiso's conduct are personal elements: the civility of the conduct and even of the disobeyer himself is stressed and a great effort is invested in showing that there is a genuine conflict of values. The aims which the acts of *insumisión* were seeking – to alter the law and policy of the government[8] – do not feature in the reasoning. Insumisión is thus conceptualised in terms of a strong conflict between morality and the law rather than a conflcit between politics and law.

The drawback of this emphasis on the moral dilemma is that it makes civil disobedience almost a personal matter rather than a political societal conflict. The potential for constitutional debate and interpretive discourse is lost, or at least diluted in the presence of strong moral reasons or moral-legal objections, stressed by the judges and perhaps even shared by them.

It must not be forgotten that the aim of civil disobedience is not necessarily that of avoiding the imposition of a sentence but rather that of erradicating from the legal order those laws or policies originating in the public authority which, in the *insumisos*' (civil disobeyers') view, violate fundamental constitutional values: non-discrimination, peace, political participation, freedom of conscience, dignity of the person, free development of personality, participation, the right not to be forced to live outside one's culture and language during a considerable period of time, or even the right to education.

Civil disobedience and therefore *insumisión* should not be regarded as a right but rather as a means or instrument of last resort in the defence of fundamental rights, an extreme case of self-protection of fundamental rights. At best, it can be construed as a defence or a justification for the breach but that in no way turns it into a (subjective) right to disobey.

5. Constitutional disobedience as paradox

The criminal law discussion under the plea of necessity turns the civilly disobedient act into a personal moral act which might constitute a defence or a justification excluding the presence of a legal type or its unlawfulness. The public and political dimension of civil disobedience which engages in constitutional debate is thus lost. The first paradox is sketched: the civil disobeyer obtains a favourable response from the legal system (the law and the officials) but his or

diciembre 1994, juzgado de instrucción nº 2 de San Sebastián; Sentencia nº 75 del 6 de marzo de 1992, del juzgado nº 4 e Madrid.

8 There are over 3000 cases of registred *insumisión* in Spain. The *insumisos* in question have made it plain that their aim is to fight against a law that is unjust, discriminatory, militarist, etc. It is worth noting, in this regard, that the Spanish Conscientious Objection Movement MOC, which represents the greatest number of *insumisos* held a press conference following the order of the San Sebastian judge. The movement praised the reasoning of the judge but reminded that their main objective was not to be personally exempt from military service but rather to achieve demilitarisation.

her action loses political impact because it is reconducted into a personal act. **Law does not debate politics** and if the civil disobeyer insists on the political meaning behind his or her act and refuses to reduce it to a morally justified defence, then the law might have no other safety valve to accommodate for the particular form of civil disobedience and will most certainly penalise the act. The disobeyer will then be punished in spite of the civility as constitutionality of his disobedience, in spite of the moral justification of his action and in spite of his willingness to engage in constitutional debate.

Paradoxically, it is this tragic situation which will give civil disobedience all its symbolic potential and public attention. Without necessarily wanting to do so, the legal system will refuse to engage in the constitutional debate. The political forum will then be the only context left for discussion of civil disobedience, of the aims it seeks and of the constitutional justification it relies on.

Thomas D. Campbell, Canberra

Communication Rights: Defaming Free Speech

It is one of the drawbacks of court-administered human rights that they provide yesterday's solutions to today's problems. Interpretations which are achieved in one set of cultural and economic circumstances, continue to be followed in very different circumstances. Often this means that even where human rights discourse enables us to put our finger on the significant values at issue, the remedies they offer often do not relate to the securing those values in present rather than historical conditions.[1]

Nowhere is this more true than in the case of freedom of expression, perhaps the most fundamental of fundamental civil and political rights, especially in its hallowed and influential formulation, the First Amendment to the constitution of the United States which declares that "Congress shall make no law abridging the freedom of speech. Or of the Press". This very proper attempt to ensure that the federal government of the day did not censor by way of prior restraint was posited on the then plausible view that government was the only powerful enemy of freedom generally and freedom of expression in particular. Religious authority was and is another source of speech restrictions but was to be feared in the North American situation mainly in its official guise as state enforced religion. The First Amendment, of course, goes on to proscribe the establishment of religion.

These conditions no longer prevail. The threats to free expression values are now as much private and commercial as they are public and political.[2] Moreover many of the solutions to private restraint involve the use of public power. That is one of the better reasons for having states. This makes the prohibition of government regulation of speech a principal obstacle to freedom of expression in the contemporary world of corporate controlled media dominance in which the most powerful means of communication are in a very limited number of private hands and are overwhelmingly devoted to economic gain, an objective whose attainment requires deference to the requirements of the advertisers more than devotion to the provision of significant information and argument.[3]

The utilisation of the First Amendment to inhibit effective freedom of speech is evident. It has been used as an instrument to protect newspaper owners against having to offer a right of reply.[4] It has been used to outlaw attempts to limit the dominant influence of money in election campaigns.[5] It is currently argued in the support of cable television owners to enhance the profits to be made through control of the electronic media: the Turner Broadcasting Corporation

1 See, Tom Campbell "The Rationales for Freedom of Communication", in Campbell and Sadurski (editors), *Freedom of Communication* (Dartmouth, 1994).

2 See Owen Fiss, 'Why the State?' 100 *Harv. L.Rev* 781, (1987), at 787: "Terror comes in many forms"; also Cass Sunstein, *Democracy and the Problem of Free Speech*, New York; The Free Press, 1993.

3 Thus, C. Baker, *Advertising and a Democratic Press* (Princeton University Press, 1994).

4 *Miami Herald Publishing Co. v. Tornillo,* 418 US 241 (1974).

5 *Buckley v. Valeo* 424 US 1, 48–9 (1976).

argued that the First Amendment renders unconstitutional the "must carry" rules of the Cable Act 1972 which prevent them shutting out programs which, for instance, rival their own in the relevant ratings or from which they derive most profit.[6] Interestingly even the American Council of Civil Liberties when it uses the slogan "money is speech", does not mean that empowering speech requires providing potential communicators with money, but that preventing someone buying TV time is equivalent to silencing them, and hence an infringement of the First Amendment. Not to be outdone, the Australian High Court used the occasion of a (perhaps not very well designed) democratically devised attempt to neutralise some of the determinative force of money in election campaigns, to conjure up an implied right of freedom of political communication in a constitution whose creators overtly turned their backs on entrenching such rights. The High Court took this breathtaking step on the initiative of a commercial television company whose revenue would have been diminished by the Act in question. Following U.S. jurisprudence to the effect that government regulation of communication is an abridgment of speech whereas economic abridgment is not, the High Court simply assumed that the only restrictions on speech that count are restrictions enforced by government.[7]

This is the sort of thing that gives free speech a bad name, as a negative and unimaginative right that inhibits rather than nurtures the values of truth, self-expression and democratic dialogue whose realisation it should rightly promote. My sub-title – "defaming free speech" is intended to convey the need to mount a rescue operation on behalf of free speech values and reconstitute the significance and import of the right to communicate in a way which does something to rescue our sources of information and comment from pervasive commercialism and the magnate manipulation which makes us take notice when we learn that Mr Rupert Murdoch is backing Mr Tony Blair or Mr Kerry Packer is displeased with Mr Paul Keeting.

Although the phenomena that concern us are palpably practical ones concerning the social and economic forces that have captured free speech discourse and threaten to swamp free speech values, the reconstitutive path commences in philosophical reflection. Some conceptual analysis and weighing of normative arguments and empirical postulates are prerequisites to formulating any plan for a New Deal in free speech.[8]

An important initial point to make is that, surprisingly for such a basic right, the most powerful arguments for communication are instrumental ones. Of the seven or more rationales that can readily be identified all bar one are based on consequentialist considerations: communication serves the causes of truth, promotes informed democratic decision-making, fosters accountability, enables individuals to achieve their objectives and nurtures tolerance.[9] Only the non-instrumental aspects of self-expression stand out as having a deontological

6 *Turner Broadcasting v. Federal Communications Commission*, No. 93–44 (1994).

7 Tom Campbell, "Democracy, Human Rights, and Positive Law" 16 *Sydney Law Review*, 195–212, 1994.

8 Cass Sunstein's catch phrase, op.cit., chap.2.

9 See Frederick Schauer, *Freedom of Speech: A Philosophical Enquiry*, Cambridge University Press, 1982.

flavour, but even here further analysis suggests that it is successful purposive uses of language that is primarily cherished. Evaluative debates are not settled by counting arguments, and communication for its own sake may still be selected as the factor which gives free speech its overriding normative force. However, the central rationale for freedom of expression is the argument from truth, both in its own terms in which justified belief is the justificatory value for freedom of communication, and in its role in the argument from democracy, as the means for the provision of information and the achievement of participatory agreement. To this extent, at any rate, we can go along with U.S. free speech jurisprudence and its incantation of the attractive, if insidious and ultimately misplaced metaphor, the "market place of ideas".[10]

Another important theme is that the central arguments for freedom of communication have no inner logic which commits them to a negative view of freedom of speech as having to do solely with the absence of legal prohibitions or legally mediated sanctions against expresssion. If truth is the value, for instance, then it is important that the communication of views is not limited to those who can pay to have them published or those whom other will pay to read.[11] Or, more frequently now, those which advertisers will pay to have published. The freedom of expression that fosters truth must be one which enables the availability of all contributions that might contain an element of truth. Only in a society where the street corner and the cheap leaflet are central impact mechanisms can a mere negative right, let alone one which proscribes only government restrictions on expression, have a great deal of relevance. Further, the process of finding out is prior to the process of communicative truth-oriented speech, and research, as we know, can be expensive. There is certainly no clear rational distinction between Freedom of Communication and Freedom of Information.[12] So, in one way or another, as Owen Fiss points out there is no such thing as free speech in much the same way as there is no such thing as a free lunch. "Money is speech" should indeed be reinterpreted as the thesis that significant speech requires money. We should therefore be wary of any free speech policies which are reputed to be costless.

So much, for the moment, for free speech values and mechanisms. What I want to concentrate on is more to do with defamation values and the rationales for the protection of reputation, particularly as these relate to free speech matters. The traditional position here is that defamation law is one of those perfectly proper limitations on freedom of speech which the American founding fathers, following in the British tradition, did not consider for one moment to be contrary to the First Amendment, and which presents no problem for the common lawyer who has a concern for the citizen's historic rights of free speech. Freedom of expression, the traditionalist contends, just does not include the right to say (or more especially write or broadcast) whatever you like about other people.

10 *Whitney v. California*, 274 US 375 (1927); *Furman v. Georgia*, 408 US 238, 467 (1972); *Red Lion Broadcasting Co. v. FCC* 398 US 367,392 (1969); *New York Times v Sullivan*, 376 US 254, 272, 279 (1964) etc.

11 See Sunstein, op.cit.

12 See Peter Bayne, "Freedom of Information and Political Free Speech", in Campbell and Sadurski, Op.cit, pp. 199–220.

There are in fact two ways of accommodating the defamation exception to freedom of communication. The first is to say that freedom of expression is concerned with general ideas not particular facts, so that there is really no incompatibility between protecting reputation and promoting speech. Any social and political view can be aired but this does not include unsubstantiated negative assertions about the conduct and character of particular identifiable individuals.

This contrast between freedom for abstractions and control for particulars is not persuasive. Many social and political views are generalisations induced from the behaviour of individual persons. We cannot hope to convince our listeners that academics are lazy unless we are prepared to idetify those that are. Empirical generalisations cannot be substantiated or dismissed without establishing the truth about the conduct of particular persons at particular times. Further, it is not only historians who have a legitimate interest in concrete events. Quite apart from the independent significance of historical truth as history, the actions and speech of individuals may have great political significance, both in relation to electoral choices which involve assessing the qualities of individual persons, but in relation to the desirability of competing policies which often generate from beliefs about the situation and conduct of individual persons and have to be assessed by reference to their consequences for these or other persons. Significant truths and important political choice are not all about abstractions and generalities.

This takes us on to the second approach to the allegedly combatant interface of defamation law and free speech rights, which is to regard the former as a legitimate limitation on the former. Remedies for defamation must to some extent simply override what would otherwise be protected under the rubric of freedom of communication. Thus, it is argued, the protection of a person's good name must limit freedom of communication and law may be used to compensate for and deter publication of defamatory speech. In other words, free speech and defamation represent different and conflicting interests between which a balance or compromise must be reached.

I argue that to base our thinking on this simplistic opposition is once again to defame free speech, this time not by making it a mere negative right, but by giving it an undeserved bad name as an intrinsically incompatible with defamation law. Just as important, it is also to defame defamation law, for it is unfair to the reputation of defamation regimes to hold that they necessarily compromise free speech values. Indeed defamation regimes may and can serve free speech. This means that defamation law as well as free speech are denigrated by setting up a false antithesis between them.

There are plenty of reasons for holding that the defensible values underlying acceptable defamation law are conducive to or overlap with free speech rationales. After all, the sort of reputation that matters is a justified or merited reputation, one that has withstood, in J. S. Mill's terms, "constant critical questioning".[13] If we regard a purpose of defamation law as providing a framework in which reputation can be challenged and defended in a way which serves truth in this important area of human concern then defamation and free

13 J. S. Mill, *On Liberty.*

speech rationales come together, and do so in a major way. All the more so once we discard the first defamation that freedom of communication is a matter of controlling states rather than controlling economic power. A New Deal for freedom of expression may point to a new emphasis within rather than the annihilation of defamation law.

And what might this emphasis be? Everyone seems to agree that defamation reform is required.[14] Australia has its particular problems over multiple jurisdictions and litigation happy public persons (officials and figures). In most places existing law is used by those with power and money to block often well founded criticism or certainly matters which deserve an airing. Defamation law is not an instrument which is within the means of the ordinary citizen whose personal life becomes a matter of interest to the media. Political debate is inhibited by the costs of defending and persuing defamation actions, many of which are initiated not to win but to gag, while the absolute privilege of Parliamentary debate clearly contributes to the abysmal quality of much of what goes on in that forum. Obscenely large sums of money are paid out to some who have suffered little harm as a result of what has been written about them, although overall the situation here is not half as bad as is usually made out. Even for those who can afford defamation litigation (or pretrial preparation for the same) are rarely satisfied by the outcome. One has to be careful here. Newspapers are not nearly as vulnerable to the chilling effect of defamation actions as they make out in that they could afford to resist such pressures if they wished, and often fail to do so for purely commercial reasons.

So, where do we go on defamation, particularly in relation to freedom of communication? Those who see the situation as one of absolute conflict, a zero-sum game in which one or other objective (protecting reputation or freeing up speech) has to win out over the other, may argue quite convincingly for the delegalisation of defamation. To points about the ineffectual operation of the law in relation to its assumed objectives (compensating those who really have been unfairly damaged or hurt) may be added the seeming impossibility of formulating rules and finding procedures which would have the desired results. Libel law it seems cannot be saved from "abuse".

It is indeed very difficult to positivise defamation regimes. The slippery nature of language and the intangibility of "reputation" are just two reasons why defamation rules and proceedures are unfathomably complex. The term "defamation" itself seem to invite inappropriate value judgments from judge and jury alike by its historic connection to what how "right thinking" people would react to often elusive words in ambiguous contexts.[15] The swamp of technicalities of the formal rules here contrasts with the gut reactions of the adjudicators to the merits of the parties, be they sensationalist journalists, celebrity heroes or captains of industry. All this is not good law. It might however be improved by a more determined effort to define legal defamation in terms of the actual reaction of the audience through which the defamatory harm is mediated. But this would

14 For just one powerful critique, see Donald M. Gillmor, *Power, Publicity and the Abuse of Libel Law*, New York: Oxford University Press, 1992.

15 John Fleming, *The Law of Torts*, 8th edn., Sydney: Law Book, 1992.

involve identifying and quantifying the harm of an injured reputation, matters which our existing regime ignores by not requiring proof of injury to the plaintiff, an interesting anomaly in the domain of tort law.

Another basic improvement would be to make more objectively justiciable the distinction between statements of fact and opinion which is so crucial on defamation law where statements of opinion may be protected (as fair comment) while statements of fact are not.[16] Analytically we may make headway by distinguishing factual statements from evaluative ones (for all the flack that has been taken by that distinction in contemporary philosophy) but that leaves out the no-man's land of speculative and not so speculative views about what might be the case, which are the stuff of everyday "opinion".[17] Further, patent value judgments such as "Smith is a disgrace to human nature" are, as lawyers know but juries very reasonably don't follow, taken as statements of fact if they are not overtly a comment upon some matters of fact.[18] No more does the fact/value distinction help us to understand decisions like that which says that a magazine identifying the wrong person as a criminal suspect is a matter of opinion (and may therefore be fair comment, whether true or not) simply because it is printed in a book review rather than reported as news.[19] And, although we may more readily share the view that a cartoon depicting events may not be intended to refer to real rather than fictional events[20] fiction is not opinion in any normal sense any more than is hyperbole.[21]

It is sometimes suggested that "fact" is or should be taken as a matter that can be settled by evidence (something like verifiability) while opinion is not settlable by citing evidence, and so is unverifiable. But not only does this leave out the class of unverifiable facts, which is infinite, it could serve to exclude matters of fact from the tests of open debate, for, once the evidence is in, the matter can be taken as settled. We need free speech for opinion but not, at least so much, for facts. Maybe this assumption lurks behind the idea that defamation is not a matter for free speech. Yet, if free speech is for the unverifiable only, is it ever going to settle anything?

I am not saying that progress cannot be made here, but this is tricky ground and it would be nice to avoid it by delegalising defamation. Moreover delegalisation may be economically justified in that the cost of litigation is disproportionate to the objectives achieved. Costs outweigh damages awarded and the process generates disillusionment all round. It would be tidy to be convinced that defamation law always undermines freedom of expression and do away with such a problem area. On the other hand, better laws may be formulated, and

16 Thus, *Gertz v. Robert Welan Inc.*, 418 US 323 (1974).

17 Hence the problem over opinion which is based on false facts – still liable under *Bose Corporation v Consumers Union*, 466 U.S. 485 (1984).

18 See Geoffrey Robertson and Andrew Nicol, *Media Law*, 3rd edn., London: Penguin, 1992, p.80.

19 See also Frededrick Schauer, "Language, Truth and the First Amendment" 64 *Virginia Law Review*, 263, 279 (1978).

20 *Falwell v Hustler* 108 S.Ct. 879 (1988).

21 For instance, "blackmail" when it is not meant literally. See Titus "Statement of Fact v Statement of Opinion – a spurious dispute in Fair Comment" 15 *Vanderbilt Law Review* 1203 (1962) note 144.

there are questions of justice involved, justice relating here to that meritorian concept which calls for compensation to be paid, for instance, by those who negligently report defamatory falsehoods about other people.

Moreover do we really wish to be without the constraint on sloppy sensationalist journalism that is provided by the threat of defamation? The parties may not like present systems, and we may not like the parties, but the system may benefit nevertheless. Delegalisation might save us from the unfortunate chilling effects which inhibit honest and careful investigative journalism, but we may not want to defrost the irresponsible journalism that will emerge from the freezer once the constraints are lifted.

There are two directions for liberal reform we may choose. One is the US track of *New York Times v Sullivan* and the freedom to defame at least public persons (officials and figures). That I think is, in itself, a false step which diverts attention, and money, to the investigation of journalistic practices. The other is to devise a defamation regime that is centred on the public discovery and affirmation of truth, provided this can be done in a way which provides justice for the defamed. This latter approach (exemplified in the Annenberg proposals in the US[22] and in aspects of the New South Wales Law Reform Commission discussion paper of August 1993)[23] is one which does provide some principled guidance.[24]

Given that mud sticks and that journalism is above all business, it is not evident that truth or democracy is served by reducing the rights of the individuals on whom the media focuses for its own purposes. How can we at once complain that the corporate media are the paramount threat to truth and reputable democratic dialogue in the modern world and then commend a reform which enhances their corrupting power? Under the New Deal for free speech will we not want to take (perhaps costly) steps to broaden the base of effective communication rather than reduce the accountability of those in control of massive communicative power?

This line of thought takes up idea that defamation law already has elements of, and has potential for considerably more, mechanisms for enhancing truth promoting activities. This is to follow the famous but underdeveloped affirmation of Brandeis that the answer to bad speech is more speech, but pointing out, with New Deal realism, that establishing the truth about particular matters requires something more than speech, it requires money. The most evident extant elements of what I have in mind are those (somewhat rare) cases where the truth or falsity of the factual component of a defamatory assertion becomes the matter at issue, as when truth (perhaps plus public interest) is led as a justification for the published libel. Also, the way in which the publication of a reply may be taken into account in the assessment of damages. Retractions and apologies I am less

22 The Report of the Libel Reform Project of the Annenberg Washington Program, *Proposal for the Reform of Libel Law*, Communication and Policy Studies Northwestern University, 1988.

23 Discussion Paper 32: *Defamation*, August 1993.

24 But see the recent Australian constitutional cases *Stephens and Others v. West Australian Nespapers* Ltd (1994) 182 CLR 211; *Theophanous v. Herald Weekly Times* (1994) 182 CLR 104.

sure about, at least in our current regimes, since these may be motivated by a desire to avoid costly litigation rather than a genuine change of mind, and may be perceived as such.

Of course, these elements form part of particular litigation contexts. Truth is argued by the plaintiff as a defence or justification. Publishing a reply plays its part in the mitigation of damages, but both can be viewed as aspects of enhancing dialogue and we can extrapolate from them to a bolder and more thorough strategy for using reputational disputes to further truth-oriented debate. Thus the Annenberg proposal for a declaratory judgment as opposed to monetary compensation might become the central focus of the New Deal defamation process.

The Annenberg proposals are "designed to encourage the dissemination of truth in the public realm and to facilitate the prompt, efficient resolution of defamation disputes by emphasising remedies other than money damages".

The Act (l) requires every plaintiff to have sought a retraction or an opportunity to reply from the defendant before filing suit. If this is complied with (and a retraction can be insisted on) then there can be no suit. (This would be little benefit to speech in itself if it was backed by a threat of further expensive legal action).

(2) If there is an action then either party can opt for a declaratory judgment, in which case there are no money damages and no first amendment protections for public persons etc. This means a quick, less expensive trial (within 120 days) while the matter is still fresh and reputation can be salvaged.

(3) Only by consent can there be a suit for actual damages roughly under current rules, but without presumed or punitive damages.

The attraction of this approach is that both parties, in so far as they can claim legitimate motives, have an interest in establishing the truth of the matter, an interest which may well be shared by others to whom the matter has significance. This confronts the fact that defamation is not simply a private matter, but is of concern to others in the same communicative community, evidently in the case of public ofificals and figures, but also in a more limited way in any case where any reputation is at stake, for reputation involves the responses of other people, and these responses matter not only because of their impact on the lives of the defamed persons.

Vindication is important and vindication is a matter of a credible procedure for establishing or giving an informed opnion on the matters of fact on which evaluative judgments are based. Here the open free market of ideas may be quite inadequate since newspaper readers etc are unable to get close enough to the evidence on which such assertions are based. Courts may therefore be important not simply as delivering a judgment but as doing so on the basis of more first hand assessment of relevant evidence. A sort of representative truth finding body, a mini Royal Commission.

There are many objections to this proposal, with respect to its realism and its costs, but it is the most promising direction for libel law reform discussions to go.

Ben Crum, Amsterdam

Legal Deliberation about the Right to Free Speech*

Introduction

There are probably few political principles that appear as deeply entrenched in liberal-democratic societies as the right to free speech. Citizens in liberal democracies generally take their right to free speech for granted in everyday action. However, sometimes they may find statements they have made contested. While these statements may have been made under the presumption that they would be protected under the right to free speech, the possibility appears that punishment will be imposed for them. Moreover, one's right to free speech may be affected in that it will be prohibited to make similar statements in the future.

The need to invoke the right to free speech arises exactly at the point where one's speaking freely is found to conflict with claims of others. Sometimes conflicting parties are able to avoid a head-on collision of their claims, but if they do not, they are likely to bring their conflict before the court. In such cases the right to free speech is sure to be invoked. Few will deny its validity, but the meaning this right is to have, the implications that can be derived from it, may be far from clear. Here the problem I want to address is posed: while on the one hand the right to free speech is not determined as an unqualified rule, it is still expected to guide our judgements.

The background against which I will develop this argument is Stanley Fish's claim "There's No Such Thing as Free Speech and It's a Good Thing, Too". More specifically Fish argues that the proclamation of the right to free speech has never provided "any normative guidance for marking off protected from unprotected speech; rather the guidance we have has been fashioned (and refashioned) in the very political struggles over which it then (for a time) presides. In short, the name of the game has always been politics (...)" (Fish 1994: 111). Against Fish's assertion I want to demonstrate that the right to free speech does provide normative guidance. Still his argument has to be taken seriously as it is provoked not merely by widespread sentiments regarding the right to free speech, but also by two of the leading theories of law in our times: legal positivism and the work by Ronald Dworkin that we may label 'moral constitutionalism'.

The classical, positivist approach to free speech is that it can be protected by a system of rules in which all cases can be categorised. Rules are to define the limits of free speech, and in turn further rules may be developed to allow for exceptions to these rules. In the long run the system of rules is to expand until it leaves no open texture whatsoever (Hart 1961). Fish capitalises on the by-now common critique of legal positivism that legal rules and principles do not

* An earlier, under-developed version of this paper was presented at the Working Group on the right to free speech at the 17th IVR-World Congress in Bologna June 18, 1995. Besides the comments received at that occassion it has benefited from commentary by Günther Frankenberg, Karl-Heinz Ladeur, Steven Lukes, and Rory O'Connell.

determine how they are to be applied. However, it is one thing to point out that the right to free speech is underdetermined relative to cases to which it may be applied, it is quite another to suggest that under the right to free speech 'anything goes' or that the legal decisions are in the end up to the whim of the judge or whoever has the power to rule, as Fish does.

The 'moral constitutionalism' of Ronald Dworkin enriches our understanding of the law by highlighting the importance of basic rights and by providing a theory of legal interpretation that is susceptible to moral considerations (1977; 1986). He starts by arguing that in principle rights are to trump most other claims. Still he recognises that there are limits to such rights as the right to free speech (cf. Dworkin 1977: 200). He argues that these limits can be discerned by way of a process of interpretation which is to be guided by the reigning morality of our societies. In our societies 'liberalism' is the name of this morality, and it is to direct us in finding the 'right answer' in all legal conflicts. Similar conclusions have been reached by Robert Alexy in his theory of basic rights. Since the legal norm guaranteeing the right to free speech cannot be applied as a 'hard' rule, the right should be regarded as a principle with prima facie-force, which may be overridden in cases in which greater weight has to be attached to other values or principles (Alexy 1985).

The problem with both Dworkin's and Alexy's account is that they determine 'the right answer' or 'the right balance of values' mainly by appealing forcefully to our moral intuitions. However, in the end the interpretation processes by which they decide such balancing exercises appear rather particularistic and ad-hoc. Thus it is open to Fish to argue that they are merely pushing one side in the conflict.

Rights in Deliberation

In my view the right to free speech does provide guidance to legal judgement as it constitutes a reason in public deliberation about political and legal conflicts. In societies in which the right to free speech is recognised there is a common presumption working in favour of it, as it is associated with a wide range of common goods, such as the pursuit of truth, the value of self-expression and the exercise of democratic self-government. In this essay I simply assume that the entrenchment of the right to free speech in liberal democracies can be justified by such arguments (cf. Mill 1859; Meiklejohn 1965; Schauer 1982). As persuasive as this general justification may be, it does not turn the right to free speech into a stipulative, absolute rule. There may well be reasons that dominate it. At this point the challenge I want to deal with arises: How can the right to free speech accommodate countervailing reasons without standing in an all-or-nothing-at-all relationship with them or subjecting them to the opaque practice of balancing?

A first step towards a satisfactory answer to this question is to distinguish rights as reasons from the claims they are meant to support. This distinction derives from Joseph Raz's definition of rights: "'x has a right' if and only if x can have rights, and other things being equal, an aspect of x's well-being (his interest) is a sufficient reason for holding some other person(s) to be under a duty" (Raz 1986: 166). A right, according to Raz, provides a reason for holding someone to be under a duty, or in other words (and assuming the Hohfeldian logical correspondence between claims and duties (Hohfeld 1919)) a right validates a claim. Raz's definition further warrants the important observation that a right is only a reason for a duty "which, if not counteracted by conflicting considerations, justifies holding that other person to have a duty" (Raz 1986: 171; cf. Melden 1977: Ch. 1).

Raz allows a certain indeterminacy into the operation of rights: whether the reasons given by the right dominate is conditional upon possible countervailing considerations that cannot be determined at the outset for all cases in which a right might apply. This indeterminacy does, however, not correspond to irrationality. The question whether a right dominates or not is not open to whim but has to be decided on the balance of reasons. Hence, by differentiating rights from claims, Raz retains a moment of judgement in deliberation.

Being entrenched in liberal democracies the right to free speech poses a pre-emptory reason in favour of the claims for which it is invoked. Thereby it defines the tasks of both parties involved in legal or political conflict. The party invoking the right has the lighter task of reconstructing the relationship her claim has to the common goods generally associated with free speech. The antagonist faces the more difficult task of demonstrating that the duty imposed upon her in the case at hand cannot reasonably be accepted by any one. Thus, initially, given the invocation of the right to free speech, the burden of argument is on the latter. As a consequence, the right to free speech becomes embedded in a range of arguments with, on the one hand, arguments articulating its common good functions and, on the other hand, arguments articulating the costs that may be implicated in the claims the right validates.

The analysis of concrete legal arguments can demonstrate how such processes of deliberation proceed. By reconstructing the arguments on both sides we can test, on the one hand, whether the status of the right to free speech operates indeed as a pre-emptory reason, ruling by default when arguments on the opposing side fail to convince. On the other hand, we can also analyse what it takes for these latter arguments to qualify as succeeding in changing the burden of argument. If the actual practice of legal deliberation can be demonstrated to conform to our intuitive understanding of the justified status of the right to free speech and the importance of the burdens of reasons, we have a strong argument holding against Fish that there is such a thing as a right to free speech and that, indeed, it is a precious and rational thing.

Two Cases under Deliberation

I want to reconstruct two processes of legal deliberation involving the right to free speech, one from Great Britain and one from Germany. In the British case *Telnikoff v. Matusevitch*, two Russian émigrés, both employed by radio stations based in London and broadcasting to Russia, quarrelled over a letter that the latter had written to 'The Daily Telegraph'. Reacting to an earlier article by Telnikoff, Matusevitch maintained among other things:

> "Mr Telnikoff demands that in the interest of more effective broadcasts the management of BBC's Russian Service should switch from professional testing to a blood test. Mr Telnikoff is stressing his racialist recipe by claiming that no matter how high the standards and integrity of 'ethnically alien' people Russian staff may be, they should be dismissed."

The Zwangsdemokraten-suit involved the late German politician Franz Josef Strauß, who claimed to be defamed by the following passage in an interview with the publicist Ralph Giordano in the German weekly 'Stern':

> "Stern: You have coined the expression "Zwangsdemokraten".
> G.: That I consider to be those people who had themselves converted to democracy only by force or for opportunistic reasons and who uphold this system of government merely formally. Franz Josef Strauß is for me the personification of this type.
> Stern: The political Vita of Bavaria demonstrates, however, that we are better democrats than we appear to be - since he has not made it yet.
> G.: It is true that Strauß has not attained his goal. The second German democracy has domesticated him. But that does not change any thing to the fact that this type – I would like to de-personalise this, because it does in no way refer to Franz Josef Strauß alone –, that this type is very much alive in the Federal Republic. For sure, its trees have not reached the sky, the remaining longing for a strong man, say the federal-German version of the National- Socialist Führer-cult, has not asserted itself; this notwithstanding, I hold this type of forced democrats for very dangerous. Not that they could take over the democracy, but they could do damage to it.

Notwithstanding the many similarities between the two cases, there are some differences between them that should not be ignored. First of all, in the German case the victim of libel is a person well known to the public whose general reputation as a politician is affected. Moreover, the disagreement in the German case reflects certain major divisions of the German political debate. Depending on one's general political sympathies, any observer is soon drawn to one of the two sides: Strauß represents the political 'right' who in any case are more likely to cherish an articulate conception of 'personal honour', Giordano, on the other hand, stands for a more leftist, critical political position. The particular prominence of Strauß only goes to increase the political impact of any judgement on the conflict (cf. NJW-RR 1990: 1436 IV.3).

Comparatively the social resonance of the conflict between Telnikoff and Matusevitch is much less, since it does not even relate as much to British as it does to Russian society. As deeply divided as these two men may be on the particular issue at stake, their conflict arises against a particular experiential background in which few people can share to the same extent: they are both emigrants working for Russian broadcasting services in Britain.

The Public Interest in Free Speech

As I asserted earlier, free speech is often considered to serve certain public interests. Political philosophers have argued for a number of public interests in free speech. John Stuart Mill (1859), for instance, regarded free speech as a necessary requisite for the social quest for truth, while Alexander Meiklejohn (1965) has defended free speech as a necessary pre-condition for democratic self-government. If the right to free speech serves a public interest and if this public interest amounts to any thing more than the mere aggregation of individual interests, institutional provisions must be made to guard it. Constitutions are often regarded as fulfilling such a role, to protect public interests against the whims of individual preferences. Hence the right to free speech is laid down in Article 5 of the German Basic Law:

> "(1) Everyone shall have the right to freely express and disseminate his opinion by speech, writing and pictures and freely to inform himself unhindered from generally accessible sources. The freedom of the press and freedom of reporting by means of broadcasts and films are guaranteed. There shall be no censorship."

However, this right is not absolute. Other interests have been identified by which it may be restricted. These are enumerated in the following paragraph:

> "(2) These rights are limited by the provisions of the general laws, the provisions of law for the protection of youth, and by the right to inviolability of personal honour."

The last provision provided the ground on which Franz Josef Strauß could go to court. Both the Trial Court (*Landgericht*) and the Appeal Court (*Oberlandesgericht*) held that Strauß' personal honour had actually been violated by Giordano's statements. Thus these statements were classified as malicious libel (*Schmähkritik*). The Appeal Court sought to accommodate the right to free speech, however, by coming to a decision that would have minimal impact upon Giordano's right. It only prohibited the use of the exact wordings of the interview and added that it could not be said at the outset whether similar statements by Giordano in different future contexts would be permissible.

Even though this verdict might have had very little impact on the rights on which Giordano could act in the future, he decided to appeal to the Federal Constitutional Court since the decision of the Appeal Court demanded him to abandon his considered statements. Giordano's first objection was that in general the Appeal Court had failed to heed properly the full extent of the defence that the constitutional right to free speech provides, in particular since his statements were made in the context of a relevant public debate. Secondly, the Appeal Court was mistaken to classify Giordano's statements as malicious libel. It had reached this conclusion on the basis of a wrong interpretation of the passage concerned. The Federal Constitutional Court decided that these objections held ground and overruled the decision of the Appeal Court. The limits of the right to free speech would only be surpassed if it could be established unambiguously that the statements lacked any substantial content and that the speaker acted not so much with the intention to engage in a public debate but to maliciously libel his victim (BVerfGE 82: 272).

In Great Britain, as is well-known, the right to free speech is not established as part of a constitutional Bill of Rights. This notwithstanding, a commitment to free speech has been entrenched in certain moral and legal norms. Such a commitment is most notably expressed in the legal provision of 'the defence of fair comment' on which the leading compendium on British law states that it is "in the nature of a general right, and enables any member of the public to comment on matters of public interest." (Halsbury's Vol. 28: §131) As another authority has remarked, the defence of fair comment "is generally regarded as a bulwark of free speech" (Committee on Defamation 1975: §151).

When *Telnikoff v. Matusevitch* came before the House of Lords, Lord Ackner stressed this special status of free speech in his dissenting opinion [1991] 4 All ER 830. He considered that the freedom of speech is one of the fundamental freedoms, and referred to the decision of the Court of Appeal in *Lyon v. Daily Telegraph* [1943] 2 All ER 316, in which it was argued:

> "The reason why, once a plea of fair comment is established, there is no libel, is that it is in the public interest to have free discussion of matters of public interest."

Though such a principled view may be more and more common in the British legal system, it did not prevail in this case. In Great Britain, the defence of fair comment is most of the time regarded as serving above all the individual interest of the speaker. Hence the legal deliberation proceeds in terms of an individual conflict. The added weight of a public interest is hardly ever invoked.

The Statements' Meaning

The initial verdict of the Munich Appeal Court started with establishing that Giordano's statements were pure statements of comment and not of fact. In this the Court relied on the ruling of the Federal Constitutional Court by which it held that comment is characterised by the three elements of *Stellungnahme* (making a stand, position taking), *Dafürhaltens* (belief) and *Meinens* (opinion).

Even though the question of the truth of the facts maintained did not apply any more, the meaning of the comment still had to be established. The crucial passage in this respect became the statement that „the remaining longing for a strong man, say the federal-German version of the National- Socialist Führer-cult, has not asserted itself". The Appeal Court read this passage as referring directly to Strauß. This verdict was overruled by the Federal Constitutional Court , which considered a second interpretation of this passage. In this interpretation the passage refers not to Strauß but to a part of the German population, which merely may regard Strauß as a candidate to fulfil their longing for a strong man. If this interpretation applies, then the defamatory effect for Strauß is put in doubt.

The Federal Constitutional Court emphasised that the statements were not to be classified on the basis of an assessment of their (semantic) form and meaning in isolation, but that their meaning had to be brought out by reference to the whole context, including the book Giordano had published on 'forced democrats'. At the same time the Court relied on the impression the statements would make on an unprejudiced average reader. On this basis the Court asserted that the reference to Strauß as a "forced democrat" was a sharp and exaggerated offence which severely affected his personal dignity. But given the strong conception of the right to free speech, such a statement was not necessarily inadmissible, this would still depend on the way this statement was to be interpreted.

In the case of *Telnikoff v. Matusevitch* the issues of establishing the factual content of the statements complained of turned out to be crucial. At the Trial Court Judge Drake took little trouble in deciding that Matusevitch's defence of fair comment was well grounded. Telnikoff brought an appeal over this verdict by dissecting Judge Drake's opinion on three grounds and demanding further justification for them. Telnikoff's most fundamental challenge read that there was "reasonable doubt as to whether the words are statements of fact or comment". Secondly, even if it were asserted that the letter contained mere comment, then still it could not be regarded as fair in the sense that a fair-minded man could have written it in reaction to Telnikoff's initial article. Finally, Telnikoff claimed that, in making his statements, Matusevitch had actually been motivated by express malice.

The claim that the words complained of contained defamatory statements of fact and not comment was extensively considered before the Court of Appeal. Lord Justice Lloyd eventually delivered the following opinion:

> "... it is well settled that a comment does not lose its quality as such merely because it is stated as a fact, providing it is apparent from the context that the fact so stated is an inference from the facts on which the comment is based"

and he ruled:

> "The words are comment, and are not reasonably capable of being understood as statements of fact" [1990] 3 WLR 732/3.

This ruling raised a new issue, namely: was the letter to be read in context or in isolation? Notably it appears that the German courts generally favour a contextual reading. During the initial hearings both parties before the Court of Appeal agreed that in deciding the question „fact or comment?" the Court was confined to consider the letter alone. The main reason that both solicitors gave for this opinion was that someone might have read the letter without having read the article, or without being able to remember what the article said.

However, the Court directed the deliberating process by resuming hearing on a later date to have further argument on this particular point. Only then Matusevitch's solicitor, Mr. Garnier, decided to submit that Telnikoff's original article might actually be taken up by the Court for the sake of constructing the content of the letter. This position the Court of Appeal actually adopted against the continued insistence from Telnikoff's side that the Court should confine itself to consideration of the letter in isolation. Lord Justice Lloyd's reaction to this submission was:

> "I do not agree. When any question of construction is involved the courts always have regard to the context. In other words, the courts have regard to the document as a whole." [1990] 3 WLR 731.

As Telnikoff appealed to the House of Lords, Lord Keith of Kinkel speaking for the majority, overruled the decision of the Court of Appeal: „In my opinion the letter must be considered on its own." Against Lord Justice Lloyd's reasoning for the opposite, Lord Keith observed:

> "The writer of a letter to a newspaper has a duty to take reasonable care to make clear that he is writing comment, and not making misrepresentations about the subject matter upon which he is commenting. There is no difficulty about using suitable words for that purpose" [1991] 3 All ER 823.

Lord Keith moreover asserted that:

> "... if the letter alone is looked at it would be open to a reasonable jury properly to find that the offending paragraphs contained statements of fact" [1991] 3 All ER 826.

The only dissenting opinion of Lord Ackner failed:

> "It is not always easy to draw the distinction between an expression of opinion and an assertion of fact [...] whether the words complained of were reasonably capable of being understood as comment or a statement of fact must depend on a consideration of the whole of the words used, their context and the circumstances of publication" [1991] 3 All ER 827.

The Speakers's Intention

The main issue the Munich Appeal Court initially considered was whether Giordano's statements classified as malicious libel. The constitutional right to free speech does permit a wide range of personal criticism. Malicious libel, however, is not warranted. The Court relied on a formulation by the Federal Constitutional Court which had held that statements classify as malicious libel when they contain an excess of defamation which cannot be unsaid and justifies its prohibition (NJW-RR 1990: 1436). The primary test is whether the libelling statements have been made with the express aim to hurt somebody's personal honour.

The Appeal Court ruled initially that Giordano's statements established a close relation between Strauß and National-Socialism and implicated that Strauß would have continued the National-Socialist Führer-cult, if the opinion of the German majority had not been against him doing so. Such an assertion was regarded as a most serious infringement of the right of personal dignity. Furthermore, the Court regarded this remark as having been made arbitrarily and not as part of the substantial argument. Even though these statements were made in the spontaneous context of an interview, the Court assumed that Giordano had considered the issue well enough to realise the implications of what he was saying.

Overruling this verdict of the Appeal Court, the Federal Constitutional Court accepted Giordano's assertion that throughout the interview his primary aim had been to point to the threat that 'forced democrats' pose for the democratic order. Even if the interpretation of the Appeal Court was adopted whereby Giordano's statements on "the Federal-German version of the Führer- cult" referred directly to Strauß, one could not interpret them as expressly meant to hurt Strauß' personal dignity, instead of sticking to the (though passionate and exaggerated) argument. At the re-trial, the Munich Appeal Court followed the Federal Constitutional Court and asserted that it could not be ascertained whether Giordano intended to maliciously libel Strauß. Hence his right to free speech prevailed (NJW 1992: 1324).

In the case of *Telnikoff v. Matusevitch*, both Judge Drake at the Trial Court and the Court of Appeal were not convinced by Telnikoff's claim of express malice. However, before the Court of Appeal Telnikoff claimed that even if the comments did not classify as express malice, it still had to be demonstrated that they were fair. Initially in the appeal Telnikoff had phrased this question as that

„the judge should have left to the jury the question whether the comment was on its face (and regardless of the issue of malice) such as could be made by a fair-minded man on the plaintiff's article“ [1990] 3 WLR 727. This test is called the „objective test of fairness“. The Court of Appeal established that Matusevitch's statements did meet this test, but then Telnikoff's solicitors introduced another, „subjective“ test of fairness into the deliberation. By this test Matusevitch would have to show that the comments represented his honest opinions.

On this issue there were different legal authorities contradicting each other. For instance, one of the main textbooks, 'Gatley on Libel and Slander', even appears to contradict itself, stating in paragraph 729: „The law does not protect the expression of an opinion not honestly held, even if it is an opinion which someone else might have honestly expressed“, while it says in paragraph 789: „the defendant who relies on a plea of fair comment does not have to show that the comment is an honest expression of his views“.

Lord Justice Lloyd ruled:

> "In my judgement the correct view of English law is that where the defendant's comment is fair by the objective test, it is presumed to be the honest expression of his view unless the plaintiff pleads and proves express malice" [1990] 3 WLR 737.

Thus Telnikoff failed to establish that Matusevitch's statements were not fair.

However, as we saw, when the case came before the House of Lords, the majority adopted a restrictive conception of comment, excluding statements which could be regarded as statements of fact and not even allowing for an interpretation of them on the basis of the context in which they had been published. As the jury at the re-trial actually found that some of Matusevitch's statements amounted to statements of fact, which he moreover failed to justify, it was ruled that he had to pay Telnikoff damages amounting to £240,000.

Discussion

The reconstruction of the different arguments adopted by the parties in the two cases, displays that actors reacted to each other's arguments and how these changed in the course of their legal trajectories. This shows that the law as it stood did not provide the parties with a strict recipe for action. Moreover, these incidents can be read as indicators of the attempt to search for reasonable understanding, if not from the opposing party then at least from the judges and jury.

My categorisation of the different arguments shows that in both legal systems a number of similar concerns were raised bearing upon the cases involved: public interests, meaning and intention. Still the differences between the two legal systems are striking and one can note that these go much beyond the obvious differences in statutes and the fact that in Germany the right to free speech is recognised in a written constitution while in Great Britain it is not. Witness, for instance, the way the common distinction between fact and comment is applied in both countries. In principle if statements of fact can be identified they are open to proof which demonstrates them to be either true or false, while statements of comment, on the other hand, are not open to such a truth-test. The British courts sought to isolate fact from comment, and subjected the former to a strict test of truth. In Germany there appears a more general scepticism towards facts. A statement classifies as comment relatively easily, if only it meets the three elements of *Stellungnahme* (making a stand, position taking), *Dafürhaltens* (belief) and *Meinens* (opinion). Moreover, no attempts are made to isolate statements from each other. The judges rather refer throughout to the context in which the statements were made to establish the different possible interpretations which they might allow.

The legal means by which the speaker's intention is to be determined also show some marked differences. Here the strongest test is the "subjective test" proposed by Telnikoff which would require the person speaking to demonstrate that his statements reflect his honest opinions. The British courts actually decline to apply this test. Instead they rely on the "objective test" by which a statement is found to be fair if "a fair-minded man" could have made it. The way in which this test is applied can obviously remain contested. Moreover, it contains a presupposition in favour of the speaking person, as it puts the burden of proof on the plaintiff. The conclusions that this test yields may in the end not be markedly different from the focus of the German Federal Constitutional Court on the question whether the statements at issue could be interpreted as being part of a substantial argument.

One might want to consider, hypothetically, whether the cases would have been decided differently if each of them would have been dealt with in the other system. In Britain the jury found Matusevitch eventually liable to pay damages amounting to £240,000, while the Munich Court found that there were no valid charges against Giordano's statements. Indeed, much suggests that both cases would have been decided the other way around! In Germany by way of the Basic Law and its active guards of the Federal Constitutional Court the right to free speech is established as an almost inviolable principle. As a consequence Matusevitch would most likely have won his case in Germany. In Britain, on the other hand, even though the right to free speech is generally acknowledged, there is a notable concern with the limits that reasonably have to be imposed upon this right. Precise conceptual distinctions are upheld which differentiate between cases that are not tolerable and cases that are. It appears all too likely that the British courts would have found Giordano's remarks unjustifiable.

What do these observations leave of the rationality of the right to free speech? Is Stanley Fish right in saying that in practice the right to free speech cannot provide any normative guidance? Can there be such a thing as free speech any way? For a start, we should not underestimate the rationality of these judgements concerning the right to free speech. Each of them, in their own particular context, may well be right, or rational at least (cf. Wellmer 1986: VII). Moreover, even if one cannot fully agree with these judgements, still one can appreciate some of the grounds which may go to justify them.

Notwithstanding that there is little reason to regard ourselves better judges than the ones actually appointed as such in these cases, there are some critical observations to be made. The comparison of these two cases confirms that, corresponding to the absence of the constitutional codification, the basic right to free speech is (legally at least) much less entrenched in Britain than in Germany.

Matusevitch, relying on the right to free speech, has a heavy burden of argument to discharge and as he is found to fall short in doing so, he eventually loses the case. Under these circumstances one indeed comes to wonder whether there is any sense to impute the right to free speech, as it is generally regarded to be at the heart of any liberal democratic system, to Britain. In the case of Giordano, on the other hand, we find the Federal Constitutional Court fully asserting his right to free speech, while almost bypassing the countervailing arguments raised. Here one comes to wonder what, if any, arguments the Constitutional Court would recognise as carrying the burden of reasons against a claim validated by the right to free speech (cf. Ladeur 1993).

The conception of the basic right to free speech here proposed recognises the great value that is generally attributed to free speech, not only for the individual interests it serves directly, but also for the constitutive function it has for liberal democratic society at large. This value is expressed as the right operates as a pre-emptory reason in political deliberation. However, in the end deliberation proceeds by rationally assessing the force of reasons against each other; it therefore has to leave open the possibility that indeed actors may raise reasons that dominate those underlying the right to free speech.

References

Alexy, Robert (1985), *Theorie der Grundrechte*, Nomos, Baden-Baden.

Committee on Defamation (1975), *Report of the Committee on Defamation*, HMSO, London.

Dworkin, Ronald (1977 [1987]), *Taking Rights Seriously*, Duckworth, London.

Dworkin, Ronald (1986), *Law's Empire*, Belknap Press, Cambridge, Mass.

Fish, Stanley (1994), „There's No Such Thing as Free Speech, and it's a Good Thing, Too", in: *There's No Such Thing as Free Speech* : Ch. 8. Oxford University Press, New York.

Hart, H. L. A. (1961 [1990]), *The Concept of Law*, Clarendon Press, Oxford.

Hohfeld, W. N. (1919 [1964]), *Fundamental Legal Conceptions*, as Applied in Judicial Reasoning, Greenwood Press, Westport, Connecticut.

Ladeur, Karl-Heinz (1993), „Meinungsfreiheit, Ehrenschutz und die Veränderung der Öffentlichkeit in der Massendemokratie", in: *Archiv für Presserecht* , 2: pp. 531–536.

Meiklejohn, Alexander (1965), *Political Freedom: The Constitutional Powers of the People*, Oxford University Press, New York.

Melden, A. I. (1977), *Rights and Persons,* Basil Blackwell, Oxford.

Mill, John Stuart (1859 [1991]), *On Liberty and Other Essays*, ed. by John Gray, Oxford University Press, Oxford.

Raz Joseph (1986), *The Morality of Freedom*, Clarendon Press, Oxford.

Schauer, Frederich (1982) *Free Speech: A Philosophical Inquiry*, Cambridge University Press, Cambridge.

Wellmer, Albert (1986), *Ethik und Dialog, Elemente des moralischen Urteils bei Kant und in der Diskursethik*, Suhrkamp, Frankfurt am Main.

Court Decisions

Telnikoff v. Matusevitch [1984 T. No. 964]: 4 All E.R. [1991]: 817 (= 3 W.L.R. [1991]: 952 ; 1 Q.B. [1991]: 102); 3 All E.R. [1990]: 865 ; 3 W.L.R. [1990]: 725; 2 A.C. [1992]: 343.

Lyon v. Daily Telegraph [1943] 2 All ER 316

Zwangsdemokraten: BVerfGE 82, 272; NJW 1992: 1324; NJW-RR 1990: 1436.

Filimon Peonidis, Thessaloniki

Remarks on a Philosophical Defence of the Right to Freedom of Expression

A. Introduction[1]

In this paper I would like to express some thoughts that in my opinion constitute a necessary prologue to a plausible philosophical theory defending a right to free expression. It is not my intention to say anything about the details of such a theory, although it is evident that the preliminary remarks that follow will rule out certain accounts of freedom of expression. In parts (b) and (c) I undertake the task of meeting the challenge set by antitheoretical and critical tendencies. Unfortunately, their discussion can only be selective and limited. Finally, in part (d) I briefly discuss certain general conditions which should be met by any adequate free speech theory.

B. Anti-theoretical Tendencies

Which are the basic elements constituting an anti-theoretical tendency? I will start with a negative answer. A scholar does not express an anti-theoretical attitude in respect to free speech issues, if he is convinced that one or more of the normative theories that are usually adduced to highlight the special significance of certain utterances are mistaken.[2] The number of principles moral and political philosophers appeal to may be limited, but there is an impressive variety of argumentative strategies that can be used for purposes of criticism and defence. Thus, disagreement with a particular consequentialist or deontological justification of a free speech principle should not entail an overall rejection of theoretical approaches. On the contrary, the distinguishing mark of an anti-theoretical

1 This paper is part of a book-length work in progress on the philosophical foundations of freedom of expression and some arguments appear here in a condensed form. Although I believe that the term freedom of expression is more apposite for the purposes of this paper, I will use the terms freedom of expression and freedom of speech interchangeably. I am indebted to Stelios Virvidakis, Wayne Norman, X.J.Paparrigopoulos and Roy Allan for their valuable comments and assistance. I also thank T. Campbell, B. Crum, R. A. Shiner and the other workshop participants for the discussion that followed the presentation of the paper.

2 See Lawrence Alexander and Paul Horton, “The Impossibility of a Free Speech Principle,” *Northwestern University Law Review* 78 (1983):1319–57 and esp. 1346–52. The authors give the impression that they regard a general philosophical theory of free speech impossible since “consequentialist or deontological theories are either (1) wrong, (2) too narrow in their theoretical ambit or practical application to support a principle of general application, or (3) not about “speech” or “freedom of speech” as an independent Principle at all, but rather about concepts or activities in which speech or freedom of speech is only a lesser and completely included subcategory” (1352). However, the sample of theories considered is very small and their discussion too cursory to warrant conclusions (1) and (2), whereas I cannot see why conclusion (3) undermines a theoretical approach.

approach is a complete distrust of the use of normative theories and principles in free speech debates.

Normative theories have been recently under attack.[3] The most common charges are that they lack motivational force, that they are based on abstract and obscure principles that mean little to ordinary people, that they are insensitive to context, that they restrict moral reflection by ignoring the multiplicity and heterogeneity of values, and that their basic tenets are presented as objectively valid and universal, whereas in reality they reflect nothing but the subjective preferences of their authors. Along these lines Stanley Fish has recently accused of hypocrisy all those who are concerned with the articulation and defence of free speech principles.[4] The charge is that, while they boast of being tolerant in respect to a variety of utterances, they take a completely different attitude when they come across an utterance posing a threat to whatever values they happen to cherish. In other words, despite the usual rhetoric, it turns out that free speech is valued only instrumentally and it cannot be otherwise.

> "[I]f you are engaged in some purposive activity in the course of which speech happens to be produced, sooner or later you will come to a point when you decide that some forms of speech do not further but endanger that purpose".[5]

One could agree with Fish that free speech cannot have value *per se*, but only in relation to the higher-order principles it promotes.[6] However, this does not render theoretical approaches redundant or self-refuting. On the contrary, it reveals the need for serious theorizing. There are values that allow a vast array of utterances and others that set strict limits to permissible speech. One could claim that "political speech should promote only the aims of the Soviet people's revolution"; another "political speech is valuable because it enables citizens to act as autonomous agents". One could promote her values without the use of speech at all, as in the case of the religious person who believes that she can reach God through meditation; another could consider freedom of expression as an indispensable means to the realization of her projects, as happens with the opposition leader in a constitutional democracy. The point worth making against Fish is that it is possible for someone to start with an intuitively favorable attitude towards expression and then seek a justification protecting the greatest possible number of categories of expression. Undoubtedly, there would be some exceptions, since expression does not have intrinsic value (as Fish correctly points out, that would amount to valuing "the right to make noise"). However, this

3 This attack is explicit in the work of Michael Walzer, Bernard Williams, Alasdair MacIntyre and Annete Baier.

4 The most recent statement of his views is included in the collection of essays *There's No Such Thing As Free Speech And It's A Good Thing, Too* (New York : Oxford University Press, 1994), chapter eight. For a different critique of his "nihilist" conception see Joshua Cohen, "Freedom of Expression," *Philosophy and Public Affairs* 22 (1993):238–41.

5 Ibid., 107.

6 It should be noted that one of the most urgent problems any conception assigning intrinsic value to speech has to face is that of balancing free speech interests against other interests favoring suppression. This balancing cannot yield any satisfactory results without the aid of a general normative theory that would explicate the privileged position of free speech interests. For a detailed account of this problem see Alexander and Horton, op. cit.

does not imply that the person engaged in the admittedly onerous task of setting legitimate exceptions merely pays lip-service to the value of free speech or contradicts herself.

Fish does not acknowledge this possibility and after expressing his dissatisfaction with the results of First Amendment scholarship makes his own suggestion :

> [The] alternative is *politics*, the realization...that decisions about what is and is not protected in the realm of expression will rest not on principle or firm doctrine but on the ability of some persons to interpret-recharacterize or rewrite-principle and doctrine in ways that lead to the protection of speech they want heard and the regulation of speech they want heard and the regulation of speech they want silenced.[7]

In an effort to be charitable to Fish one can take this statement as descriptive. This is the way politics is conducted, we all know that politicians and their lawyers often twist constitutional and democratic principles to achieve immediate political gains. However, this impression is dispelled a few lines below when the reader encounters the following statement:

> The question of whether or not to regulate will always be a local one and we can not rely on abstractions that are either empty of content or filled with the content of some partisan agenda to generate a "principled answer". Instead we *must* consider in every case what is at stake and what are the risks and gains of alternative courses of action.[8] [Emphasis added]

Several objections could be raised against this method of deciding free-speech issues. For instance, one can express one's worries about the identity of those agents who decide free speech issues and question their authority, but I do not wish to pursue this line of criticism. Instead, my response to Fish's anti-theoretical attitude is that on a closer examination his position turns out to be a theoretical one. In fact, it can be characterized as an exemplification of what moral philosophers call *act-consequentialism*. According to this view – which has been the subject of extensive debate – a particular act is right if and only if it has the best overall consequences. The agent has to weigh the available courses of action, assess their expected outcomes in order to determine which one meets his moral standards best and finally perform the one yielding the best possible result. This is a "principled" position, although it differs significantly from other positions giving priority to well-defined abstract rules. In sum, it appears

7 Op. cit., 110. In an earlier version of the same essay one reads : "...on the ability of some persons and groups to so operate (some would say manipulate) the political process that the speech they support is labelled "protected" while the speech inimical to their interests is declared to be fair game." [Paul Berman (ed.), *Debating P.C. : The Controversy of Political Correctness on College Campuses* (New York : Laurel, 1992), 242.] This was quite puzzling. In the absence of any free speech principle, one could wonder why groups should regard utterances contravening their interests as "fair game". The most natural reaction, as we know from experience, would be to try to silence those who conveyed them. Perhaps Fish meant that a tolerant stance towards views which one finds threatening should be inculcated in every citizen, but this presupposes a "principled" treatment of free speech issues and a minimal consensus on its value. The revised version avoids all these difficulties.

8 Ibid., 111.

that Fish does not put forward any decisive arguments against a systematic and theoretical treatment of the right to free speech.[9]

A similar anti-theoretical stance underlies the work of Douglas N. Husak who has criticized traditional philosophical defences of free speech for being under the strong but rarely acknowledged influence of legal practice.[10] A distinguishing mark of the latter is that it attributes special value to speech *per se* by "legislative or judicial fiat". Moral philosophers, however, should realize "that most limitations on state authority typically enacted on behalf of a moral principle of freedom of speech can be retained without supposing that speech is entitled to a degree of protection not afforded to other forms of conduct[11]".

This becomes evident if moral philosophers abandon the common view that speech in principle requires more protection than action, and replace it with a theory of attribution specifying "whether and under what circumstances persons may be blamed or held accountable for an ensuing harm[12]". This theory suffices to blame A when she lies to B to the effect that the bridge the latter plans to cross is safe, with the intention of getting rid of him; it also suffices not to blame A when on another occasion she merely mentions to B that C's death would be a good thing and then B proceeds to kill C. What is essential here is to specify the author of the ensuing harm and this can be achieved without any special reference to the value of speech per se. In both cases B acted under A's influence, but in the first A manipulated B's decision-making procedure to her advantage, whereas in the second she treated him as an autonomous agent. Husak does not deny the existence of gray areas and problematic cases, but he is absolutely convinced that his approach yields results which are in conformity with our intuitions. On the contrary, he argues, had one followed the standard method assigning speech a privileged moral status, one would have encountered insurmountable difficulties in showing that in the first case A is to be blamed for B's plight. This is confirmed by the scholarly practice – common in the U.S. – of categorizing certain forms of (allegedly) harmful conduct (such as the publication of obscene material) as "non-speech" to deny them First Amendment protection.[13] All these lead Husak to believe that most traditional philosophical free speech defences rest on defective grounds.

9 In a postscript (ibid., 116–7) Fish acknowledges the possibility of conflict between "principled visions" of speech, but regards them as exclusively political ("politics is the source of principle, not its opposite"). To this one can reply that all the justifications offered are not necessarily political (in the sense of being dictated by the exigencies of current politics), but even if they are of this kind, one can develop a theoretical account to make one's position more convincing.

10 "What is so Special about (Free) Speech?" *Law and Philosophy* 4 (1985):1–15.

11 Ibid., 3.

12 Ibid., 3.

13 Ibid., 13. For instance, Frederick Schauer discussing obscenity maintains that "it contains none of the properties that are defined by the technical sense of the word "speech", and is thus outside the scope of the Free Speech Principle" [*Free Speech : A Philosophical Inquiry* (Cambridge : Cambridge University Press, 1982), 183]. Recently, Catharine A. MacKinnon [*Only Words* (Cambridge, Mass. : Harvard University Press, 1993)] claimed that for women pornography cannot be regarded as expression of ideas, but as an act of sexual subordination.

In response to Husak, first I would like to make a point similar to the one made earlier against Fish. In so far as it is unnecessary to conceive free speech as intrinsically valuable in order to produce a philosophical defence of it, it is equally unnecessary to start with the assumption that speech requires more protection than other forms of conduct. It is extremely difficult, if not impossible, to find arguments in favour of either of these positions.[14] It should not escape our attention that the overwhelming majority of the relevant philosophical defences emphasize the significance of speech *only in relation* to the promotion of other higher-order values. The attainment of truth, the proper functioning of democracy, social utility, tolerance, free competition of ideas, liberty and self-realization (or a combination of them) are some of the values scholars appeal to when they set out to lay the foundations and determine the scope of a satisfactory free speech principle.

Second, Husak's account raises the following query : On the assumption that there is nothing special about speech *per se* possessing as it does only instrumental value, is his theory of attribution of blame adequate to deal successfully with all the traditional free speech issues? I think it is not, since philosophical defences of speech don't have as their sole objective the identification of those that should be blamed for being disrespectful to (a particular conception) of free speech. They also aim at convincing people about the value of free speech and propose certain measures to enhance speakers' and listeners' opportunities for expression and reflection.

Consider the following example : It has been suggested that governments should subsidize newspapers covering political and social issues to make them less vulnerable to the demands of advertisers. This, it is argued, will provide citizens with food for thought thus strengthening "civic deliberation and true popular sovereignty".[15] This proposal is controversial, but it is an undeniable fact that more is at stake here than holding someone accountable. Besides, the harm inflicted, in case no measures are taken, gains significance only in the context of a particular free speech theory. In the absence of the latter, no one can be blamed. It might be true that we can realize that someone is harmed by being lied to without any reference to a free speech theory, but there are harms that are closely connected with a particular conception of free speech the agent happens to endorse. This shows that there is more to be said than a theory of attribution of blame that deliberately ignores any philosophical justification of speech can say.

14 It is worth noticing that Schauer, one of the few scholars who believe that "speech is less subject to regulation than other forms of conduct", no longer holds this view. However, although he finds the hypothesis that speech always causes lesser harm than action untenable, he expresses his satisfaction that the arguments in favor of free speech are now to be understood as arguments "about liberty in general". See his "The Phenomenology of Speech and Harm," *Ethics* 103 (1993):635–53.

15 See Cass R. Sunstein, *Democracy and the Problem of Free Speech* (New York : Free Press, 1993), chapter three.

C. Critical Attitudes

One could seriously wonder what form a plausible position that is hostile to free speech could take, assuming that views prescribing complete silence cannot be taken seriously. A possible reply is to regard claims such as "public speech should be consistent with the aims of the Soviet people's revolution" as denying freedom of speech, since they leave a vast array of utterances devoid of legal protection.

However, the same holds with the more popular view that public speech should have "social value as a step to truth" to fall within the bounds of First Amendment protection.[16] It goes without saying that the second account is less restrictive, since now more utterances are protected, but this is merely a quantitative difference. And it would be entirely arbitrary to specify a minimum number of types of utterances a theory should protect to be characterized as promoting freedom of expression. Another suggestion would be to dub critical those views which by allowing content- based restrictions are distinguished from those which regulate only the place, time or manner of expression. However, this suggestion cannot fare any better, for one can devise a system of freedom of expression focusing exclusively on the latter type of restrictions that would result in an almost complete suppression of public speech. Finally, one could see an indication of disapproval of free speech in the existence of heavy penalties for speech-crimes, but this depends to a great extent on factors that do not form part of a philosophical theory about the value of speech such as the prevailing conception of punishment.[17]

It seems to me that certain passages from the political writings of Hegel and Spinoza give us a better insight into the essentials of an arguable philosophical position that opposes freedom of speech.

Thus, according to Hegel :

> Freedom of public communication ... is indirectly guaranteed...by its innocuous character, which it owes chiefly to the rationality of the constitution and the stability of the government, but also to the publicity of the assemblies of the Estates. It is rendered innocuous by the latter because these assemblies give expression to sound and educated insights concerning the interests of the state, leaving little of significance for others to say, and above

16 This was the majority opinion of the U.S. Supreme Court in *Chaplinsky v. New Hampshire*, 315 U.S. 568 (1942).

17 Torbjörn Tännsjö in his "Against Freedom of Expression" [*Political Studies* 33 (1985):547–59] claims that freedom of expression is an untenable ideal, since it failed to achieve its most significant objective, namely to contribute to "sound mass communication" (growth of knowledge, pluralism of ideas, and equal access to mass media). He blames privately-owned western mass media for establishing a cultural imperialism and for monopolizing information. This might be true, but it is hardly a reason for abolishing freedom of expression. Rather, it is a reason for pressing for more responsible, public-spirited, pluralistic and objective mass media. Freedom of expression is not in principle incompatible with state regulation of broadcasting. For detailed arguments see among others : Sunstein op. cit. and Owen M. Fiss, "Why the State?" in *Democracy and the Mass Media*, Judith Lichtenberg, ed. (Cambridge : Cambridge University Press, 1990), 136–54.

all denying them the opinion that what they have to say is of distinctive importance and effectiveness.[18]

Spinoza two centuries earlier wrote in the final chapter of his *Tractatus Theologico-Politicus* that he had shown the following :

> II. That this freedom [of speech] can be granted to everyone without infringing the right and authority of the sovereign; and that everyone can keep it without infringing that right as long as he does not use it as a license to introduce anything into the state as a law, or to do anything contrary to the accepted laws. III. That it is no danger to the peace of the state; and that all troubles arising from it can easily be checked. IV. That there is no danger to piety either.[19]

Passages like the above lead me to the hypothesis that the distinguishing mark of an extreme critical view must be its emphasis on the *harmless* and *inefficacious* character of protected speech. In particular, its basic principle could be formulated as follows : A particular utterance is legally permissible only in so far as those affected by it unanimously agree that it invades none of their interests.

In effect, this doctrine leaves people speechless, given the fact that the long-term struggle for freedom of speech was conducted to grant people the right to express views that are critical, heretical and disturbing. But, setting history aside, why must the above doctrine be rejected by a philosophical defence of free speech? The answer should be sought in the normative character of the latter. Endorsement of a free-speech principle implies endorsement of at least one underlying general normative principle. Yet, sincere acceptance of a particular moral standpoint requires by definition a willingness to suffer certain harms stemming from the frustration of desires and the invasion of interests incompatible with the requirements of the above standpoint. This is the price any agent has to pay by abandoning egoism and entering the moral realm. For instance, if I believe in liberty or equality, I am under obligation to abstain from certain actions that would endanger the liberty of others or create undeserved inequalities, although on many occasions I would be better-off by not discharging my obligations. Similarly, if I am convinced that the protection of certain forms of speech can receive an adequate moral justification – say, because they are necessary for the exercise of popular sovereignty – I have to tolerate utterances of this type that I find critical, embarrassing, distressing, patently offensive or absolutely mistaken. In addition, I have to suffer various ensuing harms, such as to be ousted from power in the next election, and to suppress my natural desire to resort to violence in order to silence my political opponents.[20] It goes without

18 *Elements of the Philosophy of Right*, translated by H.B. Nisbet, edited by Allen W. Wood (Cambridge : Cambridge University Press, 1991), 356.

19 *The Political Works*, edited and translated with an introduction and notes by A.G. Wernham (Oxford : Clarendon Press, 1958), 241–3. My reference to Spinoza is not intended as a criticism of his work and it shouldn't conceal the radical character of his thought.

20 Consider Jonathan Rauch's *Kindly Inquisitors : The New Attacks on Free Thought* (Chicago: The University of Chicago Press, 1993). The author's critique of the "fundamentalist" and the "humanitarian" conception of expression is premised upon the claim that the advancement of knowledge is necessarily harmful to those who are criticized or proved wrong. His defensive strategy is on the right track, although one can entertain serious doubts as to whether an exclusive emphasis on the value of knowledge can provide reliable guidance in every free speech issue. On the unavoidable costs of free speech see also Cohen, op.cit.

saying that the acceptable harms caused by speech (as well as the unacceptable) vary from theory to theory and they cannot be assessed independently of a particular justification of free speech. What is of utmost importance at a preliminary level is to realize that em- phasis on the harmless nature of speech is tantamount to rejection of free speech.

D. Conditions

Having identified and reviewed several anti- theoretical and critical conceptions, it remains to set out certain *necessary* conditions for a plausible philosophical theory underlying the right to free speech.[21] The first two derive from the discussion in sections (b) and (c). It should be noted that the following account seeks to elaborate, justify and qualify when necessary the widespread (at least in the West) pre-theoretical intuition that freedom of speech is something valuable to humans and should be protected even at a high cost.[22]

Condition one: *Speech should not be assigned intrinsic value, but should be evaluated within the context of a general moral framework.*

Condition two: *Any plausible theory should tolerate certain harms agents suffer due to particular forms of expression that promote or respect its basic tenets.*

Condition three: *Although unconditional freedom of speech is morally objectionable, any theory that aspires to gain superior plausibility over its rivals should protect more categories of expression than they do.* This condition partly satisfies the pre- theoretical belief in the unqualified value of speech. Still, the ultimate objective of a plausible theory should be the attainment of a reflective equilibrium between our positive pre-theoretical attitude to free speech and the reasonable restrictions on it a moral justification would warrant.

Condition four: *Any restrictions on expression should not only be well-argued, but be justified by the same higher-order principle (or principles) that justifies freedom of expression.* This condition aims at avoiding the weighing of the principles validating freedom of expression against other principles speech is supposed to violate. This weighing, as it was claimed before, could lead to a complete suppression of speech.

Condition five: *Any plausible theory of free speech should ascribe to agents the putative right to remain silent, if they so wish.* Were the idea of speaking freely to have any meaning, it must include the possibility of remaining silent. An agent speaks freely (in a metaphysical sense) only if she could have done otherwise but had no intention of doing so. Thus, if we want citizens to speak freely (in a political sense), we must grant them the putative right not to speak and remove most legal barriers obstructing its exercise. By the same token, all theories

21 For different sets of conditions see Alexander and Horton, op. cit., 1353–4 and Cohen, op. cit., 232–4.

22 This intuition is dramatically encapsulated in Salman Rushdie's words : "'Free Speech is a nonstarter', says one of my Islamic extremist opponents. No, sir, it is not. Free speech is the whole thing, the whole ball game. Free speech is life itself." *Imaginary Homelands : Essays and Criticism 1981–1991* (London : Granta Books, 1991), 439.

refusing to confirm the above right must be left out of the account.[23] However, it appears that this right should be overridden in certain cases as when one is summoned to testify to what came to one's attention in respect to a serious crime, but any detailed discussion concerning the limits of the above right should take place within the confines of a specific free speech theory.

Undoubtedly, the above conditions do not address crucial questions concerning the scope of expressive acts, the grounds for their protection, the role of the state in free speech regulation, the rights and the obligations of speakers and audiences and so on.

Moreover, they deserve a more detailed discussion that cannot be offered in this paper. However, it seems to me that even in their present form conditions 1–5 (and perhaps others consistent with them) prepare the ground for the formulation of theories that would elucidate our pre-theoretical intuitions concerning the overriding importance of free speech considerations, offering a deeper and broader understanding of their content.

23 These considerations bear upon the discussion of the legal right not to incriminate oneself. See Alan Donagan, "The Right Not to Incriminate Oneself," in *Human Rights*, Ellen Frankel Paul, Fred D. Miller, Jr. and Jeffrey Paul, eds. (Oxford : Blackwell, 1984),137–48.

Roger A. Shiner and Matthew Stephens, Edmonton, Alberta

Advertising, Free Expression, and Public Goods[1]

1. Introduction

The extension of constitutional protection under a freedom of expression clause to socalled commercial expression or speech is a relatively recent phenomenon. The U.S. case establishing the doctrine was decided less than two decades ago,[2] the analogous case in Canada less than one.[3] In Europe the idea is barely gaining a foothold.[4] All the same questions may validly be raised about the justification from the point of view of political morality for the doctrine.

Traditional liberal theory identifies three grounds for the constitutional protection of freedom of expression – the contribution of free expression to robust democracy, to a competitive market-place of ideas which enhances the search for truth, and to personal growth and self-realization. Each of these three grounds bases constitutional protection of freedom of expression on some value of such protection to the individual. At first sight, however, constitutional protection for freedom of commercial expression protects organizations, or corporations, and not the expression of individuals. Moreover, such protection guards their strictly commercial expression – that is, expression or speech whose motivation is to improve the position of the organization or corporation in the real economic market-place, not the so-called 'market-place of ideas'. The initial intuitive question may therefore be fairly raised: If the point of constitutional protection for freedom of expression is to protect the truth-oriented, or political, or self-realizing expression of individuals, why are courts protecting the commercial expression of organizations and corporations?

Many defences of the commercial expression doctrine take the form of arguing that, despite appearances, the doctrine really does directly protect or foster the expression of individuals in one or more of the three traditional ways. These arguments raise a host of different questions, and invite a host of different responses. In this paper we leave those issues aside.[5] In a recent article,[6] Joseph Raz develops an argument for the constitutional protection of freedom of expression from the point of view of freedom of expression as a public good.

1 The research on which this paper is based is supported by the Social Sciences and Humanities Research Council of Canada.

2 *Virginia State Board of Pharmacy et al v Virginia Citizens Consumer Council Inc et al* 425 US 748 (1976)

3 *Attorney-General of Quebec v Irwin Toy Ltd; Moreau et al, Interveners* [indexed as Irwin Toy Ltd v Quebec (Attorney-General)] (1989) 58 DLR (4th) 577. For a critique of the Court's current approach, see Shiner (1995), pp. 190–1.

4 *Barthold v Germany* 7 EHRR 383 (1985) (ECtHR); *Markt Intern and Beerman v Germany* 12 EHRR 161 (1989) (ECtHR); *Autronic AG v Switzerland* 12 EHRR 485 (1990) (ECtHR).

5 See Shiner (1994) and the literature considered in the article for a discussion of these different arguments and responses, including some scepticism about whether commercial expression can be defensibly protected on individualist grounds.

6 Raz (1994)

The standard economists' definition of public good[7] turns on the characteristics of such goods as 'non-rival' (the quantity consumed by one person does not limit consumption of the good by others) and 'inexcludable' (if the good is provided at all, it is available for all and none may feasibly be excluded from enjoying it). Raz suggests that, if autonomy is a fundamental value, then living in a society which preserves many options with respect to such things as careers and forms of sexual relationship fosters autonomy. But the good which consists of the availability of those options is not a matter of individual right; no other individual has a duty to provide some given individual with the fact of such options. The availability of options is a public good in the technical sense in that society (pp.52–3).

Since commercial expression or speech takes place in the essentially public realm of the economy, it is intuitively tempting to contemplate a 'public good' argument for freedom of commercial expression. We shall consider whether a 'public good' argument in the form proposed by Raz for freedom of expression generally can indeed be constructed for the defence of constitutional protection for specifically commercial expression or speech.

2. The public good argument for freedom of expression

Let us first summarize Raz's public good argument for freedom of expression. He gives two normative arguments for freedom of expression as a public good. The first (p.12 ff.) is this, the argument from toleration and encouragement of validation. Through freedom of expression as described, ways and styles of life are validated. A great service is thus rendered to people's well-being, in three ways. i) Validation of a way of life helps peoples' identification with their way of life and so their integration into society. ii) Such validation is important for making ways of life real options for people. iii) Public validation is an essential element in the process of cultural transmission, preservation and renewal.

The second argument is the argument from censorship as insult. The 'public good' aspect of freedom of expression creates an added disvalue of censorship. Being able to identify with one's society is normally vital for personal prosperity. A significant number of activities through which people prosper (or not) involve engagement with larger groups. Full membership in society is necessary for free participation in activities of such groups. Content-based censorship and criminalization are harms not only to the specific interest of the rightholder whose right to freedom of expression is denied. They are additionally every time harms to the common interest of all. Citizens as a whole have an interest in the society in which they live being harmonious and without alienation. Content-based censorship and criminalization 'constitute official condemnation of the way of life aspects of which are censored or criminalized' (p.15).

In short, the public good argument for the value of, and so a right to, freedom of expression is this. A society such that its members despite their diversity can readily identify with it makes a unique and special contribution to the well-being

7. Cf. e.g. Peston (1972), pp.12–14.

of those members. Thus conditions which contribute to such a society existing and continuing are public goods. In a pluralistic society, where lifestyles are many and a wide range of opportunities for identification are necessary, freedom of expression contributes uniquely and materially to the provision of such opportunities. Therefore it too is a public good.

3. Is advertising a public good?

We turn now to the applicability of this kind of argument to the case specifically of freedom of commercial expression. We are going to restrict the discussion to so-called 'lifestyle advertising'. These are advertisements whose content is primarily not informative but symbolic, portraying ways of living in acts of endorsement or advocacy that do not involve discursive promotion of a product. They rely for their effect and for their 'message' far more on visual or auditory imagery and emotional association than on language and explicit content. Some typical examples are:

i. Chanel no. 5. The images are of wealth, romance and beauty, of rich and elegant people in rich and elegant surroundings; the only speech is the call to 'Share the fantasy'.

ii. Marlboro cigarettes. A clean-cut and fit-looking cowboy is shown smoking a cigarette on a horse amid a gorgeous western landscape.

iii. Microsoft. Microsoft's new ad campaign, captured under the slogan 'Where do you want to go today?' The associated sights and sounds suggest that Microsoft's products are integral to a new movement of mass computer literacy, and that the accompanying empowerment of the world's youth is to some degree creditable to this company.

iv. Nike. Nike's 'Just Do It' ads.Simple, elegant, to the point. A superbly composed picture of a sprinter in the starting blocks is complimented with a simple, catchy phrase.

There are two main questions which have to be settled, for there to be a public good argument for freedom of commercial expression:

1. Is advertising technically a public good?
2. Does advertising promote the values which underlie Raz's public good argument for freedom of expression?

I will address these issues in turn, beginning with the first for the remainder of this section.

A person sees an ad in a magazine or on television. Apart from the fact that, barring library reading-rooms, screens in airport lounges and the like, the person has to purchase the magazine or the television set, their enjoyment of whatever good the reading of the ad as such brings them is not subject to voluntary control by anyone else. Once the ad is published or broadcast, it is equally available to any reader/viewer, and one viewer/reader's enjoyment of it does not interfere with similar enjoyment by another reader/viewer. The economist Fritz Machlup (1984, p.154) writes about what he calls the 'awareness effect' of some public goods:

> Advertising may make an otherwise unchanged product a more highly valued good merely because its users are made aware, perhaps falsely, of some special feature of the product. Sometimes the information or awareness effect may account for a large part of the value of the good. In the case of some goods, information, knowledge and awareness are not merely part but the whole of what makes them goods, that is, useful and valuable. And in certain cases the 'use fulness' may not in any but a very indirect sense affect the recipients of the information, the persons becoming aware of it; they may simply be glad to hear it or read it.

It is clear that any good essentially linked to the provision of an awareness effect will be a public good in the technical sense. One person's enjoyment of the effect will not interfere with the enjoyment of the effect by others, and the provision of the effect at all is the provision to anyone.

It is also clear that Raz's public good argument for freedom of expression relies on making the most of an 'awareness effect' of acts of portrayal of lifestyles. The three different beneficial results of performance of the three-fold validation function peoples' identification with their way of life and so their integration into society; the making of ways of life into real options for people; cultural transmission, preservation and renewal – all are consequences of the awareness effect of portrayals of lifestyles, rather than of any further effects of the appearance of such portrayals. Let us therefore turn to the second of the three questions above, and consider whether lifestyle advertising has an awareness effect of the kind which would license a public good argument like Raz's for freedom of commercial expression.

4. Lifestyle advertising and the public good

The striking point about the cases of lifestyle advertising (i)–(iv) above is the absence, or virtual absence, of any explicit informational element. In (i), no information is presented in the ad relevant to the product being offered for sale, and the only explicit speech or expression is the imperative 'Share the fantasy'. The fantasy we are enjoined to share is just that, a fantasy, not a lifestyle that many of us currently enjoy. In (ii), the information is presented that cowboys smoke Marlboro cigarettes, but beyond that the content is entirely imagistic. In (iii), there is a straightforward call to action: buy software, improve the world, but scant informational content. Nothing at all is said explicitly about the properties of Microsoft software. Rather, the associated sights and sounds suggest that not buying Microsoft's progressive software constitues resistance to a worthy humanitarian goal. In (iv), fitness is portrayed in a fashion that embodies many existing values: sexual attractiveness, stoic nobility, and so forth. Reference to the product (in this case, running shoes) is muted.

(i)–(iv) do communicate a message in some sense. Moreover, they do it via the portrayal of a lifestyle, and furthermore the portrayal of the lifestyle in a favourable light. Thus to a degree they seem to constitute the validation of a lifestyle. The Marlboro ad, for example, would seem to do for Marlboro smokers exactly what the TV serial East Enders does for people living in the East End of London, in terms of validating their lifestyle. It therefore may seem as though a Raz-style public good argument is available for the protection of lifestyle advertising as it is for portrayals of lifestyles in television sitcoms.

We shall now try to show that this impression is illusory. We have three different counter-arguments to present, which I shall call the Suppression of Interpretation Argument, the Unreality Argument, and the False Implication Argument. We shall consider these in turn.

The Suppression of Interpretation Argument turns on an account of the associational mechanism which underlies the value for advertisers of lifestyle advertising. As R. Moon has well shown (1991, p.108 ff.), 'a lifestyle advertisement is meant to affect consumer behaviour while discouraging conscious realization of this effect' (ibid., p.115). The Chanel ad invites the reader to assume the wealth and glamorous lifestyle depicted will be theirs if they use the perfume. The Microsoft ad invites the viewer to believe they are contributing to the empowerment of youth by purchasing Microsoft software. The Marlboro ad invites the reader to believe that masculine strength and handsomeness, and a healthy outdoor life will be theirs when they smoke Marlboro cigarettes. Put like that, of course, the claims are ridiculous. None of those things will happen. The ads are successful only insofar as interpretation of the real message conveyed is suppressed in favour of going unthinkingly with the emotional association. The Nike ad says it perfectly: Just do it. Thinking about the 'it' will interfere with the very possibility of realizing the (unreflectively) worthwhile goal.

This very feature of lifestyle advertising, however, means that it is singularly unsuited to perform the three validating functions of expression identified by Raz the familiarisation function, the reassurance function, and the validation function stricto sensu. The public good argument for freedom of expression presupposes an 'awareness effect', a level of up-take of the material being read which involves understanding and appreciation, responses which are at least in part in some sense cognitive. There must be appreciation of the lifestyle portrayed as a lifestyle of such-and-such a kind, before the public at large can be 'familiarised' with it, or before the stamp of public acceptability can be imposed. There must be conscious recognition of the lifestyle portrayed as being one's own lifestyle before reassurance can occur that one is not alone. Lifestyle advertising works precisely to suppress this kind of interpretative appreciation. Advertisements based on associating images function best when such associations are absorbed uncritically, so that viewers will begin, quite unconsciously, to associate the advertised product with some other good they currently endorse. Lifestyle advertising therefore cannot serve the validating function on which the public good argument for freedom of expression is based.

The Unreality Argument is best illustrated by the Chanel ad and the honesty of its entreaty, 'Share the fantasy'. The lifestyle portrayed is fantastic, not in the sense that as a matter of empirical fact many people fantasize about living such a lifestyle. It is fantastic, in the sense that it cannot be realized by anyone. Tricks of make-up, of lighting, of photographing, and so forth create a false world, an unreal world. Consider the number of times a television ad follows a display of the remarkable agility of an automobile with the swiftlyshown proviso, 'Professional drivers; do not attempt'. The ad shows nothing which is ever going to appear in the life-history of anyone who will actually purchase the product in question. And we know that. To the extent that lifestyle advertising portrays an unreal or unrealizable way of life, then it cannot serve to validate actual ways of life as the public good argument for freedom of expression demands.

The False Implication Argument is typified in the Microsoft advertisement. The implication of the advertisement is not only 'inform and empower yourself through our products'. It embodies also the idea that not buying Microsoft's progressive software constitutes resistance to a worthy humanitarian goal – something like: 'Don't deprive your kids of the software we all, as human beings, now have a right to'. The ad is effective because it links the product with highly favoured values like knowledge, democracy and pluralism (not to mention power, adventure, creativity, etc.). It is more effective than a simple informed appeal to current software consumers in that it creates a series of powerful, emotional appeals to draw in the sceptics, Luddites and romantics who have thus far resisted the call to information mobilization. It is an ad which appeals to the broadest of our community's values, in the hopes of extending its market to the entire community.

The ad portrays values held by most citizens, and the product itself has prima facie claim to status as a good as it seems to contribute to progress. However, it is not difficult to have obvious misgivings about these sorts of claims. Society has, after all, done pretty well without Microsoft to fulfil the sort social goods (such as progress, creativity, sharing of information) suggested in its ads. Electronic empowerment is, after some scrutiny, something we all can take or leave. In short, the appeal of the ad turns on the false implication that purchase of Microsoft products is essential to realize valued social goals. The lifestyle of computer literacy and software use is presented in a false light. The public good argument for freedom of expression requires at the very least that the lifestyle portrayed be truthfully portrayed. That does not happen in the case of lifestyle advertising.

5. Conclusion

In conclusion, We have argued that the way that lifestyle advertising communicates the messages that it contains is incompatible with the presuppositions of a Raz-style public good argument for freedom of expression as a value. That argument depends upon the expression which is paradigmatically protected by the argument being informative expression which fosters well-being through an awareness effect on the part of hearers, readers and viewers. By contrast, lifestyle advertising aims to suppress its awareness effect; it presents unreal lifestyles, and false implications of portrayals of lifestyles. It may rightly be pointed out that the argument has the form of generalizing to all advertising of a certain kind, lifestyle advertising, on the basis of certain select examples. This is true. We do rely on the reader's perception that the examples chosen are typical, and would sustain such an extrapolation. We are content to do so.

Bibliography

Machlup, Fritz. 1984. *The Economics of Information and Human Capital.* Princeton, NJ: Princeton University Press.

Moon, R. 1991. "Lifestyle Advertising and Classical Freedom of Expression Doctrine." *McGill Law Review* 36:76–129.

Peston, Maurice. 1972. *Public Goods and the Public Sector.* London: Macmillan.

Raz, Joseph. 1994 <1991>. "Free Expression and Personal Identification." In *Free Expression: Essays in Law and Philosophy*, ed. Wilfrid J. Waluchow, 1–29. Oxford: Clarendon Press.

Shiner, Roger A. 1994. "Freedom of Commercial Expression." In *Free Expression: Essays in Law and Philosophy,* ed. Wilfrid J. Waluchow, 91–134. Oxford: Clarendon Press.

–. 1995. "Advertising and Freedom of Expression." *University of Toronto Law Journal* 45:179–204.

Emilios A. Christodoulidis, Edinburgh

What Re-discovery of the *polis*?

Some Thoughts on Rights, Conflict and the Politics of Identity

Political and legal theorists have recently been proclaiming the return of the political.[1] Just as it seemed that the realities of western politics were about to 'liberate' us from politics,[2] there has been a proliferation of theories of 'strong democracy', 'adversary democracy', republicanism in its many guises, drawing from sources as diverse as Aristotle, Durkheim, and Hegel, that 're-discover' the ideal of an empowered citizen – the republican polites – and his habitus: the political community.

Within the ambit of the "re-discovery" of civil society and its community there is a crucial split. This split has too often been ignored. It divides the re-discoverers into, on the one hand, advocates of associational democracy, on the other, advocates of republicanism. What is crucial to the division is the distinction that each broad category employs as significant to the re-discovery they claim.

Associational democracy views the State as the significant other of civil society. Theorists of associational democracy focus on social groups and voluntary associations as embodiments of partisan solidarities, ideological and interest group affiliations, partisan beliefs and interests, competing, overlapping, even mutually undercutting. This commitment to a pluralist democratic culture unites theorists that warn against subsuming this heterogeneity under State political institutions and processes and writers from and on eastern Europe whose obvious target is still the nightmare of collective harmony under the watchful State. What is significant to this position is that it does not view dissonance and fragmentation as undermining civil society's self-discovery and therefore *assigns no integrative function to State-sanctioned processes*; in fact the latter would prove erosive to that heterogeneity that is constitutive of civil society.[3] In this view associations are conceived of primarily as countervailing forces to the State.

The civil society that *republicans* have in mind is one that conceives of *the State and civil society on a continuum*. Michael Walzer writes characteristically: "Only a democratic state can create a democratic civil society; only a democratic civil society can sustain a democratic state."[4] Far from being the "significant other" of civil society, the state is its pre-supposition in this formulation. Walzer's argument here is reminiscent of that powerful current in communitarian theory that understands deep allegiance to the State and commitment to one's community as interchangeable. The "atomism" of liberalism and pluralism replace the state as civil society's significant other. The individualist underpinning of these theories, claim the republicans, with the consequent emphasis on issue-

1 Mouffe, *The Return of the Political*. London: Verso, 1993
2 Wolfe, *Whose Keeper?*. Berkeley: U California Press, 1989, 1
3 In this respect see Sullivan, 'Rainbow Republicanism', in 97, *Yale L J*, 1988, 1539
4 Walzer, 'The Ideal of Civil Society', in *Dissent*, 1991, 302

based memberships and pre-political interests, misunderstands the value of the integrative function of political participation itself.

What is perhaps the single most surprising feature this strand shares is that the re-discovery of civil society is accompanied not by a rejection of the State but by its re-conception as benign guarantor of the democratic process. No resonances here of the "bourgeois state" to "be seized", "occupied" or to "wither away"; as guarantor of civil society the state is not defined in opposition to civil society. Here the empowerment of civil society gains its leverage from State law and indirectly thus recognises state law as guarantor and vessel of the political discursive process.

The rhetoric of lost community worries me when it comes accompanied by the State and its law. Because all too often the rhetoric of lost community projects an abstract community as citizenry and entrusts the State sometimes with its protection, in republicanism with its realisation. In its legal abstraction republican community both depends on and realises an overcoming of the divide between citizen and state. As forum of rational discourse, as reason, the law purportedly allows a community to work out its normative commitments for itself and in the process of that dialogue realise itself as a community of people who come together in *their* reasoning of *their* practices. Notice how this common commitment to rational discourse as substantiating community within the ambit of the legal forum unites theorists like Dworkin who calls citizens to participate in legal argument and elevates the community's constitutive commitment to argument from the battleground of politics to the forum of principle that is law; Habermas with his advocacy as rights and democracy as 'co-original' and his treatment of legal discourse as an instance of general practical discourse; and the American civic republicans with their commitment to 'jurisgenerative' politics, a politics that draws its inspiration and gains its leverage from law. In the sway of the re-awakening of civil society law is recruited to effectuate the dream of social solidarity and community.

Against associational democracy the republican legal theory argues that what needs to be resisted is the *pluralist* deeply held assumption that politics is a bargaining process where interests battle for recognition and superiority. According to the republicans, the pluralists view *the public sphere as a political market* that functions on the lines of the economic market.[5] Individual preferences and interests seek a mechanism to best accommodate their competition. Groups are nothing more than organisational forms through which individuals pursue their individual interests more effectively. What wins the competition is conceived as approximating public interest, and the market logic underpinning the political process guarantees democracy's self-correcting capacity. What the republicans most oppose is this conception of the political actor projected from within the logic of the homo economicus that pulls away the ground from any possibility of conceiving an objective public interest in politics that transcends individual and group interests.[6]

5 The market-place of ideas formula has dominated Constitutional theory and practice and motivates much 1st Amendment literature. Typically associated with O.W. Holmes, the market place of ideas is conceived as the medium of competition of ideas and the mechanism of striking a balance.

6 This is a pluralism most associated with Bentley, Buchanan, Tullock etc.

So what is wrong with political pluralism? Nancy Rosenblum summarises it: "Individuals bring interests ready-formed to groups, which simply amplify them; interests are partial and contingent and thus without significance to moral identity; liberal pluralism is based on scepticism about our ability to communicate needs and values in a fashion that moves others towards consensus."[7] The republicans are very sceptical of the pluralist commitment to the sovereignty of associations and their superiority over state sovereignty, because this would erode the fundamentally integrative role of the democratic deliberative process and the production of authoritative public norms.

Republican legal theory steps in to remedy the pluralist misconception by stressing the importance of *participation* in the public sphere. By joining the dialogic-deliberative practice citizens engage in politics. During the communicative exchange principles to guide public life are hammered out. Arendt's own definition of politics sounds very apposite here: "The realm of politics," she says, "is the organisation of the people as it arises out of acting and speaking together, and its true space lies between people living together for this purpose." [8] As Luhmann would say, Arendt (and the republicans) conceive society as a politically constituted system.[9] The most important element here is that membership in the political community is not seen, as the pluralists would have it, as means to an end, the pursuit of partisan choice, but instead it is in the very process of participation as its own end that perspectives engage with one another and conceptions of a good that is common are hammered out. Whereas in the pluralist world-view, politics is about promoting diverse goods and thus relies on bargaining within a framework of rules neutral to the bargaining parties, the republican picture of politics is one of the pursuit of the *common good.* In their account, the heterogeneity of interest associated with pluralism gives way to the heterogeneity of perspective.[10] Bargaining gives way to arguing, and such participation in the public realm in turn feeds back to, as it were, "interpellate" the individual as political actor in a synthesis wherein lingers the communitarian argument about embeddedness in the community.[11]

Having established their opposition to the theory of political pluralism in the broader framework, the republicans then direct the debate to *law.* The republicans oppose an understanding of constitutional provisions as simply placing limits on political bargaining; the republican rebuttal of pluralism is a rebuttal of a misconception that understands law as external to politics and community. Instead politics is the site where communities strive for self-determination and the constitution, claim the republicans, hosts the political process, it hosts the deliberative practice of a community, of a dialogue of all about all. As Macedo

7 Rosenblum, 'Democratic Character and Community', in 1, *The Journal of Political Philosophy*, 1994

8 Arendt, *The Human Condition*, Chicago: Chicago University Press, 1968, p198

9 See Luhmann, *Ecological Communication*. Cambridge: Polity Press, 1986, pp84ff

10 This shift allows the republicans to claim "*civic virtue*" for their politics, a tenet so central as to be characterised by both Michelman and Sunstein as the "animating principle" of civic republicanism.

11 Not only regarding the 'social construction of the self', but also in the argument that although citizenship is a universal category the dialogue into which it facilitates entry is specific to the historical community .

summarises it: "critical reflection is a public commitment, a commitment, most fundamentally, to a way of deliberating publicly about what our political arrangements should be. Constitutional institutions are forums that structure and sustain the ongoing debate."[12] The entry into the public sphere through citizenship, the legally backed capacity to partake in the political dialogue, mediates the assumption of social identity. Citizenship holds up the mirror for each participant to make sense of his/her identity in community, and republican politics is about the intrinsic value of citizenship because "the self is constituted by, or comes to itself through, such engagement." [13]

This is a re-statement of popular sovereignty in no uncertain terms. Having argued the meaning and significance of their three key notions – *participation*, *common good* and *civic virtue* – republican legal theorists can now celebrate having established a connection between the embedded *self*, where the form of that embededness is participation in a dialogue, that at once both constitutes the realm of *politics* and substantiates *community*, and finally and most significantly *law* as enabling the dialogue in the constitutional forum. By putting forward these inter-relationships, republican legal theory invites us to reconceive communal dialogue as legal dialogue, and all that is political as legal.

I want to argue that the republicans can only claim this because they rely on an inadequate theory of conflict; were they to take conflict seriously, their endeavour to contain and empower the political from within the law would fail even aspirationally. And I will focus this discussion on possibly the most crucial area of the republican argument concerning the ideal of community by looking at the question of *collective identity in its connection to conflict*. The hallmark of the republican thesis is the empowerment of community. I want to argue that the republican attempt to account for (let alone empower) community through law fails because the reliance on law as lever of the endeavour imposes reductions on the possibilities of conceiving of meaningful 'we'-descriptions; why? Because it severs the constitutive connection of identity and conflict.

The relationship between conflict and society has been sociologically elaborated in two basic ways: one orientation sees conflict as constitutive of society, the other sees the relationship as an equilibrium of interrelated functions. Without acknowledging the debt, republican theory draws from the second orientation but discusses it in a way that obscures many of the insights of both. Most importantly it obscures the rather obvious point that, more often than not, entry into public space is mediated through conflict. Because conflict furnishes the kinds of commitments that are strong enough to sustain an entry and provide a sense of public persona. And the fact that such entry is effected conflictually, in solidarity to one group, in opposition to another, allows conflict theory to claim that public space is structured around a number of (often mutually exclusive and denying) cleavages, so that society *is* its conflictual self-reproduction. Typically here Marxist theory claims class cleavage and conflict as constitutive of society but the battlelines can be extended to include race, ethnicity, gender, etc. The proliferation of the literature on New Social Movements marks an awareness of

12 Macedo, *Liberal Virtues*. Oxford: Clarendon, 1990, 12
13 Michelman, "Law's Republic", in 97, *Yale L J*, 1988, 1493, 1503

precisely this proliferation of battlelines. Social Movements struggle primarily to re-assert collective identity, whether that takes the form of "defensive" withdrawal or that of the creation of societal counter-models. The insistence on collective identity is not accidental. The "political" is related to a certain "quality of association." In that sense, a movement represents a very distinct moment of intersubjectivity, marked out by a distinct level of integration, sociality and imagination in the pursuit of politics. It is what the French, in more inspired days, called "la verité du movement"; what Sartre refers to when he defines the group by its undertaking and by the constant movement of exclusion and integration which tends to turn it into "pure praxis";[14] and it is that undertaking that Willener claimed was re-situated as both form and content of politics in the events of May.[15] [16]

In all the above conflict sets a context within which political identity becomes meaningful: conflict makes who we are and what we are pursuing relative to an opponent that is attempting to hinder the realisation of our project and appropriate its stake. Conflict allows us to conceive all three, identity, opponent and stake, as setting the context against which politics is played out.[17] The three components do not in themselves suffice to describe a social movement if they are not conceived of *as interdependent*. The interdependence must be total. Only together do the components constitute the field of reference against which context each of them in turn draws for meaning. If we conceive of the relation between actor and stake without the opponent then what we are describing is not the stakes of a struggle, a conflict, but a society as a single actor striving for an objective that can be described e.g. as progress or modernization.[18] The linkage between Opponent and Stake on the other hand is what reveals the aspect of ideological domination in society, in the sense that the actor is excluded from the definition and the pursuit of the stakes which become determinable by the opponent, and it becomes impossible to resist the appropriation and compulsion of meanings. At a more fundamental level, the identity of the actor-in-community only becomes that in contestation, in conflict with an opponent over the stake of the struggle, always presupposing that interdependence.

The crux of the matter is that the "total interdependence" (the integration of the three components in the three dimensions) is what forms the political context, within which collective identities, movements and their struggles make sense. Withdrawing from this context, the social relation within which they are situated, leaves the struggles politically undetermined. And *this is precisely what the law*

14 Sartre, *The Critique of Dialectical Reason*. London, 1976, pp256ff

15 Willener, *The Image Action of Society*. London: Tavistock, 1970, passim and 281–98. Willener argues that at the period of upheaval the emergent (instituant) had only the most tenuous links with the established (institué).

16 Of the two elements that Melucci identifies as characterising the ideology of the movement, the first is "the negation of the gap between expectations and reality. The birth of a movement is marked by "moments of madness" when all things seem possible ... Ideology thus overcomes the inadequacy of action." (Melucci : 'Challenging Codes', in 31, *Thesis 11*, 1992, 133) For the relationship with Utopia cf the work of Francesco Alberoni.

17 My discussion here draws on the work of Alain Touraine.

18 The point has been elaborated by Melucci in 'Réponse à Alain Touraine', in Touraine A (ed) *Mouvements sociaux d'aujourd'hui*, Paris: Editions ouvrières, 1982

does: within the categories of legal discourse (i) the actors are not defined in their class (or other) conflictual relationship, (ii) their field of struggle and the stake is defined independently of them. *By abstracting from that interdependence*, the interdependence that stems from the situation of the parameters in conflict, *law severs the political basis of collective action.*[19]

This is what I am arguing then: that legal discourse submits the political self-understanding that groups have of their identity to such abstraction that it annihilates it. The question we are seeking to answer is how actors conceive of themselves, of their identity. It is trivially true that a pre-condition for collective action is the possibility of identifying with the other members of the group, the self-reflexive capacity that allows actors to say 'we'. That in turn means that the group or movement must constitute a field of reference wherein identity is formed. In conflict it is conceived as a tight interdependence of the parameters of identity, opposition and stake; within it the common identity is articulated through identification with the stakes of the conflict. Collective identity is conceived as emergent property of collective action. There are neither fixed identities nor determined ascribed memberships prior to their generation in 'totalised' conflict. But in contrast to this focused commonality, the law's projection of the universal category legal subject/citizen screens off the forcefield where identity is shaped, by defining out the significant Other: the opponent. The category provides no purchase into partiality[20] and opposition, where partiality is what underpins political identity. By disarticulating this frame of reference, severing the connection with conflict, the legal discourse renders the political opaque to itself and political praxis meaningless.

19 Alberto Melucci, a student of Touraine's, has extended and enriched this analysis by focusing it on the cultural and symbolic reproduction of collective action. "The very idea of a social conflict," he stresses, "implies the opposition of two actors struggling for the same resources, symbolic or material. The adversaries share the same field but they interpret it in opposite ways... They identify themselves with the whole field while denying any role to the opponent." The point here is the one that Touraine suggested before: that individuals within the movement "construct" their action in ways that are incompatible to outsiders' understandings and in the process appropriate the relational field of conflict (they "reify" it according to Melucci). To append meta-political categories to such understandings of action, conflict and identity, and to fix the conflict through categories alien to the parties involved, cancels out the understanding that the movement has of its identity and action. But more importantly, Melucci discusses the New Social Movements in a way that raises the central question of whether there are forms of conflict that are being directed against the logic of complex systems. He designates not only solidarity and engagement in conflict as definitional elements of a social movement, but designates as a necessary feature that "a social movement breaks the limits of compatibility of a system." The system Melucci has in mind is the one the republicans have in mind too: the legally constituted political system of participation. What defines a movement is a conception of its opposition to a system. The "expressive politics" in which it engages as a continuous source of identity consolidation, is an exercise in defying the dominant codes of participation, the institutional forms of politics. The movement draws for self-understanding from its very resistance to the containment of its identity in law.

20 As Sullivan writes in her defence of partiality, "[i]ntermediate organizations not only facilitate individual self-definition and expression but also keep the state from replicating itself by nurturing deviance, diversity and dissent. These functions depend on subgroups' private status – on their detachment and distance from the all-inclusive State." (Sullivan, op.cit., 1988, 1721)

The ego/enemy opposition ceases to be in law the decisive factor and the key to deciphering conflict. Law introduces an exclusive focus on the issues that divide the parts, the parts themselves retreating to mere neutral "points of allocation" of claims that may be operationalised in law concerning the issues at hand. This shift in law severs the connection with conflict; it withdraws from conflict conflict's constitutive importance for political identity because it disassociates a community from its constitutive involvement in conflict, i.e. the drawing from conflict of its (the community's) standing, of its form and the strength of its binding. One's entry into the public space of "citizenship" is not effected conflictually, in solidarity to one group, in enmity to another, over a stake that can accommodate such total confrontations. I would warn here both against the *absence* of a political frontier altogether as well as against *establishing it as a legal one*: when republican legal theory *does* talk of conflict it is always-already a conflict *a priori* bridge*able,* therefore too weak to 'carry' the kinds of commitments that might sustain partisan collective identities. The instrumental role that law reserves for identity renders social-conflictual identity irrelevant. There is a crucial area of politics that is defined away in this "irrelevancy": we may designate it as the *politics of identity.*

In a situation of conflict questions of the definition of identity are absorbed into conflict itself. Conflict dictates what significant features underpin the self-understanding of the common "we" and more generally, under what capacity or in the name of what cause the political actor enters the public sphere. The important correlate is what one attributes as identity to Alter. It *does* matter whether, in a strike say, the opponent is designated as an employer, with whom we have entered a contractual relationship, or the owner of the means of production who appropriates our surplus production; whether the opponent is designated as a formally equal party to each employment agreement in which case the strikers are ganging up on him, or a member of a class to whom the workforce relates in class-conflictual terms. The freedom to designate these identities, to contest them, to be reflexive about them, is withdrawn in law where identities are either rigidly fixed (in essence invisible as mere operators of rights) or at least restricted to a limited pool of alternatives (where law has to some extent "re-materialised"). The assumption of the legal persona as presupposition of legal conflict withdraws the contestation of the identity of the enemy from the conflict itself; in law identity becomes a semantic artifact, a neutral container. The two aspects of conflict that are screened off in law are relevant (i) to the freedom to choose the description under which one enters the conflict – in the name of what ego wages the struggle, and (ii) the correlate freedom to deny the identity of Alter, which includes the freedom to choose how to identify Alter. These are the two aspects of the politics of identity that do not resonate in law. And the republicans, by relying on law to voice politics, lose sight of how this important aspect of the political is legally annihilated.

There are numerous examples where the political is played out on the terrain of identity. Marxism provides the obvious example and both the rise and defeat of a type of insurrectionary politics in the 60s is testimony of the importance of the politics of identity. Insurrection by the radical groups involved in the university uprisings was conceived as a means only, to serve as catalyst for the emergence of class consciousness and working-class solidarity. Such strategic use of conflict turned on the assumption that the State would not fail to rise to meet this challenge and in the process reveal its real nature as an instrument of class oppression; that would in turn trigger processes that would foster class-consciousness.[21] Importantly for the present discussion, it was through law that this politics was defeated. It was defeated because in law the logic of this politics was screened off. Movements as a whole have no legal personality, no point of entry into the legal world. Entry can only be effected by disintegrating and defusing that which is constitutive of the movement – its collective nature – and the basis of its claim to legitimacy – the collective claim to which individual actions are only instrumental. The law screens off all else and focuses directly on the latter by initiating selective prosecutions on individualistic grounds (how could *mens rea* apply to the group?). The legal system collapses the understanding behind collective action. It does not give voice to that which is essential to the politics of collectivities: the corporateness of the group that underlies its politics. It is no surprise then that an invitation to learn from the "repeated lesson of many struggles" comes from Marxists. Picciotto, for example, writes:

> "Substantive gains are achieved through collective struggles building up class solidarity: the channeling of such struggles into the form of claims of bourgeois legal right breaks up that movement towards solidarity, through the operations of legal procedures which recognize only the individual subject ... Of course we have learned and must go on struggling to overcome this: in criminal prosecutions through collective defence strategies and solidarity groups, [etc] ... But these merely enable us to probe the limits of bourgeois law as a social form. To transcend those limits ... involves a determination to struggle within but also through and beyond those legal forms, or around and in spite of them."[22]

Law offers a "we" beyond politically constituted differences. Law "stills" identity in a way that allows political conflict to be played out around "material" stakes neither affecting nor affected by the politics of identity. It is not that the law "intends" this in any way, only that it cannot evade assumptions that are in-built in the system's most fundamental premises. Outwith (and in spite of) this "innocent" observation politics continues, and the party that takes the conflict to law may be seen by the opponent as performing a discursive manoeuver aiming to obscure the identities of the parties, as performing, that is, an ideological/mystifying move. Taking to law is not an innocent move in that understanding of conflict. By assuming and propagating the naturalness and innocence of law's perception of collective identity, republican legal theory is conspiring to the silencing of politics in a way that transposes the ideological/mystifying moment from the level of practice to the level of theory.

21 See Collins, *Marxism and Law*. Oxford: Clarendon, 1982, pp125ff

22 Picciotto, 'The Theory of the State, Class Struggle and the Rule of Law', in Fine (ed): *Capitalism and the Rule of Law*. London: Hutchinson, pp171–2

William L. McBride, Lafayette

The Rights of 'Aliens' and of Other Others

The English word "alien", which is used to designate all non-citizens of the United States as well as of other countries in which this language predominates – a British citizen is an alien in the United States, and a United States citizen is an alien in the United Kingdom, for example – is of course etymologically rooted in the Latin "alienus" and "aliena", meaning "other". The same English word has come to be used, with great frequency in this age of science fiction, to designate imagined life-forms, particularly intelligent life-forms (usually represented, faute d'imagination, as humanoid), from planets other than Earth or galaxies other than the Milky Way. Meanwhile, the word in the earlier sense of non-citizen has been very prominent in recent discussions of new legal initiatives in the United States, most notably with respect to a referendum that was approved by a majority of voting citizens in the State of California in early November 1994; this referendum would have the effect of excluding from state-provided educational services and most state-supported medical care all aliens who lack the legal right to be within the borders of the United States, and would even compel medical and educational personnel to report to appropriate authorities the names of those within their jurisdiction whom they suspect of seeking such services without that legal right.

For the sake of accuracy, although nothing further in this philosophical paper will depend on the details of this referendum and its attempted implementation, it should be noted that most of it is not being implemented, as of January 1995, and that it is expected that most of it will not be implemented soon if any time in the foreseeable future, because the courts have concurred tentatively with immediate challenges that were made to its Constitutionality under the terms of the United States Constitution. But what is of great interest for a number of issues in the philosophy of law and of politics with which I shall be concerned here is the following two features of the discussion surrounding this referendum and the issue of the presence of large numbers of so-called "illegal aliens" that led to its having been proposed: first, during the campaign leading to the vote on it a number of proponents, including the Governor of the State of California himself, admitted that aspects of it were probably unConstitutional but said that that did not significantly inhibit their advocacy; and second, some subsequent discussion, since the vote, in Washington and throughout the country has pointed to the possibility of prohibiting the provision of some federally-supported services even to legally resident non-citizens, or "resident aliens".

I am of course well aware that initiatives of a broadly similar sort have been undertaken or at least proposed in a number of other countries besides the United States in recent years: Germany, Switzerland, and France are among the countries about which this can be said. A comparison between the California referendum and one or more of the situations in Western European countries would be very valuable, both from a legal and from a philosophical point of view, but it would be far beyond the purview of a brief paper such as this one. Indeed,

I regret the fact that my using an American legal development and focusing on the peculiarly English-language word "alien" as my point of departure in this paper may well appear to reinforce the obvious hegemony of American intellectual and cultural concerns and especially of the English language that is all too evident in the preliminary organization of this conference. I hope, however, that some of the conclusions towards which I shall be drawn will at least partially mitigate the appearance of such reinforcement, which I consider highly regrettable.

My brief reflections on the phenomena and events I have just summarized will be developed in the following sequence: (1) The rule of law, or Constitutionalism; (2) the relation between rights and citizenship; (3) dialectics of Otherness and alienation; (4) groping towards possible new world orders or disorders. Because of space limitations, my remarks will appear more didactic and less discursive than I would prefer them to be.

(1) *The rule of law, or Constitutionalism.* It is to be expected that at a congress such as this, at which the philosophy of law is heavily emphasized, the notion of the *Rechtsstaat* would be highly valued and valorized. It has in recent years been revived by, among others, Jürgen Habermas, in an effort to forfend some of the centrifugal and xenophobic implications of rising nationalist extremisms. It is of great significance and, to advocates of the rule of law, concern to note the extent to which many individuals in the contemporary United States, as elsewhere, who identify themselves as "conservatives" now frequently disassociate themselves from such advocacy. Not only have attitudes like that of the Governor of California which I mentioned, namely, that it is perfectly all right to support legislation that may at least in part be unConstitutional in order to serve some political purpose of "sending a message" to one's opponents, become commonplace (the same thing has been said recently in the American Congress when rules to require a 60% instead of a bare majority vote for legislation to increase taxes, a possibility nowhere envisaged in the U.S. Constitution, have been proposed by the new leadership); in addition, there have been some quite positive reactions to suggestions that individual States within the United States might consider refusing to implement federal laws – for example, some environmental regulations – that they consider burdensome or simply not to the liking of the majority of their own citizens.

Would a divided American Federal Government be likely to imitate the Russian government in Chechnya if the State of South Carolina, for example, refused to enforce federal guidelines concerning, let us say, welfare funding? This is most unlikely. This is not 1861, when the United States Civil War broke out upon the decision of South Carolina and other Southern states to secede from the Union after their claims of "States' Rights", including the alleged rights of individual states to nullify federal laws within their own territories, were rejected by the Federal Government. Already under the Reagan Administration more than a decade ago, the enforcement of many civil rights laws and guidelines was deliberately not carried out on the grounds that, while these laws were formally valid and could not, for practical reasons having to do with the division of party dominance between the Legislative and the Executive branches of the government, be rescinded, they were not favored by the Executive Branch: "they are not our laws." Similar language is frequently heard from opponents of the current U.S. President: "he is not my President." A famously "conservative" United States Senator, now Chairperson of the Foreign Affairs Committee of the Senate, actually warned against a visit by the President to the Senator's own State of North Carolina, on the ground that his life would be in jeopardy because he was so much disliked; very similar statements by less powerful individuals have in the past been interpreted as death threats. In short – and I regret having to devote so much time and space to summarizing some of the salient facts about contemporary American political life, but I have felt it necessary to do so in order to make my point – the notion of the Rule of Law is not being taken seriously by many in my country who consider themselves "conservatives". I will not enter here into the question as to whether this is an appropriate label for them.

If such a spirit of contempt for the rule of law is widespread within the United States, among government officials to say nothing of ordinary citizens, towards domestic laws, what is one to expect of their attitudes towards international law? The U.S. government's notorious refusal to accept the World Court's judgment concerning its mining of Nicaraguan harbors manifested a willingness to flout and undermine the decisions of international organizations whenever they contravene United States leaders' perceptions of their national self-interest, at least in any matters considered important. As the spokesmen for the Athenians said, in response to the appeals to virtue and the gods by the powerless Melians, whom they were soon to eradicate from the earth during the Peloponnesian War: "Of the gods we believe, and of men we know, that by a necessary law of nature they rule wherever they can." I do not endorse this position, but many of my fellow citizens and especially of our current ruling circles obviously do.

But of course such flouting of the rule of law considered as a universal ideal is carried out highly selectively; in instances in which it seems favorable to a certain political ideal, legality or "law and order" are very strongly favored indeed. In the case of the California referendum to which I have referred, supporters who concede that its implementation would do great harm to innocent children, reinforce racial bigotry, cause much needless suffering from lack of medical care, and in short do enormous injustice to individuals who have, often enough, been exploited by wealthy employers taking advantage of their lack of legal status in order to pay them very low wages earned under poor working conditions, eventually fall back on a single argument to justify such a punitive set of measures: "But, after all, they are here *illegally;* they have broken the law."

It is such blatant selectivity and inconsistency as this that has led to the enormous suspicion with which the ideal of the "rule of law" has been regarded by various elements of the political Left, including in particular proponents of Critical Legal Studies within the contemporary American intellectual spectrum, as well as of the Right. It would be facile to conclude simply that both ends of the spectrum are unreliable, and that the Aristotelian ideal of the rule of law, as a Golden Mean, has thereby been vindicated. But to leave it at this would be to overlook the most fundamental question about the rule of law considered as an idea, namely, "The rule of which law?" I propose to approach this question and some implications of a clear answer to it by means of a discussion of *i diritti*, rights, that may at one and the same time support or oppose *il diritto*, the law, in any particular set of circumstances.

(2) *The relation between rights and citizenship.* In the early days of the historic Western emphasis on rights, signs of confusion were already evident in the title of what is arguably the most important document of the time, the *Déclaration des droits de l' homme et du citoyen.* Exactly what is supposed to be the force of the connective, the "et"? Is it supposed to be the case that two quite distinct sets of rights exist simultaneously, or rather that the rights of man and of the citizen are coimplicative in some way? Marx, attempting to sort out these two sets of rights in *On the Jewish Question* with a view above all to demonstrating the anti-communitarian individualism of the so-called "rights of man" and hence criticizing, as the Marxian tradition has continued frequently to do since Marx's time, rights-talk as such, only compounds confusion about the relation between the two sets of rights – or so it seems to me. Even the *Universal Declaration of Human Rights,* for all its brave gestures towards universality, was written in such a way as to give full recognition to the separate nation-states which had to endorse it in order for it to secure some validity, and to which, for the most part, the world must still look for the enforcement of these rights. But is it not obvious that, in this situation, the two sets of rights will frequently be inconsistent with one another?

A salient example of an implicit inconsistency which is, in fact, practically explicit – that is, inconsistent in practice – is the Universal Declaration's assertion (Article 13) that a person should be free to leave any country, including his or her own, and to return to it. But this presupposes, as a practical matter, that there must be at least one other country to which every citizen of every country is free to move – and not just for a period of a few months, let us say. This presupposition clearly runs counter to existing reality, in which the citizens of many countries, particularly of the vast majority that are poor, are not at all welcome to stay in most other countries, and indeed are often not even welcome to visit them. (It should be observed, in passing, that decisions about whom to welcome and whom to bar as visitors are often made in a highly idiosyncratic and arbitrary fashion by individual Consular officials and that, at least in the case of the United States, this lack of uniformity is sanctioned by the law itself. In this respect as well, then, an important component of the Rule of Law ideal is simply not respected. But to explicate and reflect on this point would take us too far afield.)

It is precisely this inconsistency, of course, that lies behind the events in California to which I have alluded. The American law, valid in California as elsewhere in the country, bars permanent residence to large numbers of individuals who, for various reasons but in particular in order to escape conditions of poverty and joblessness in their countries of origin, would like to enter the United States and (usually) to try to find employment there. Large numbers of these persons have managed to escape enforcement of this law and thus to exercise their right to leave their own country. They then, often enough, proceed to attempt further to exercise their supposedly universal rights (as enumerated in the Universal Declaration) to decent health care, adequate education, and so on, within the United States. A majority of California voters, goaded by conditions of relative economic scarcity there by contrast with previous conditions, presumably made the judgment, as reflected in the previously-mentioned referendum that they should indeed be denied these rights. This judgment is often defended on the ground that citizens' rights take precedence over "abstract" human rights and above all, as I have already noted, that "the law" is superior to claims about "rights". This can be done in the English language without even opening up the possibility of experiencing a twinge of bad conscience, such as *might* occur to a speaker of Continental European languages in which the word for a "right" and for "law" in general is the same – *diritto, droit, Recht,* and so on. But many, including no doubt the majority of the citizens of the richer Continental European countries, would reply that there is no call for feelings of bad conscience about this – that the world is organized according to nation-states, which confer whatever real rights may be said to exist, and their respective citizenships, and that this is as it should be. In order better to understand some of the implications and consequences of this commonplace assumption, we must turn now to a consideration of Otherness in general, and of the treatment of "aliens" in particular.

(3) *Dialectics of Otherness and alienation.* There have been approaches of the most diverse sorts to the problem of the Other in twentieth-century philosophy, especially in France; a paper by Yvanka Raynova, published in the *Bulletin de l'Association Américaine de Philosophie de Langue Française* and recently presented at my university, which has in part inspired the present paper, well summarizes this diversity. It is also important not to dismiss the voluminous literature, both in philosophical psychology and in the vast spectrum of critical theory, that has appeared on the subject of "alienation" during the same, now waning, century. It is only in light of these concerns, it seems to me, that the question of the rights of "aliens" can properly be understood. On the one hand, every fellow human being is an Other to me, and there is a profound sense in which oneself is also an Other, as the title of Paul Ricoeur's book, *Soi-même comme un autre,* implies. Otherness is therefore ingredient in the human condition, not per se an evil. On the other hand, alienation in the sense of Hegel's and Marx's *Entfremdung*, though not necessarily in the sense of *Entaüsserung*, betokens a parlous state of affairs, one that is widespread in our societies and that would be eliminated in a more ideal world. The weight of connotation of the English noun, "alien", meaning above all "non-citizen", lies closer to this meaning of "alienation" than to the more neutral one of "Otherness".

It is ironic, though not a novelty from an historic standpoint, to find hostility towards "aliens" being displayed in the contemporary United States. The irony stems, of course, from the fact that the vast majority of United States citizens are descendants of persons who arrived from completely other continents than North America, at a time when the separation or otherness of continents from one another was much greater than it is today. Yet antagonism, often of a violent sort, towards those who were not part of the politically dominant group(s) at various times in American history – towards the Native Americans, massacred systematically and in large numbers; towards Africans, most of them first brought to that continent as slaves, and towards their descendants; towards Irish a century ago; towards women as soon as significant numbers of them began to claim political rights for themselves; and towards many other classes of Others – has been a leitmotif of that history. Of course the United States is not unique in this respect. But the dialectical interplay of opposition and desired reconciliation between expressed ideals and real practice has perhaps been more exaggerated, more extreme, in American experience than in the experiences of other nation-states.

The role of U.S. law, especially of Constitutional law, has been Janus-faced in this regard. A certain historical tone was set in that provision of the original United States Constitution (Article I, Section 3) which counted each Black slave as three-fifths of a person for purposes of determining the populations of those States in which they lived – thus allowing those states, largely in the South, to claim more inhabitants for purposes of obtaining greater influence in the so-called "representative" institutions of government while at the same time not having to acknowledge that their slaves were full human beings. Thus the extreme alienation of enslavement was given the appearance of scientific, or more aptly pseudo-scientific, precision by this fundamental law. Unfortunately, slaves in fact enjoyed far less than three-fifths of the rights of U.S. citizens; as the Supreme Court majority opined less than a century and a half ago in *Dred Scott* v. *Sanford*, "Negroes...had no rights or privileges but such as those who held the power and the Government might choose to grant them." At other times the courts, especially this Supreme Court which is charged with interpreting the law and Constitutionality, have contributed to mitigating some of the most alienating treatments of Others within American society – for example by declaring "suspect", and thus helping to end, some practices of racial discrimination in property sales, education of children, access to public facilities, etc. However, as far as those legally defined as "aliens" are concerned, the American courts have usually interpreted very narrowly indeed the rights that they may be accorded, and have typically deferred to the stated policies of the Legislative and especially the Executive Branches of the Federal Government, particularly whenever the latter have invoked "national security" interests against rights claims on behalf of such individuals. Recent dismissals of such claims for Haitian citizens seized, while fleeing in boats from their homeland, by American authorities on the high seas are an excellent example of judicial deferral to executive policy. Appeals to universal human rights on behalf of these Others bear exceedingly little weight in the American legal process. Moreover, there exists a legal presumption, embodied in U.S. immigration law, that aliens seeking to enter the United States for limited periods of time are to be considered as being in bad faith with regard to their announced intentions unless they can demonstrate otherwise. In other words, a condition of alienation lies at the basis of the relationship between the U.S. legal system and non-citizen Others; for to presume bad faith is almost a definition of "alienation".

Is an alternative to this state of affairs conceivable?

(4) *Groping towards possible new world orders or disorders.* What might be the legal and political consequences of universally enforcing the declared right of any human being to leave the country in which he or she is living, with its implicit correlative right of moving to some other country? "Total disorder," many would say. As I write the final part of this paper, the American President is said to be planning a very large increase in expenditures, at a time when the fiscal deficit is large and funds are scarce, for the purpose of greatly increasing police activities against "illegal aliens". It is a policy designed to reduce "disorder" within

the country – it is true that the number of such individuals is, as I have already noted, quite large and that up to the present time many of them, once inside the United States territorial borders, have lived and worked in low-paying jobs with comparative impunity despite their illegal status – but at the same time it will contribute to *greater* disorder – more unemployment, intensification of poverty, increased political unrest – in the countries, especially Mexico but also Ireland and many others, from which they have come. (It will have such effects, that is, if it is effectively and even-handedly implemented, about the likelihood of which one has good cause to doubt.) It was Mr. Clinton's predecessor, President George Bush, who proclaimed the dawning of a New World Order; while this is of course merely a slogan, I think that it points to some important new historical realities, realities that can best be encapsulated in the assertion that ours is very rapidly becoming more and more "One World". But there is no guarantee that this "New World Order" will be a better or happier or less chaotic one, and there are many indications to the contrary.

My proposal is that one important step towards the development of a more decent and more truly orderly "One World", a step that is in keeping both with classical liberalism's emphasis on the rights and freedoms of individuals *vis-à-vis* governments and the socialist Left's traditional insistence on the necessary connection between freedom and economic equity, be taken by in fact eliminating emigration and immigration restrictions worldwide, just as the Universal Declaration of Human Rights implies. I do not see this as a prescription for chaos with respect to any of the objections most likely to be raised against it. For example, funding for the increased social services that would be required in some localities could be met by transferring monies no longer needed for immigration enforcement, together with some other imaginable innovations in the delivery of such services that it would be beyond the scope of this paper to enumerate. A few simple regulations to uphold existing workers' rights to work, also asserted in the Universal Declaration of Human Rights, would prevent the chaos of widespread unemployment, while the migrations that would be likely to take place would create many more employment needs. Increasingly sophisticated electronic communications among police forces around the world should allay the fear that the elimination of migration barriers would enable genuine criminals more easily to escape apprehension, while not necessarily reducing local autonomy or raising the spectre of a world police state beyond what is already in place.

Indeed, I see my suggestion as contributing to mitigate the growing possibility that a single hegemonic government, culture, and economic structure, those of the United States (together with, in the economic sphere, the major multinational corporations), may soon totally dominate all others and become in effect the world government and "policeman", despite all demurrers. A United States with truly open borders would be less insular, more inclined to view the Others of this world as equals rather than "aliens"; consequently, its citizens would themselves be less alienated. And some of the most salient injustices on the global level would most likely be, not eliminated, but reduced – injustices of vastly disproportionate resources between nation-states and between social classes. For the redistribution of global resources and power is a moral and political imperative, if any such imperative exists.

In the United States as in, no doubt, many other parts of the world there have been times at which non-citizens were not treated as so rigidly distinct a group as they are today – when, for example, in certain states and localities, "aliens" who were residents were encouraged to vote in local elections. If this and other implications of my proposal were to become a worldwide practice, it would not put an end to local and regional differences and cultures; for the love of one's homeland and its culture, at present so cruelly and unfairly connected to nationalist excesses in the minds of many people in many places, is a very widespread sentiment, one not likely to disappear. But it *would* involve a major change of perspective both with respect to the meaning of "rights" – the "rights of man" (in the generic sense) articulated in the Universal Declaration or some roughly similar new document would at last take precedence over the "rights of the citizen" – and with regard to ordinary individuals' perceptions and evaluations of *all* Others. And that would be an important step towards a less unjust and more law-respecting world.

Lukas H. Meyer, Bremen

Can Actual Future People Have a Right to Non-Existence?[1]

Many of us, if asked, would want to defend the view that we do not have an obligation to procreate out of regard for the interests of possible future people. Not to bring about the existence of future people does not harm any interest of 'these people'. I should like to examine the question of whether the widely held belief that possible people cannot be said to have, against us, a right to existence is compatible with another widely held belief: Prospective children have an interest to the effect that their parents not act in a way likely to lead to their birth where the parents are in a position to know that the life of the child, should the child be born, would not be worth living.[2] All children may well have a right vis-à-vis their parents to the effect that their parents not act in such a way. We should, then, under certain circumstances refrain from procreating, namely, owing to the plight of the would-be child. We might be under an obligation not to procreate under certain circumstances – people may have a right to non-existence where, if born, they would lead lives not worth living.

I will argue that a person-affecting approach makes it possible to hold both beliefs. A person-affecting view regards only the interests of people as morally relevant whereas an impersonal view would attribute value to states of affairs quite independently of how these states affect the interests of people. A person-affecting approach requires that only the interests (and rights) of actual people are to be regarded as morally relevant. In some decision-making contexts we relate to future people as *actual* future people: If we make a decision about an action or a policy and the likelihood of the existence of future people is (relatively) independent of our performing the action or carrying out the policy, then these future people are, for us, actual future people with respect to their existence and in this decision-making context. In other decision-making contexts we relate to future people as *possible* future people: If we make a decision about an action or a policy and the likelihood of the existence of future people is (highly) dependent on our performing the action or carrying out the policy, then these future people are possible future people for us with respect to their existence and in this decision-making context.[3] David Heyd argues for adopting a person-

1 I wish to thank Joseph Raz, Stanley L. Paulson, Barbara Reiter, David Heyd, Thomas W. Pogge, Catherine Framm, Wieslaw Lang, Hendrik Ph. Visser't Hooft and the participants of the IVR Working Group 'Various Rights' for valuable criticism.

2 Some people deny that we can know whether or not another person´s life is worth living. They claim that a person can only judge his or her own life in these terms. In the following discussion I will assume that we can make such judgments about other people´s lives. Assuming that we can, I will ask whether this is of relevance to the question of how we should relate to our possible children.

3 In characterizing this important distinction I follow the accounts given by David Heyd, *Genethics. Moral Issues in the Creation of People* (Berkeley and Los Angeles: University of California Press, 1992, 97–103) and Trudy Govier (in her 'What Should We Do About Future People?', *American Philosophical Quarterly* 16 (1979), 105–113, 106).

affecting approach to genethical problems. He claims that in the context of making decisions on procreation we relate to future people as possible future people. Thus, in this decision-making context their interests do not count. Future people can have a right neither to existence nor to non-existence.[4]

1. Refraining from Bringing a Child into Existence out of Regard for the Child

I believe that a helpful way of accounting for both beliefs is to distinguish two decision-situations.[5] First, assuming that we have no reason to doubt that our possible children would have a reasonable prospect of normal development and thus, would have a life worth living, what considerations arise where as possible parents we take a decision on whether or not to reproduce? Second, once a decision is made in one way or other, what reasons might a moral agent have for changing his or her mind?

I shall consider, first, how possible parents make a decision on whether they ought to have children – assuming they have no reason to doubt that their possible children would have a reasonable prospect of normal development and, thus, a life worth living. When we decide whether or not to reproduce, the

4 In chs. 1 and 4 of *Genethics* (n. 3 above), Heyd discusses whether we can be under an obligation not to procreate out of regard for the interests of the prospective child . Whether future people can be said to and have a right to non-existence under certain circumstances is the central issue of 'wrongful life' cases, which are to be distinguished from both 'wrongful birth' and 'wrongful pregnancy' cases. The latter two concern interests of *parents* in not giving birth to a defective child and in not having an unwanted pregnancy, respectively. 'Wrongful life' cases concern the interests of *children* in not being brought into existence under certain circumstances.
On the basis of an impersonal approach one could account for the asymmetry of our procreational duties – the asymmetry, on the one hand, of our having no obligation to procreate out of regard for the interests of possible future people and, on the other, of our having an obligation not to beget children who are going to be miserable – by some version of negative consequentialism (giving priority to the prevention of evil and suffering over the creation of good and happiness). Alternatively, an impersonal approach could deny that we have no duty to beget children and could argue instead that we have a *prima facie* duty to promote over-all happiness by creating new well-off people. For problems with these accounts, see Heyd, *Genethics* (n. 3 above), 59 f., and Parfit, *Reasons and Persons* (Oxford: Clarendon Press 1984), ch. 17, respectively.
Since the publication of Narveson's seminal paper 'Utilitarianism and New Generations' (*Mind* 76 (1967), 62-72, and see his 'Moral Problems of Population', *Monist* 57 (1973), 62-86), many have contributed to the debate on whether a person-affecting approach can account for the asymmetry of our procreational duties. Heyd discusses several such contributions in *Genethics* (n. 3 above), 111–14, arguing that they typically rely on assumptions that are incompatible with a person-affecting approach. Specifically, they either rely on comparing the value of possible lives or on comparing the value of 'nonexistence before conception' with the value of 'life not worth living'. My account of the asymmetry as presented in this paper does not rely on these assumptions.

5 To my knowledge, Govier was first to suggest that distinguishing between these decision-situtations is helpful in the context of procreation. See her 'What Should We Do About Future People?' (n. 3 above), 111.

probability that a child will be brought into existence is very largely dependent on what we decide to do. In deciding whether or not to reproduce, the possible child's interest in being brought into existence cannot be a factor of decision-making. We cannot harm an interest in survival (or any other interest) by hindering the coming into existence of a bearer of an interest in survival. A possible person's existence and corresponding interests cannot properly be used as a basis on which the decision on whether or not to reproduce is made. Such interests cannot be weighed against the probability of the possible person's coming into existence, since the probability of this crucially depends upon whether we decide to reproduce or not. Instead, we make a decision on the basis of the interests of those already alive; it is the actual people's lives that would be affected by whether or not the child comes into existence.

Once a decision is made on the basis of weighing these interests, what reasons might a moral agent have for changing his or her mind? First, let us imagine that the possible parents decide in favour of having a child. The prospective parents now learn that this child, if born, would have a life not worth living. Should they revise their decision to have the child out of regard for, *inter alia*,[6] the child itself? Yes, they should (1a).[7] And this for the reason, as Trudy Govier puts it, that "the typical and intended effect of deciding to have a child is that there will be a child to consider."[8] If the prospective parents' decision is successfully implemented, their child will be an actual person. Thus, they ought to consider the interests of this "child-that-is-to-be".[9] Actual people have an interest in having the chance of living a life worth living. They may even have a right to the chance to have a life worth living. We can harm a person by bringing that person into existence under circumstances that will not allow the person to live a life worth living. One might even want to say that prospective parents would violate a right of this would-be child in bringing it into existence: Every child has the right that its parents not act in a way likely to lead to the child's birth in circumstances in which they could know that the life of the child, if born, would not be a life worth living.

Second, let us imagine that the would-be parents decide against having a child. Once again, the possible parents now learn that the life a child of theirs would have, if born, is not worth living. Should they revise their decision not to have a child out of regard for, *inter alia*, the child? Obviously they should not (1b). Having decided not to bring about the existence of a bearer of an interest means

6 They have good reasons from refraining to cause the existence of this child out of regard for themselves and all those people who will be negatively affected by the existence of a child whose life is not worth living. See Heyd, *Genethics* (n. 3 above), 96 f.

7 Heyd denies this. See his *Genethics* (n. 3 above), 102, 105 f., 241 f.

8 Govier, 'What Should We Do About Future People?' (n. 3 above), 111. However, one might want to ask whether prospective parents who very strongly desire offspring that share their genetic makeup can reasonably be expected to refrain from conceiving their own biological offspring when they learn that the plight of prospective offspring is likely to be very serious. This is a question to be answered by the psychology and ethics of parenting. See Nancy S. Jecker, 'Reproductive Risk Taking and the Nonidentity Problem', *Social Theory and Practice* 13 (1987), 219-235, 221 f.

9 Govier, 'What Should We Do About Future People?' (n. 3 above), 111. I will refer to what Govier terms 'child-that-is-to-be' by 'would-be child'.

that they do not have to consider the interest of a possible child. We cannot provide benefits for people through acts of forbearances that assure that these people shall never exist.

Alternatively, after having made a decision whether or not to procreate, the would-be parents now learn that their possible children, if born, would have far more than the ordinary 'reasonable prospect' of having a life worth living. First, let us imagine that the possible parents have decided in favour of having a child. Should they revise their decision to have the child out of regard for, *inter alia*,[10] the child itself? Obviously, they should not (2a).[11] Nor do parents who have decided against having a child have a reason to revise their decision out of regard for possible children when they learn that their possible children, if born, would have far more than the ordinary 'reasonable prospect' of having a life worth living (2b). We can neither benefit nor harm people through acts of forbearances that assure that these people shall never exist.

2. Causing Harm to a Child by Bringing It into Existence

There are systematic ways of objecting to the account as presented in the previous section. These objections concern, in particular, the claim that after having made a decision to have children, prospective parents should revise their decision *out of regard for their would-be child(ren)* when they learn that the prospective child(ren) would have a life not worth living. I shall assume that we can judge another person´s life to be not worth living and that we can specify what it means to have a life worth living. Then the claim under consideration may be understood as saying that an important reason for parents to refrain from having a child is that they can expect this child, if born, to fall below a certain standard of well-being, namely, the standard of having a life worth living.

Why, under these circumstances, should parents revise their decision to have children out of regard for the children? For the reason that they would act wrongly towards the would-be child. To inflict a wrong on someone is to harm that person. When prospective parents learn that their child would have a life not worth living, they should refrain from having it, for by bringing the child into existence they would cause harm to it. In bringing about a child's existence we

10 Again, knowing that one's would-be child would have a far greater than ordinary 'reasonable prospect' of a life worth living is likely to change our estimation of how the parents´ and other actual people´s interests would be affected by the future child.

11 I have restricted myself to the question of whether the prospective parents have a reason to revise their decision out of regard for the child. Thus, it is not incumbent upon me to discuss whether under the circumstances described they would have additional reasons, namely, reasons based on the interest of the child, to bring about the child´s existence. Although I believe that people can live lives that are not worth living, I am highly sceptical about comparative judgments on the relative value of lives all of which are worth living. See also Robert Elliot, 'Identity and the Ethics of Gene Therapy', *Bioethics* 7 (1993), 27–40, 39 f. (Elliot argues that there are person-regarding reasons for preventing the coming into existence of persons whose lives are not worth living and at the same time he denies that such reasons are applicable to choosing among lives that are worthwhile to different degrees).

can harm this child (3). To be sure, some have denied this.[12] They argue that the judgment, to be meaningful, presupposes, first, the commensurability of the values of 'life not worth living' and 'nonexistence before conception'[13] for a person when this person is brought into existence.[14] Second, the judgment presupposes that we can assign the states 'nonexistence before conception' and 'existence' to a person when this person is brought into existence. I shall argue here that we do not have to make comparisons of the values of 'life not worth living' and 'nonexistence before conception' in order to be able to claim that we can cause harm to a person by bringing about that person's existence. Further, I will show that we can assign the states 'nonexistence before conception' and 'existence' to a person when that person's existence is brought about.

Here, everything hinges on the notion of harming someone. As Joseph Raz points out in *The Morality of Freedom*:

> Roughly speaking, one harms another when one´s action makes the other person worse off than he was, or is entitled to be, in a way which affects his future well-being. So much is a matter of meaning.[15]

Derek Parfit suggests that in the context of causing harm to a person by bringing about that person´s existence, we should draw an additional distinction. We should distinguish between causing harm to someone by making this person worse off than he was and 'worse off than he would otherwise at that time have been.'[16] Thus, in what follows, I shall analyze the implications of three different notions of harm for understanding the claim that by bringing about the existence of a child, we can cause harm to this child.

(I) We harm someone by doing *x* now, at a time t_1, only if by acting in this way we cause this person to be worse off at some later time t_2 than the person was before we acted in this way, that is, before t_1.

(II) We harm someone by doing *x* now, at a time t_1, only if by acting in this way we cause this person to be worse off at some later time, t_2, than, other things equal, the person would have been at t_2 had we not acted in this way.

(III) We harm someone only if, after our having acted in a certain way or omitted acting in that way at a time t_1, we cause this person to be worse off at t_2 than the person should then be.

Choosing among these notions of harm is crucial for understanding the claim under consideration. When these notions are used to explicate the claim that by

12 See, e.g., Heyd, *Genethics* (n. 3 above), 122 and see 117–26.

13 Instead of my 'nonexistence before conception´ one often finds 'prenatal nonexistence' in the literature. The prenatal nonexistence of a person is a period of time that includes a person's nonexistence before conception as well as the normal nine months of the development of an embryo before birth. The question of whether we can harm a person by bringing about his or her existence can be separated from the question of the moral status of the embryo. Every position we might want to take on the latter question is compatible with both our affirming or denying that we can harm a child by bringing about the child´s existence.

14 Heyd seems to believe that applying the notion of a 'life not worth living' within the context of procreation presupposes the commensurability of 'life not worth living' and 'nonexistence before conception'. See *Genethics* (n. 3 above), 121f., 31f.

15 Raz, *The Morality of Freedom* (Oxford: Clarendon Press, 1986), 414.

16 Parfit, *Reasons and Persons* (n. 4 above), 487–90.

bringing about the existence of a child we can cause harm to this child, each of these notions can be shown to presuppose a different set of assumptions ((a)-(d)), as stated below. Notion (I), employed to explicate the claim under consideration, commits us to presuppositions (a), (b), (c). Notion (II) commits us to presuppositions (b) and (c). Notion (III) commits us to presuppositions (c) and (d). I shall argue that propositions (a) and (b) are, to say the least, doubtful. Given that it is only the third notion of harm that does not presuppose either (a) or (b), this notion seems to be most apt for explicating the claim that we can cause harm to a child by bringing about the existence of this child.

(a) That which is in the state of nonexistence before conception can be said to have an interest in (not) being conceived. (I)

(b) The values of 'life not worth living' and 'nonexistence before conception' are commensurable. (I, II)

(c) We can assign the states 'nonexistence before conception' and 'existence' to a person when this person does exist. (I, II, III)

(d) We can positively describe a standard of well-being so that we violate a duty to a person when we cause this person to fall below the standard specified or when we fail to cause this person to reach the standard. (III)

Assumption (c) is presupposed by all three notions. Claiming that I harm a person by bringing about this person´s existence presupposes that bringing about someone´s existence can be attributed to this person as something that happens to this person at the time the person comes into existence. Indeed, once a person exists, we can refer to this person by saying that his or her coming into existence was brought about, say, by John and Jill. We know who it is who would never have come into existence had John and Jill not brought the person into existence. In this respect, 'never having come into existence' and 'ceasing to exist' do not differ with respect to a person who exists. Just as we can refer to a person who at this moment might have ceased to exist, we can refer to the person who may well never have come into existence.[17] We can assign these states to a person when this person´s existence is brought about without thereby committing ourselves to the view that 'in virtue of acts or forbearances that assure certain people's non-existence, we (can) cause harm to or benefit these people' (4).[18] In fact, (4) does not make sense. For we cannot refer, here, to particular people. In claiming (1b) and (2b), I rely on this argument. After having decided that they do not want children the would-be parents have no reason to revise their decision when they learn that their possible children, if born, would have a far greater than ordinary 'reasonable prospect' of having a life worth living or when they learn that their possible children, if born, would have a life not worth living. Not wanting children, they presumably will not bring about the existence of a bearer of an interest in anything. Thus, there is no particular person to whom

17 Ibid.

18 It may also be noted that in assigning these states to a person when the person does exist, we do not commit ourselves to the view that nonexistence before conception and death have the same ontological status. For the long-standing debate on the ontological status of what is possible, see Ludger Honnefelder, 'Possibilien', in *Historisches Wörterbuch der Philosophie*, vol. vii, ed. Joachim Ritter and Karlfried Gründer (Darmstadt: Wissenschaftliche Buchgesellschaft, 1989), cols. 1126–35.

they could refer in revising their decision not to procreate. We cannot benefit or cause harm to people by means of actions or forbearances that assure these people's non-existence.

None of the notions of harming someone, as distinguished above, implies (4). However, (I) presupposes assumption (a). Attributing interests to an egg cell before its fertilization by a sperm does not seem to make sense. It is hard to see how an egg cell before its fertilization could qualify as a bearer of an interest. When employed to explicate the claim that we (can) cause harm to a person by bringing that person into existence, (I) presupposes assumption (a). Then, however, this notion of harm is inapplicable in the context in question.[19]

(II) presupposes (b). This notion of harm presupposes not only that one can assign the two states to an existing person but also that one can compare the values of these states for an existing person. In claiming that by bringing about a person's existence we thereby cause that person to be worse off than he or she would otherwise have been at that time – if, that is, the person had never come into existence – we are relying on the possibility of making an intrapersonal comparison between the values of 'nonexistence before conception' (in the sense of 'never existing'[20]) and 'living a life not worth living'.

Most people hold that these values are incommensurable. I shall not discuss in a systematic way the commensurability of these values. Instead, I shall only point to a source of our doubts about their commensurability. On the one hand, we believe that if a person is in a truly terrible state (that is, has a life not worth living), then this is undesirable for this person. It is undesirable in the interpersonal sense of being worse than the state of other existing people, those who do have lives worth living. On the other hand, we would resist the idea that it makes sense to say that if a person is in a truly terrible state (that is, has a life not worth living), this is undesirable for that person in the sense of being worse for that person than the state of affairs that would have prevailed had this person never come into existence.

Even if one thought that one could assign a value to the state of 'never existing' one would still have to show that the value of this state is commensurable with the value of the state of 'having a life not worth living'. It is doubtful that the value of 'never existing' can be understood in person-affecting terms. After all, to imagine that an existing person has never come into existence at all implies imagining that person's having had no experiences whatsoever. To be sure, as I noted above, we can attribute to an existing person the state 'nonexistence before conception' just as we can attribute the state of 'having ceased to exist' to this person. This does not mean, however, that never existing at all is of (dis)value for that person.[21]

19 It is not the case that this notion of harm (I) is applicable to all cases save for the case I am discussing here. Rather, as Raz shows, this way of understanding harming someone cannot account for harming another person by not fulfilling one's positive duty to this person. See *The Morality of Freedom* (n. 15 above), 414.

20 Here I assume that to compare an existing person's current state of well-being with the state of this person had the person not been conceived is to compare an existing person's current state with this person's 'never existing'.

21 But see Persson, 'Genetic Therapy, Identity and Person-Regarding Reasons', *Bioethics* 9 (1995), 16–31, 28 f. (arguing for assigning "zero-value" to never existing; his account seems to presuppose proposition (4), above).

In this respect, death seems to be different from never existing at all. Life can be understood as an ongoing project that consists of more particular projects that are defined in part by goals and whose completion requires time.[22] If a person's life is cut short, this can be contrary to this person's interests. Through death, the person is hindered from bringing his or her projects to fruition. As far as carrying out these projects is concerned, there may not be anyone else in a position to take this person's place. On the other hand, the fact that my pursuing certain projects makes my life worth living for "me" does not mean that it would necessarily have been undesirable for me not to have ever been given the chance to form the idea of any meaningful projects, namely, by having never been brought into existence at all. 'Never existing' is of (dis)value for no one.[23]

The third notion of harm distinguished here relies on the idea that we have a general duty to people not to cause them to be worse off than they should then be. We can cause a person to be worse off than that person is entitled to be by our actions and omissions. This third notion of harm relies on our being able to specify a standard of what any person is entitled to. As I explained above, in claiming that people should refrain from having children out of regard for the children, when the children can be expected to have a life not worth living, we rely on our being able to define what it means to fall below a standard of having a life worth living. We assume, too, that we can judge another person's life as not worth living. If we make these assumptions, we can then use the third notion of harm for explicating the claim 'by bringing a person into existence we can cause harm to this person' without our having to confront the special ethical difficulties discussed in the previous paragraphs. In applying the third notion of harm, we compare the values of 'having a life worth living' and 'having a life not worth living'. Comparing these values does not present special difficulties either intrapersonally or interpersonally. Through some terrible accident a person having a life worth living might be irreversibly caused to have a life not worth living. Then we would certainly want to say that this person was better off before the accident occurred. Also a person having a life worth living is better off than another person having a life not worth living.

22 See Thomas Nagel, 'Death', in his *Mortal Questions* (Cambridge: Cambridge UP, 1979), 1–10, 8 f.; also see Heyd, *Genethics* (n. 3 above), 123 f.

23 And if so, Nora K. Bell and Barry M. Loewer are then mistaken in assuming that the value of 'never existing' is equal to the value of 'no longer existing' (i.e., death) for the afflicted child in wrongful life cases. See their 'What is Wrong with "Wrongful Life" Cases?', *Journal of Medicine and Philosophy* 10 (1985), 127–145, 137–41.
How to compare the value of prenatal nonexistence with death for a living person is a different issue. As F. M. Kamm rightly points out, where it is a question of whether we have had the chance of achieving something in our lives, our prenatal nonexistence may matter no less than our posthumous nonexistence. See F. M. Kamm, *Morality, Mortality. Vol. 1. Death and Whom to Save from It* (New York and Oxford: Oxford UP, 1993), 36.

3. What is so Special about Harming a Person by Bringing about this Person's Existence?

If the prospective parents' decision is successfully implemented, their child will be an actual person. Thus, they ought to consider the interests of this would-be child. Having decided that they want a child, prospective parents ought to revise their decision out of regard for, *inter alia*, the child should they learn that this child, if born, would have a life not worth living. The child is entitled to have a life worth living. By bringing about the existence of the child, we create a situation in which the child is worse off than it should then be.

This is, however, clearly a special case. Harming a person by bringing about this person's existence differs from many other cases of harming someone in that we cannot resolve the problem posed by this case by employing either notion (I) of harm or notion (II). When applied to this case, each of these notions of harm presupposes an assumption (b) or assumptions ((a), (b)), which I have found to be mistaken. Before having brought about the existence of a person, there is no person to whom we could attribute interests or who could be affected by values.[24] But children have an interest in their parents' not acting in a way likely to lead to their birth in circumstances in which the parents could know that the life the child, if born, would have is a life not worth living. By bringing about the existence of a person we can harm this person, namely, when we create a situation in which the person is worse off than he or she is entitled to be.

Can children be said to have a right vis-à-vis their parents to the effect that their parents are not to act in a way likely to lead to their birth in circumstances in which they could know that the life the child, if born, would have is a life not worth living? Can children, in other words, have a right to non-existence? The right to non-existence has a highly peculiar structure. The bearer of the right is the actual person. The children are thought to have the right vis-à-vis their parents. At the time prospective parents consider whether they should revise their decision to bring about the existence of a child, there is no right bearer of the right to non-existence. But this does not mean that the parents could not act in light of an interest on the part of their child in never existing at all.

In the circumstances in which bringing about the existence of a person causes harm to this person in the sense specified, the right to non-existence is violated when, quite simply, the existence of the person is brought about. The

24 In *The Moral Limits of the Criminal Law. Vol. 1. Harm to Others* (Oxford: Oxford University Press, 1984), 102, Feinberg suggests that the inapplicability of notion (II) precludes "criminal liability for 'wrongful conception'". According to Feinberg, in the context of the criminal law 'harming someone' should presuppose worsening a person's condition, i.e. setting back a person's interests. Thus, Feinberg does not consider our notion (III) a notion of harm to be applied in delineating criminal liability. However, in his analysis the afflicted child in wrongful life cases was "wronged" (ibid. and 34 f.) by having been deprived of his "birth rights" (ibid., 99) and "the wrongful progenitors ... should ... be held civilly liable to pay damages to the child" (ibid., 102). Here I do not discuss whether our notion (III) should be applied in delineating criminal liability. See also Feinberg 'Is there a Right to be Born?', in his *Rights, Justice, and the Bounds of Liberty. Essays in Social Philosophy* (Princeton: Princeton UP, 1980), 207–220, 218 f.

only way, here, in which the prospective parents can avoid the violation of the right is by ensuring that the person whose right it would be does not come into existence at all. Thus, the only way in which the prospective parents can respect the right is by excluding the possibility that the right ever becomes actual. With respect to the particular child who, if born, would have a life not worth living, the right to non-existence cannot be honoured but can only be violated. With regard to all those actual people who have lives worth living, the right has not been violated and cannot be violated.[25]

25 I should like to add that while considerations based on the rights of future people are important in accounting for our procreational duties, rights-based considerations cannot account for important concerns that most of us have for future people. As I argue in 'More Than They Have a Right to: Future People and Our Future-Oriented Projects', in *Contingent Future Persons: Philosophical and Theological Challenges*, ed. Nick Fotion and Jan C. Heller (Kluwer: Dordrecht, forthcoming), future people cannot coherently be said to have a right to existence. Further, they cannot be said to have a right to a life that is well above a minimal level of well-being or to a particular way of life. Instead, we can account for our concerns that there be future people and that they have lives that are well worth living in terms of duties towards them to which no rights of future people correspond.

Wiesław Lang, Toruń

The Concepts of Rights and the Rights of the Unborn

For about twenty years the debate on the rights of the unborn has been carried on in Europe and in America.The most controversial point of this discussion is the right to life of the human fetus with reference to abortion. The clash of the positions of prolifers and prochoicers is a clash of absolutes.[1]

The following crucial questions have been put forward in the debate: Have the conceived but unborn children all rights or at least some rights which born persons enjoy? Is the right to be born alive among these rights? Or have the unborn some special rights different from the rights of living persons? Should the unborn have legal rights granted by law on equal terms with the rights of living persons ? It is not the purpose of this paper to settle definitively the dispute between the prolifers and prochoicers and to answer the above mentioned questions. Rather I will try to assess the philosophical and methodological framework of this dispute and to analyse the relationships between the concepts of rights and the views concerning the rights of the unborn.

I. The preliminary clarification of the meanings of the term "the right to something"

The "right to something" or "right to a holding"[2] are family notions linked intrinsically with the notions of claim, power or immunity.[3]

There is a vast philosophical literature concerning the concepts of right and related notions. I will not examine all concepts of right developed in this century in jurisprudence and legal philsosophy. From the variety of concepts, classifications and typologies of rights I will choose and consider only these ideas of rights which are relevant for the topic of my paper namely for the pretended rights of fetuses.

1. "Right" is a meaningful term and the proposition "X has a right ot something" makes sense. This assumption is a necessary condition for a sensible discussion on the rights of the unborn or of any other entities. The view that the term "right" is only a verbal expression of emotions or irrational ideas makes this discussion pointless.[4]

1 L. H. Tribe, *Abortion. The Clash of Absolutes*, New York, London 1990.
2 A. Peczenik, "Morality, Law and Rights" in: *Sprache, Performanz und Ontologie des Rechts*. Festgabe fur Kazimierz Opalek zum 75. Geburtstag. Duncker & Humblot, Berlin 1993, p.150.
3 W.N. Hohfeld, *Fundamental Legal Conceptions*, New Haven 1919. Compare C. Wellman, *A Theory of Rights. Persons under Laws, Institutions and Morals*, Rowman & Allenheld Publishers. U.S.A., 1985, pp. 17–60.
4 V. Lundstedt, *Die Unwissenschaftlichkeit der Rechtswissenschaft*, Berlin 1932. pp. 268, A. Ross, "Tu-tu", 5 *Scandinavian Studies in Law* 1960.

2. The term "right" is an open term.[5] The notion of right can not be defined (by using the classical form of definition). Its core meaning as well as its penumbra can be grasped or clarified only in the context of its linguistic usages or with reference to the description of the typical situation of the rightholder (in contrast to the situation of a person being under the obligation or duty).

3. The notion of a right is a value laden and value related concept. Ethical and legal scholars widely agree that the notion of claim is intrinsic to the core meaning of the term "right". To have a right means at least to have good reasons for claiming something or to be in a position in which claiming makes sense.[6] In ethical and moral discourse this notion of right is related to the value of human dignity.[7] In the realm of law the claim oriented concept of right may prima facie seem to be a serious obstacle for predicating legal rights of embryos, newborn children, incompetent persons or animals. These beings are not able to make claims as they are not able to perform any rational actions. But this problem is easily settled by law through the institutions of legal representation and vicarious actions. Legal representatives of fetuses, the newborn,incompetent persons or animals can make legal claims and perform legal actions in their names and on their behalf. (Representation without authorisation).

In legal doctrines the concept of right has been tentatively defined by direct reference to following values: (1) the liberty, freeedom, individual autonomy[8] (2) the power of the rightholder over the things or persons (as the expression of his free will).[9] (3) the interest or the advantage[10], which cannot be overbalanced by social interest in virtue of the benefit costs analysis[11]. None of these value related characteristics captures the full meaning of the term "right" in various situations and in various linguistic contexts. But the cluster of the above mentioned values renders the general sense of the idea of right. In different usages of this term one of the above characteristics takes precedence over the others. The talk about the rights of the unborn as well as about the rights of the newly born or of fully incompetent persons makes sense if the understanding of the right is bound up mainly with the present or future interests or avantages of these beings.

4. The frame of reference of rights are human conducts, things (as isolated parts of environment) and some states of matters. The human conducts as the phenomena to which the rights refer are the actions and forbearances of the rightholders or other persons. As concerns the pretended rights of fetuses these are mainly the rights to states of matters consisting in keeping hold of life, health and bodily integrity or of future property interests.They encompass also the claim rights to forbearances or actions of other persons.

5 As concerns the notions of the open terms and open textures see H.L.A Hart, *The Concept of Law*, Oxford l961, pp. 1–17,120–131.

6 J. Feinberg, "Duties, Rights and Claims", in J. Feinberg, *Rights, Justice and the Bounds of Liberty,* Princeton, New Jersey, U.S.A. 1980, pp. 130–142

7 J. Feinberg, "The Nature and Value of Rights", in J. Feinberg, supra note 6, pp. 143–158.

8 A. Ross, *Law and Justice*, London 1958, pp 177.

9 K. Olivecrona, *Law as Fact*, London 1971, pp. 147–151 (an overview of the theories of rights).

10 K. Olivecrona, supra note 9, pp. 147 –154.

11 R. Dworkin, *Taking Rights Seriously*, Cambridge Mass. U.S.A., 1977.

The concept of a right as a meaningful notion is not redundant and cannot be reduced to other concepts or ideas.

5. In contemporary international covenants as well as in domestic constitutions and statutes various kinds of subjective rights of individuals have been formulated: right to life, to liberty, to privacy, to property,to employment, to minimal standard of welfare etc.These are the kinds of rights singled out on the basis of their substance. In legal philosophy and legal doctrine various classifications of rights based on formal criteria have been elaborated (claim rights, power rights, immunity rights etc.)[12] All of them might have some relevance for the rights of fetuses except of the power rights. The concept of the right as a power is not applicable to fetuses or other beings which are not legal or moral agents. But one formal typology of rights, only marginally mentioned in legal literature, is of a paramount importance for the pretended rights of fetuses namely the distinction of topical rights and future rights.The topical rights are the rights which the subjects enjoy at present. The future rights are contingent rights which the subject aquires at the moment but which will become legally effective and enforceable only if a definite event will occur in future. The typical cases of such rights are the property rights of the fetus based upon the rules of inheritance law.These are the future and contingent rights of beings which already do exist or the existence of which has already been initiated and has begun to develop.This type of future rights are to be distinguished from the rights of future generations, which are the contingent rights of future persons.

If they come into existence the future persons will enjoy these rights . In contrast to the fetuses which can be identified as already existing beings and potential persons, the future persons are possible persons[13]. They do not exist now as individual entities and cannot be identified. We can speak also meaningfully in this sense about the rights of the past generations.

6. The distinction of moral and legal or institutional rights is of a paramount importance for the discussion on the rights of fetuses. It is a well founded and prolific distinction[14].

This distinction makes meaningful the concept of rights of the rightless. The persons endowed with moral rights may be deprived of corresponding legal rights within a legal order. In this sense the moral rights of fetuses or animals may be considered in the realm of law as the rights of the rightless.

I will focus my considerations mainly on legal rights but taking into acount R. Dworkin's theory of the morality as the necessary background of law[15].

12 See W. N. Hohfeld, C. Wellman, supra note 3.

13 J. Feinberg, "The Rights of Animals and Future Generations", in J. Feinberg, supra note 6, pp. 180–183.

14 C. Wellman, supra note 3, pp. 81–184.

15 R. Dworkin, supra note 11.

II. The ontology of rights

The ontological status of rights is of some relevance for the discussed problem. Two main groups of philosophical views concerning the ontology of rights are to be distinguished. namely the phenomenological and the linguistic approach.

1. Phenomenological approach. A right to something is a term which denotes a phenomemon existing indpendently of linguistic utterances in which they are formulated. Consequently, rights are entities existing independently of norms rules, principles or normative systems. This view has been developed in legal philosophy in an idealistic, naturalistic, psychological or sociological version. Accordingly the right is conceived as an intrinsic ingredient of human nature, as an ideal entity (having no spatial and temporal parameters), as a psychic experience, as a social fact or social relationship.[16]

The naturalistic, idealistic and sociological concepts of rights are relevant for the rights of fetuses.

On the ground of these concepts rights are prior to norms of conducts and are discovered by reason or intuition beyond the normative systems. Law making agencies can only declare rights of individuals or groups but they do not create the rights by enacting statutes or other types of legal regulations. The statutes are not the real sources of rights but are the legal settings protecting the preexisting rights of individuals.

The psychological concepts of rights are irrelevant for the issues concerning the rights of the fetuses because in view of these concepts rights exist only in the realm of the subjective psychic experiences of individuals, consequently the discussion on the rights of fetuses or other beings becomes pointless.This is true as concerns both versions of the psychological theories of rights, namely emotivistic and rationalistic ones.[17]

2. The linguistic approach consists in considering rights as the elements of the content of a particular kind of linguistic utterances, namely the normative or the deontic propositions, assuming that these are meaningful utterances.[18] This view implies a norm related and ascriptive conception of right.

Rights do not exist beyond the realm of norms and normative systems, which is the realm of language and culture.Rights are predicated of definite categories of beings on the basis and in virtue of norms and principles forming normative systems. Rights denote ideal relationships between the rightholder and some portions of his natural or social environment, but these are the relations defined(directly or indirectly) by norms and principles.

16 K. Olivecrona, supra note 9, pp. 141–181.

17 V. Lundsted, A. Ross, supra note 4, L. Petrazycki, *Law and Morality*. Translated by W. Babb. Cambridge Mass. 1955, pp. 123.

18 K. Opalek, "The Problem of 'Directive Meaning'", in: *Festkrift til Professor Dr. Jur. et Phil. Alf Ross*. Copenhagen: Juristforbundets Follag, 1969.

III. The ascriptive theory of the right.

According to this theory the proposition "The subject X has a right to something" becomes a completely meaningful one when it is uttered in a norm and system related formula. "The subject X has a right to something or a claim against some other subjects in virtue of a norm or principle valid in a definite normative system". This type of utterance renders the prepositional meaning or the term "right". It means simply that a right conferring norm is applicable to a definte subject. The same is true with reference to the concepts of duties and obligations (as deontic notions). The ascriptive theory of rights makes sense also when the notion of right is a redundant one and on the semantic level of the analysis of language can be reduced to the negation of duties or to some combinations of commands and prohibitions.[19] But on the ground of the reductionist concepts of right the discussion on the rights of the unborn makes little sense.It must be reframed in terms of legal protection of human beings born or unborn. This type of protection differs substantially from the protection of the rights of the beings qualified as persons before law.It does not assume any idea of individual right. Legal protection of intrinsically valuable objects (pieces of art) or animals does not imply that these entities enjoy some rights.

Rights are ascribed to beings which have the status of potential rightholders within a definite normative system. So the rights are intrinsically linked with the normative status of the subjects, to whom the rights are ascribed. The relation between the rights and the status of the rightholder forms a feedback relationship. On the one hand the status of a being as a potential rightholder is a necessary logical condition for the ascription of a right, on the other hand the ascription of rights to a category of beings may constitute or change their normative status.

Two versions of the ascriptive theory of rights are to be distinguished, namely a pure normative version and a context related version.

(1) The pure normative version sets no substantive limits for the ascription of rights as well as for according the status of the right holders to various kinds of entities.The rightholder is considered as an ideal point of ascription.[20] The content of the rules or principles conferring the rights is indeterminate and the reasons for the ascription of rights are irrelevant. This theory makes the discussion on the rights of the fetuses completely pointless.

(2) According to the pragmatic version of the ascriptive theory a right is not only a norm related notion but it is also a concept related to extralinguistic situational contexts of the normative system and to the values encoded in the social and cultural environments of the system. These factors determine and constrain the content of rights and the scope of their ascription; they especially determine and justify the choice of the class of beings to whom rights may be meaningfully ascribed.[21]

19 K. Swirydowicz, S. Wronkowska, M. Zielinski, Z. Ziembinski "O nieporozumieniach dotyczacych t. zw. norm zezwalajacych"(On Misunderstandings Concerning the so-called Permissive Norms), *Panstwo i Prawo* 1975, 7. See a critical analysis of this position: M. Zirk Sadowski, "Permisssion and Pragmatic Approach", in: *Studies in the Philosophy of Law*, vol I, 1986 pp. 109–120.

20 H. Kelsen, *The Pure Theory of Law*, Berkeley l967 (transl.).

21 J. Feinberg, "The Nature and Value of Rights", supra note p. 6, pp. 143–158.

On the ground of this version the reasons for the ascription of rights to a definite category of beings are relevant for the predication of rights of these beings. It makes sense to contend that there are good reasons or no reasons for attributing rights to some categories of beings.

IV. The problem of the legal rights of the unborn

The rational perception of legal rights as meaningful and not redundant notions is possible only on the ground of ascriptive theory of rights in a pragmatic (context and value related) version, assuming the linguistic and cultural reality of rights.

Only the legal subjects can be the holders of legal rights. So the discussion on the rights of the unborn especially of their right to life is in fact the discussion on the legal status of the human fetus in different stages of its development.

Law is an autopoietic and autonomous system of social control. The concept of legal status is not identical with the notion of moral status. The moral status is relevant for the legal status of a being but it can not be logically deduced from its moral status.[22] The substantive and personal scope of the ascription of legal rights is limited and constrained by the intrinsic features of legal order (labelled by Lon Fuller as internal morality of law.)[23] Legal rights are not only declared but also protected and warranted by law (by legal procedures). That is a special feature of legal rights in contrast to moral rights.

The discussion on legal rights of the unborn may be carried on from de lege lata or de lege ferenda position. De lege lata xx ascription of rights means the contention that some or all norms in force conferring rights (in a definite legal system)are applicable to fetuses as potential rightholders.De lege ferenda ascription of rights to fetuses means two kinds of decisions: (I) the prima facie statement that the fetuses are the beings of whose legal rights can be meaningfully predicated. (2)The statement that, all things considered, fetuses ought to be accorded legal rights which living persons enjoy (all rights or at least some rights) and therefore a statute according rights to fetuses ought to be enacted or that, all things considered, fetuses can not be endowed with legal rights even if they have moral rights and there are good moral reasons for according to them legal rights. Moral arguments are very important but not sufficient reasons for according legal rights to a category of beings (all things considered).

The concepts of rights which make meaningful the predication of rights of fetuses are only prima facie reasons for according legal rights to fetuses.[24]

22 W. Lang, "The Status of the Human Fetus", *Criminal Law Forum* Vol. 3, Number 3,Camden, New Jersey, U.S.A., pp. 419–439.

23 L. Fuller, *Morality of Law*, New Haven (U.S.A.) 1969.

24 I drew the idea of the prima facie rights and all things considered rights from the publication of A. Peczenik, supra note 2.

Beatriz S. Tomás Mallén, Castellón

Belonging to a Sect as a Possible Limit to the Right of Choosing the Education of One's Children

Comment in the Light of Recent European and Spanish Case Law

I. Introduction

The aim of the present report is to reflect, with regard to recent European and Spanish Case Law about belonging to a sect as a possible limitation to the right of parents to choose their children's education.

For this we will refer, in the first place and separately, to the right of parents to choose their children's education and to the sect phenomenon. In the second place, we will analyse the possible consequences of belonging to a sect in relation to the so-called parental educational right in the light of the three judgements of the European Court of Human Rights, the Spanish Constitutional Court, and the Spanish Supreme Court respectively.

1. The Right of Parents to Choose their Children's Education

According to the unanimous opinion of contemporary writers, the right to choose the education of one's children is an essential right – in teaching matters – and the choice of religious or moral education is a part.

Those entitled are the parents and the children have the right to education. Certainly, it is about compatible rights, but if conflict arises between both, the right of the children to education must prevail. This priority is distinguished with special emphasis by the European Court of Human Rights.[1]

The recognition of the paternal educational right – as much in its wider sense as in its religious sense – in various international texts[2] confirms its importance.

With regard to the Spanish field, the Spanish Constitution (1978) does not hold with the right of the parents to choose their children's education, but it does with the most limited right to "their children receiving the religious and moral education in accordance with their own convictions".[3] Nevertheless, the first also forms part of the Spanish legislation – thougt ordinary, not constitutional – and

1 Cf. Judgement of the 7th December 1976, *Kjeldsen, Busk Madsen and Pedersen* Case, Series A, no. 23; Judgement of 25th February 1982, *Campbell and Cosans* Case, Series A, no. 48.

2 Cf. 26.3 article of the Universal Declaration of Human Rights (1948); 13.3 article of the International Covenant on Economic, Social and Cultural Rights (1966); 5.1 article of the UNESCO Convention against Discrimination in Education (1960); article 2 of the Protocol No. 1 (1952) to the European Convention on Human Rights (1950).

3 Cf. article 27.3 of the Spanish Constitution: "The public powers guarantee the right which helps parents so that their children receive religious and moral education in accordance with their own convictions".

has been recognised in the international legislation applicable to Spain by order of the Constitution itself.[4]

With respect to its nature contemporary writers are not unanimous. Without trying to be too thorough, some of the most characteristic guidelines can be pointed out. Thus, in certain legislation, the paternal educational right is included in the freedom to teach, together with other rights such as the right of all to an education and the freedom of the creation and management of teaching institutions. Another section of the legislation distinguishes between the right to an education and the right to teach, and forms the opinion that the right to teach, and forms the opinion that the right of the parents to choose the education of the child forms part of the first. Likewise, it has been defined as an autonomous right together with the internal powers of the paternal authority of the parents – despite being considered in this case as a consequence of the denial of the educational monopoly which implies the freedom to teach.[5]

2. Sects

Of course, sects[6] do not amount to a monolithical or indifferent reality, so that it is difficult to judge them, defend them or condemn them in bloc.[7] It is easier to note that they arouse great social uneasiness.[8]

It is important to distinguish sects in general from the so-called "destructive or harmful sects". The first can imply the real exercise of the basic rights of ideological and religious freedom. On the contrary, the second represent a serious danger to freedom in general and particulary to religious freedom – although they paradoxically seek protection in religious freedom – because they destroy the balance of the individual and his or her work and social emotional relationships.[9]

On the other hand, to confront oneself legally with the sects is a task whose difficulty – considerable in any case – increases at the sect follower's coming of age. This is due to the legislation, as is logical, which protects minors more intensely. For example, in the Spanish educational field, the right that helps parents so that their children receive a religious or moral education which is in accordance with their own convictions,[10] ends when the child comes of age – on

4 Cf. articles 10.2 and 96 of the Spanish Constitution.

5 Cf. A. Embid Irujo, *Las libertades en la enseñanza*, Tecnos, Madrid (Spain), 1983, p. 242.

6 We will use the term "sect" because it is the most traditional, even when it is criticised for various reasons – among which stands out its pejorative sense –. Other proposed names like "new religious movements", "alternative religious movements", "cults", etc., also raise serious inconveniences and display the additional disadvantage of a less extended use.

7 Cf. M. Guerra Gomez, *Los nuevos movimientos religiosos. (Las Sectas). Rasgos comunes y diferenciales*, Eunsa, Pamplona (Spain), 1993, p. 81.

8 Proof of this are the *Recommendations about the activity of certain „New Religious Movements" inside the European Community* of the European Parliament, document 1–47 prepared by the Youth, Culture, Education, Information and Sports Commissions of the European Parliament and promulgated 22nd May 1984.

9 Cf. M. Guerra Gomez, *Los nuevos movimientos religiosos* ..., p. 81 and foll.

10 Cf. article 27.3 of the Spanish Constitution.

celebrating his or her eighteenth birthday.[11] From this moment, the outlook becomes really complicated for those parents who try to "extract" their child out of a sect.

II. Belonging to a Sect as a Possible Limit of the Right to Choose Children's Education. Recent European and Spanish Case Law in the Matter

It is possible that the reverse may happen, that is to say, that it is the parents who may belong to a sect. In this case, we can ask ourselves if such circumstances will affect their right to choose their children's education. This matter is viewed although not always explicitly, in three recent judgements of the European Court on Human Rights, the Spanish Constitutional Court and the Spanish Supreme Court respectively, whose study constitutes the main aim of this report.

1. The Judgement of the European Court on Human Rights of 26th May 1993 (Hoffmann versus Austria Case)[12]

In the Hoffmann versus Austria case, Mrs. Hoffmann – an Austrian citizen – accused before the European Court of Human Rights of the fact of having been denied by the Austrian Supreme Court the parental authority over her children – which had been conferred on her ex-husband – because of her religious convictions, specifically for belonging to the religious community of the "Jehovah's Witnesses". To this end, she called on her right to the respect of her family life (article 8 of the European Convention on Human Rights), her religious freedom (article 9 of the Convention), and her right to educate her children according to her religious convictions (article 2 of the Protocol No. 1 of the Convention); she also invoked a discrimination based on religion (article 14 of the Convention).

Among the children's rights that the Austrian Supreme Court had tried to protect by conferring the exercise of parental authority to the father, was the right of education. In this sense, the said Court had declared: "It has also been established that if the children are educated according to do the religious teaching of Jehova's Witnesses".[13]

The European Court of Human Rights came to the conclusion that the Austrian Supreme Court had treated the claimant and her ex-husband in a „different way" with regard to the negative repercussions which could arise for the children by her belonging to the religious minority of "Jehovah's Witnesses"; and that such a difference of treatment based on religion had been discriminating because, despite pursuing a legitimate end – protecting the children's health[14]

11 Cf. article 12 of the Spanish Constitution.

12 Cf. Judgement of 26th May 1993, Hoffmann versus Austria Case, Series A, no. 255–C.

13 Cf. paragraph 15 of the judgement.

14 "Jehovah's Witnesses" reject blood transfusions, which could have given rise to the children finding their health or lives threatened.

and rights – there had not existed „a reasonable proportionate relation between the means used and the objective pursued“.[15]

To sum up, the European Court of Human Rights declared that there had been a breach of article 8 taken in conjunction with article 14 – by five votes to four – and that it did not see the necessity of ruling on the allegation of a violation of article 2 of the Protocol No. 1 of the Convention. It did not consider the necessity either of the article 8 taken alone, nor article 9, taken alone or in conjunction with article 14.

Nevertheless it has to be pointed out that there were four dissenting, or partly dissenting personal opinions, in the sense of not noticing any breach of article 8 in conjunction with 14.

It is easy to agree with many of the declarations in the same, among them that of Judge Matscher when he says that "the only criterion on which the courts should base their decision in a case such as this is the welfare of the children".[16]

Nevertheless, there are doubts in the minds of those who read such reasonings. In this sense, the one that Judge Valticos makes when he points out that "the question would surely not have arisen in the case of a different religion not having the special characteristics of Jehova's Witnesses".[17] He goes on to add that "the particularities of this religion's tenets of faith would have led to the children being set apart from normal social life and would have contributed to marginalising them and restricting their future and their development".[18]

I think that in these types of conflicts one should not generalise as, I think, Judge Valticos does, if one does not want to fall precisely into discrimination because of religion. However, if the practical consequences of the religion of the claimant had been considered in this specific case to be sufficiently predictable and negative for the welfare of the children, conferring parental authority to the father – and consequently of the parental educational right – it could not have been classed as discriminatory because of religion.

It can be deduced by all above that for the European Court of Human Rights the parents' belonging to a sect does not suppose in itself a limit to the right of choosing their children's education.

2. The Judgement of the Spanish Constitutional Court (First Chamber No. 260/1994, of 3rd October 1994[19]

The background of the judgement of the Spanish Constitutional Court can be laid out as follows. the Catalan Autonomous Government (Generalidad) issued a protection and assumption statement of the legal guardianship which affected twenty-three children belonging to seven families who lived in a community

15 Cf. paragraph 36 of the judgement.
16 Cf. paragraph 2 of dissenting opinion of Judge Matscher.
17 Cf. paragraph 2 of dissenting opinion of Judge Valticos.
18 Cf. *ibidem* .
19 Cf. Judgement of the Spanish Constitutional Court No. 260/1994, of 3rd October 1994, First Chamber. Published in the Boletín Oficial del Estado (BOE) No. 267, Suplemento, Tuesday 8th November 1994.

called "Missionary Family" ("Familia Misionera") linked to the "Children of God" ("Niños de Dios") sect. Among the reasons for adopting such measures figured mental manipulation, annulment of criticism capacity and not enrolling the minors in a school. These were being educated in the family in a very disciplined organisation and similar to the old religious schools for boarders or the classical paramilitary schools.

The minors' parents raised their opposition to the protection and assumption statement carried out by the Generalidad of Catalonia before the Court of First Instance no. 19 of Barcelona. The above-mentioned Court considered the charges made by the Generalidad of Catalonia to be correct and rejected the opposition raised, confirming thus the Generalidad's conduct. It is clear from the Proceedings that the rights of the parents for their children to receive religious and moral education in accordance with their own convictions should yield when the education given prevents or limits substantially the minor's full evolution.

Which means that the case was interpreted as a conflict between the rights of the children's education and the parental educational right, giving the first priority. Immediately after, the parents lodged remedies of appeal before Barcelona's Provincial Court, which set aside – in opposition to the Court of First Instance – proving them right. The duty to respect the parents' right so that their children receive religious and moral education in accordance with their own convictions is underlined in the Proceedings and the suitability of the parental authority should be exercised in the benefit of the children and according to their personality. Likewise it is reckoned that the teachings given had not neglected those considered basic and compulsory. Accordingly, "the natural paternal-filial harmony giving superior control of the same to the State" had been broken.

That is to say, it was not considered that there had existed any conflict between the children's right and the parent's right – educational and freedom of belief. Therefore there was no reason to limit the second by the Generalidad.

In reply the Generalidad served proceeding before the Spanish Constitutional Court with the corresponding claims of protection against the Proceedings of Barcelona's Provincial Court, considering article 27 of the Spanish Constitution (right to education and freedom of teaching) breached in relation to article 15 of the same (right to life and to the physical and moral integrity). Despite the analysis of the fulfillment of procedural requirements, "what is discussed is the breach of the basic right to receive a full education of minors".[20]

Catalonia's Generalidad argued, in first place, that not enrolling the children in officially approved institutions had, as a consequence, the deprival of the right to a full education; therefore, the Proceedings appealed to breach the basic right to education by preventing such enrollment. In the second place, the Generalidad declared that the exercise of the right of the parents to religious freedom had come before the exercise of the minors' right to receive a full education, and that accordingly the second had been breached.

The Attorney General held the contrary opinion, which did not consider it proven that the minors had not received an education directed towards the full development of the human personality in accordance with the parents own

20 Cf. paragraph 2 of the 'antecedentes' of the judgement.

convictions in religious and moral matters. Thus it maintained that the Constitution points out to the State a series of duties designed to carry out the basic right to an education, without this meaning that the individuals cannot go along different ways with the same aim and with the same results. The Attorney General, following what was determined by the Provincial Court, is of the opinion that in this case there has been a different way of teaching to that established by the State – without enrolling the minors in a school – but without having supposed a breach of the basic right.

The parents declared that full education is not restricted to the officially approved institutions, that the family is the basic element of the educational process, which is an *inalienable right* of the parents power to choose the type of education which they want to give their children in accordance with their conscience, etc.[21]

According to the Spanish Constitutional Court, the aim of protection only reaches to determine if the Proceedings of the Provincial Court – which had declared the inappropriateness of the assumption of guardianship of the minors by the Generalidad and had restored the full authority to the parents – breached the minors' right to education. And the Spanish Constitutional Court understands that it is not so; that these resolutions did not prevent the enrollment of the minors in a school nor the exercise of the Generalidad's powers in order to secure the due enrolment. As a consequence, it rejects the appeals of protection, the declaring Generalidad's conduct unconstitutional.

I think that in this specific case the fact of restoring to the parents the full authority over the minors does involve, more or less directly, not enrolling the same in a school. However, from this declaration it is not necessarily concluded that the non-enrollment breaches the right to an education and justifies depriving parental authority. This is precisely the matter – in my opinion, essential – that the Spanish Constitutional Court does not deal with.[22] Perhaps its solution is formally correct, but it does not come into the merits of the case.

Neither can it be deduced from this judgement that the parents belonging to a sect can suppose a limit to their right to choose their children's education, because at no time has the Spanish Constitutional Court evaluated that circumstance on its own.

3. The Judgement of the Spanish Supreme Court (Second Chamber)[23] No. 1669/1994, of 30th October 1994[24]

This judgement deals with from the criminal law point of view, the aforementioned.

21 The European Court of Human Rights in its judgement in the *Kjeldsen, Busk Madsen and Pedersen* Case reveals in a similar way that "it is in the discharge of a *natural duty* towards their children – parents being primarily responsible for the ´education and teaching` of their children – that parents may require the State to respect their religious and philosophical convictions"(paragraph no. 52)

22 The Magistrate Gimeno Sendra regrets this in a personal and dissenting opinion, for whom the non-enrollment does imply a breach of the right to education.

23 The Second Court of the Spanish Supreme Court is the Criminal Chamber.

24 Cf. Judgement of the Spanish Supreme Court no. 1669/1994, of 30th October 1994, Second Chamber. Not yet published at the time of drafting this report.

The antecedents were the following. A decision of Barcelona's Provincial Court had acquitted the same parents of the crimes of fraud, psychic injuries inflicted on the children, building an unlawful assembly. The Attorney General brought an action before the Spanish Supreme Court, an appeal against the discharged decision, for considering that there had existed a mistake in the weight of evidence.

The Spanish Supreme Court dismissed all the complaints alleged by the Attorney General in its decision no. 1669/1994, of 30th October 1994, confirming therefore the acquital of Barcelona's Provincial Court. The above-mentioned judgement displays unquestionable interest, hence it contains evocative statements about the right to education and the freedom to teach.

In one way, the Spanish Supreme Court emphasizes that in a democratic and plural society the principle of the freedom of instruction prevails, and does not breach its extension to the existence of certain objectives and aims. In this sense, it declares that education "should be directed towards the full development of the human personality and to train citizens in standards of tolerance and coexistence".[25] I think, certainly that these objectives do not act as limits but define the freedom of instruction itself.

In another way, the Spanish Supreme Court declares that the acknowledgment of values like religious, ideological and conscience freedoms allows parents to choose children's religious and moral training which turns out to be more in tune with their convictions. With the result that the existence of different models or educational systems can be possible. According to the declaration "further from the rejection or disapproval that the pedagogical methods based on introversion and authoritarianism could give rise to, we must maintain that the criminal right should be removed from these debates and avoid the temptation of approaching in a light, insecure and dangerous way, the everlasting discussion about the suitability of educational standards".

Now then, the religious and moral training – like education in general – should be adequate, that is to say, directed towards the full development of the human personality. We can ask ourselves if this is possible in some sects. For example, in this case there were fewer problems detected of emotional imbalance and integration difficulties with other children of their age. Likewise future problems were forecast in "adapting and integration in a competitive society". Despite this, the Spanish Supreme Court did not consider that it could charge the parents with the crime of injury for psychic damages.

Another idea highlighted by the Spanish Supreme Court is that the basic right to education commits the public powers to the task of contributing and helping towards its real fulfilment, without that implying interfering in the parental educational right. Likewise it declares that the means set up by the State are not exclusive nor excluding, "in a way standards based on the teaching in one's own abode so long as it always satisfies the necessary training of the minors."

In short, the judgement declares that the parents behaviour is not criminal, but that it could be rejected morally, ethically and socially. It even points out the

25 See article 26.2 of the Universal Declaration of Human Rights and article 13.1 of the International Covenant on Economic, Social and Cultural Rights. The Spanish Supreme Court expresses itself in the same terms.

possibility of a reaction in the framework of the civil set of rules to avoid damaging consequences for the minor.

It is true that the appeal to Criminal Law can only be justified when the sects' behaviour affects legal goods worthy of protection and it is not possible to call on other less destructive instruments of guardianship – principle of minimun intervention, fragmentary character and "ultima ratio" of the Criminal Law –. Nevertheless, the behaviour – not yet criminal – of some parents who based their "parental educationall right" not to choose an "adequate" education for their children could be viewed" as an illegal or undesirable act from other sectors of the legal set of instruments of social politics".[26]

III. Conclusions

In my opinion, the idea that the parents belong to a sect is an insufficient circumstance *on its own* to determine whatever measures in favour of the children – like the limitation of the paternal educational right – finds support in the three declarations studied. Certainly, the fact of considering such a circumstance sufficient would imply a discrimination based on religion.

Nevertheless, to assess *in the specific case* the forseeable negative consequences for the welfare of the children stemmed from the doctrine and beliefs of the sect of which the parent is a member does not bring with it a discrimination because of religion. Here is where the type of sect will have to be distinguished because not all turn out to be equally dangerous. Likewise the particular way of living the faith of the parent must be taken into consideration. All with the aim of protecting the full development of the child's personality, or more extensively, the higher interest of the same.[27]

26 Cf. J. M. TAMARIT SUMALLA, "Las sectas y el derecho penal" in VVAA, *Aspectos Socio-Jurídicos de las Sectas desde una perspectiva comparada*, the Oñati Institute for the Sociology of Law, 1991, p.279–281.

27 Precisely the higher interest of the child is the spirit that inspires the Convention on the Rights of the Child (1989).

Michael Corrado, Chapel Hill, N.C.

Self-Defense, Punishment, and the State's Right to Detain

Preventive detention is detention by the state of persons thought to be dangerous to the safety of the community. It differs from detention administered as punishment in that it is aimed neither at retribution nor at deterrence of others, but only at incapacitation of the dangerous person. It may, in practice, be limited to persons who have been convicted of crimes, but it need not be. It differs from involuntary commitment of the mentally ill in that persons preventively detained are believed to be legally sane, rational, and competent. It is true that it depends upon predictions of dangerousness, but the mere predictability of danger does not all by itself mean a lack of responsibility on the part of the actor. And it differs from quarantine in that the danger to be prevented, in the case of preventive detention, is the likelihood that the dangerous person would knowingly and intentionally cause harm, while in the case of quarantine it is the likelihood that a contagiously ill person would unwittingly communicate her disease to others.

The question is whether such practices as quarantine and preventive detention can be morally justified. They require such justification, of course, because they constitute an enormous intrusion into the personal freedom of the persons detained. While preventive detention is not intended as punishment, and may not be intended to carry any stigma, the truth is that detention as a potential criminal does carry with it much of the stigma of incarceration for past crimes. And while the legislature's intention may be to make life more comfortable for the detainee than for the convicted criminal, there are limits to what can be done to make confinement bearable.

I. Arguments against Preventive Detention[1]

A. Inaccuracy of Prediction

Among those who believe that preventive detention cannot be justified, some, like Alan Dershowitz, hold that while it might be justifiable if predictions of dangerousness could be made with relative certainty, such predictions are by their very nature unreliable. It is of course notoriously difficult to predict who will commit a violent crime in the future. Using current methods, the best estimate is that there would be at least one "false positive" for every "true positive;" that is, we would preventively detain at least one person who would never commit a crime in the future for every person we detain correctly. That rate of error would seem to many to be unacceptably high; it is much higher, for example, than the rate of error that we would find acceptable in convicting people of crimes.

1 Some of the arguments of this section are treated in much greater detail in my "Punishment and the Wild Beast of Prey," 86 *Jotnal of Criminal Law and Criminology* 778 (1996).

It may be argued, however, that since such persons are to be detained because of the risk they create, it is wrong to speak of persons who are dangerous but would not in fact commit a crime as wrongly detained; to speak in that way imports notions of desert which are out of place in a discussion of preventive detention. The point of preventive detention is to incapacitate persons who create a threat of harm; and for each of the persons who are going to be detained, there is a 100% chance that person presents a risk of harm.

In addition, the argument that we would not accept that rate of accuracy when conviction for a past crime was at issue supposes that preventive detention and punishment for past crimes are comparable in this respect; but that may not be so. When the question is conviction for a past crime, one harm is already committed and cannot be changed whatever the outcome of the judicial process; the only danger is that of convicting an innocent person, or of letting a guilty person off without his proper punishment. (Keep in mind that the purpose of punishment is to punish past crime, not prevent future ones; so the harm that may be committed in the future by guilty persons who are let off is not a consideration, when punishment is at issue.) In the case of preventive detention, however, there are other harms to be considered – harms to those who will be injured if persons who will commit crimes are let go. If there is no deeper objection to preventive detention than the inaccuracy of punishment, we should be aware that there is no reason to think of that inaccuracy as having the same consequences as inaccuracy in conviction. The state's interest in making sure that someone who has committed a crime gets his due punishment is surely much less compelling than the state's interest in preventing new injuries to an innocent victim. If a group of ten can be identified, six of whom will commit murder if allowed to go free – though we don't know which of the ten they are – then if we detain them all, we perhaps wrongly detain four; but if we let them all go, six people will die. If the only concern is the risk of "false positives," then surely the likelihood that four will lose their freedom must be weighed against the likelihood that six will lose their lives.

B. Respect for Autonomy

Are there other reasons for rejecting preventive detention, then, reasons that come into play even if the prediction of dangerousness could be made more accurate? That is, is there some reason why we should not preventively detain even the one who will commit a dangerous act in the future, let alone the one who will not? One who believes that preventive detention could not be justified even if predictions were perfectly accurate is Andrew von Hirsch. Von Hirsch bases his rejection of preventive detention upon the high value we place upon human freedom. Since preventive detention interferes with human freedom and with our ability to choose how we will live our lives, and since it deprives people of freedom for reasons they have no control over and cannot choose to change, he finds it morally unacceptable. "[S]uch a scheme would entail undue sacrifice of individual freedom and dignity."[2]

2 Andrew von Hirsch, "Prediction of Criminal Conduct and Preventive Confinement of Convicted Persons, 21 *Buffalo Law Review* 717 (1972).

Do we in fact value individual choice so highly? The evidence that we do, according to von Hirsch, is that we do not incarcerate people until they have made a choice to break the law:

> [T]he choice – whether to engage in such conduct and chance the punishment – is left up to the individual; the state will not intervene unless he is found to have violated the law. By giving him that choice, society risks that the individual will make the wrong selection, to the community's detriment. ... Nevertheless, we choose to withhold the coercive power of the law until after the event. In so doing, we may incur the costs of certain anti-social conduct that might have been precluded by state preventive action. But that is felt to be well worth the assurance given to individual freedom.[3]

But we do not in fact withhold the coercive power of the law until after the choice has been made; more and more the community is insisting on putting dangerous people away to prevent crimes not yet committed. The argument must therefore be intended to show that we *should* withhold detention until the law has been broken. The argument then comes to this: Since we value individual choice highly, we should withhold detention until a crime has been committed; it is well worth the risk.

The problem is that the major premise in this argument might support an entirely different conclusion. If our respect for freedom entails the moral imperative to increase the amount of freedom in the world – a kind of consequentialism of freedom – then preventive detention might be morally acceptable. For it might be that, by preventing crime, preventive detention would increase the amount of freedom in the world (measured, perhaps, in terms of actual alternatives available to individuals), and would increase it over every alternative available to the state.

If, on the other hand, our respect for freedom means that we must protect existing freedom, regardless of the upshot, then it may indeed conflict with preventive detention. But the extent to which we should protect existing freedom is clearly limited: we permit the state to tax, to jail convicted criminals, to educate children compulsorily, to force people to serve in the military, and for many of these things we think the good to be accomplished justifies the deprivation of freedom. What the argument lacks is some reason for thinking that preventive detention is different from these things. The burden, of course, ought to be on the other side; those who favor preventive detention ought to have to show why it is acceptable. But it is clear that the argument from the value of human freedom gives no reason to think that such a demonstration would be impossible.

II. Arguments for Preventive Detention[4]

A. Preventive Detention, Punishment, and Self-Defense

Is there then, on the other side, a good reason for thinking that preventive detention is morally acceptable? Attempts have been made to justify the practice

3 Von Hirsch, *id.*, at 746–747.

4 The argument of this section is the subject of a debate with Michael Davis, to be published in *Criminal Justice Ethics*.

either as punishment, or as a form of self-defense. Michael Davis, for one, believes that preventive detention ought to be viewed as punishment. Detention cannot, of course, be seen as punishment deserved for future crimes, differing from ordinary punishment only in being given in advance. For if the detention is successful, the future crime will never occur, and the punishment will not be deserved.

Davis, on the other hand, believes that preventive detention may be understood as punishment for a past crime – the crime of reckless endangerment. If the person who is predicted to commit very serious crimes in the future is made aware of this prediction, then (assuming that present detention is the only way to prevent those crimes) either he will offer to have himself committed voluntarily, or he will be guilty of reckless endangerment.

> [T]he wrongdoing that justifies preventive detention is not in the future. Insofar as dangerousness is a form of reckless endangerment, dangerousness is itself wrongdoing... . To be found dangerous – for example, to be found to be unjustifiably putting others in great danger of serious bodily harm – is to stand morally condemned.... Dangerousness is a moral category.[5]

If he is guilty of reckless endangerment, then he may be detained as punishment.

The sentence for reckless endangerment is of course limited; but if the sentence runs out and the detainee is still unwilling to commit himself, he may be sentenced again, and so on indefinitely. Either way he cannot complain about indefinite detention; either he has consented to it, or he is guilty of a crime. Thus the state does him no wrong if it simply chooses to lock him up involuntarily; the only question is whether civil commitment or imprisonment is the less restrictive alternative. If we prefer seeing preventive detention as self-defense to seeing it as punishment, the state does the detainee no wrong by locking him up to prevent him from continuing an ongoing harm.

Since the conclusion of the argument is that we do not wrong those we preventively detain, it would seem to follow that we do not owe them compensation either. In some jurisdictions, by contrast, compensation is provided to those who are quarantined because of a dangerous disease. The thinking, apparently, is that people so quarantined, through no fault of their own, are being confined for the common good; and therefore by analogy with the taking of property for the common good, they ought to be compensated. Schoeman, for one, has argued that preventive detention is comparable to quarantine, and has suggested (without argument) the possibility of compensation. Lionel Frankel has taken the same position, on the grounds that compensation would "serve to vindicate the compensated individual's dignity and status as a person."[6] But while he thinks compensation would be a good thing, Frankel gives no reason for believing that the state is morally obliged to pay compensation. If the dangerous person is guilty of the crime of reckless endangerment, as Davis believes, we have taken

5 Michael Davis, "Arresting the White Death," 94 *APA Philosophy and Medicine Newsletter* 92 95 (1995).

6 Lionel Frankel, "Preventive Restraints and Just Compensation," 78 *Yale Law Journal* 229 (1968); Ferdinand Schoeman, "On Incapacitating the Dangerous," 16 *Philosophical Quarterley* 27 (1979).

away nothing to which he has a right if we lock him up, and there is no reason to believe that compensation is his by right. I think that Frankel and Schoeman are right about this, and that compensation is owed. This paper is, in fact, an essay in search of an argument for that position.

B. Preventive Detention and Compensation

But setting all that aside, the key point is this: The conclusion of Davis's argument is that we may punish the dangerous person for reckless endangerment; and of course if the argument is sound it would also follow that we could act in self-defense against him, to detain him. For what punishment requires is that the person punished be responsible for a crime; and a person who continues to act in ways that make him responsible for crimes may be stopped in the name of self-defense or defense of others. But is the dangerous person responsible for recklessly endangering others? I do not think that he is.

When can our present actions make us responsible for harms that might occur in the future? One thing that would make me presently responsible for something I do in the future would be for me to cause it now, or now to make it very difficult to avoid the harm at that later time. If I take a strong antihistamine, and then proceed to drive my car in heavy traffic, where I know or should know of the sleep-inducing effects of the antihistamine, I may fall asleep and have an accident that severely injures someone. The act that makes me responsible for the harm that occurs is not falling asleep, over which I may have no control at the time; my responsibility for the harm goes back to the time of taking the medication and setting out to drive my car. It would not be unreasonable to punish me for trying to drive, even before I injured anyone; and it would not be unreasonable to stop me from driving.

But the competent person who fails to have himself detained to prevent future harm has done nothing that would make it impossible or difficult to comply later on with the law, and so has not made the harm difficult or impossible to avoid. Notice that the result would be different here if the detainee was dangerous precisely because he periodically lost all control and went on violent rampages in which he injured people. By not locking himself up now he may be said to be doing something, at this moment, that would make him responsible for the harm that would result if he were allowed to remain free. In extreme cases such a person might be punishable if he failed to detain himself (in less extreme cases he could reasonably be placed under a legal obligation to stay out of provocative situations); and we would certainly be entitled to detain him in self-defense. But that is not the case we are considering. Our assumption is that the dangerous person who is the subject of preventive detention will cause harm some time in the future freely and voluntarily, and will not be out of control. A person who is sufficiently out of control not to be responsible for his own actions is or ought to be considered legally insane; and someone who knows that he is harboring a person who is periodically insane has special obligations. But the question of preventive detention is not about commitment of the insane. It is about the sane and competent, and a sane and competent person does not now cause his future free actions; otherwise they would not be free. Therefore that cannot be the ground for saying that he is now responsible for the harm he will cause in the future.

But although he does not now cause his future actions, he does not now prevent them either. Is that enough to make him presently responsible for them? Mere failure to prevent future harm does not make us responsible for it, in the relevant sense: it does not make us morally liable to punishment and action in self-defense. It may make us liable to an action of necessity; but if the justification is necessity, something is owed to the person whose resources are seized. Since the actor is not responsible for the harm that would have occurred, the actor is wronged when his resources are seized against his will. Some sort of compensation is due.

Into which category does the dangerous person's failure to detain himself fall? Does it make him responsible for his future actions? Or is it merely a failure of beneficence? There are a variety of legal relationships that create the special obligation to prevent harm, and they can serve as a way into the moral question of responsibility. By and large, these relationships fit the following pattern: X is responsible for preventing harm to Y from an aggressor Z when: (1) Y is at some disadvantage in the matter of preventing the harm from Z; (2) X is in a better position to prevent the harm from Z; and (3) either (a) it is because of some action of X that Y is at a disadvantage; or (b) X has somehow undertaken a contractual sort of responsibility for Y's safety (e.g., he has promised to look out for him); or (c) X is responsible for the actions of the aggressor Z.

If the dangerous person is presently responsible for any harm that would befall others because of his failure to prevent it, then, is it because it falls into one of these patterns? In particular, is one of the three subparts of (3) satisfied? As to (3)(a), no present action of the dangerous person puts the person who would be harmed in the future at a disadvantage, unless it is his failure to detain himself. But to rest responsibility on the failure to detain would be to assume the thing we want to prove, and it would give everyone a special obligation to protect others from harm. If I knock someone unconscious on the road, I may be responsible if he is run over by a car; but if I merely observe someone lying on the road, I do not incur the special obligation to help just because my failure to help would have put him at a disadvantage. Otherwise there would be no distinction between cases in which the special obligation exists and cases in which it doesn't.

Nor has the dangerous person undertaken any special obligation (ordinarily) for the future victim's safety, as required by (3)(b). If there is any part of (3) that applies to this case, it must be (3)(c); the dangerous person is presently responsible for the actions of the aggressor – who happens in this case to be himself. But if we could assume that the dangerous person was presently responsible for his future actions, we would not be on this chase in the first place. The person who argues that we have a responsibility for (in the sense of being presently punishable for) our future free actions has the burden of showing why that is so; and we have been down a list of possible candidates so far without success. And if there were some reason for thinking us responsible for our future actions, we would not need to rest responsibility on our failure to prevent the harm. I conclude that the mere failure to prevent future harm does not make the dangerous person presently responsible for harms he will cause in the future, unless we have already shown that he is responsible for his future actions.

I suppose it may be objected that I am trying to explain what is straightforward through what is obscure. Perhaps what makes us responsible for our future actions is simply that they are ours. But is there any argument to support this suggestion? An argument might proceed like this: Though the likelihood of future harm does not arise out of any present choice (as it would have, had I already done something to cause it, or had I failed in some special obligation I had to prevent it), it does arise out of the character of the dangerous person. It is his character – that is, the collection of tendencies he has to act in certain ways in certain circumstances – that makes him likely to harm others. Now it is at least conceivable that I could in part be responsible for the character of individuals – I may in part be responsible for the character my son has, for example – and to the extent I am responsible for their characters I would be responsible for what they do. But though it is conceivable, it is very unlikely that I could be responsible enough for someone else's character to make me responsible, through that fact alone, for his voluntarily committed crimes; and in any case we are much less likely to be responsible for our own characters than we are to be responsible for the character of another.

To make the character argument is to hold people responsible for their characters, and I do not think that is a plausible position. Indeed, if we could hold people responsible for their characters, we could punish them for their characters, and would not have to worry about responsibility for future crimes at all. But that is an abhorrent outcome. I do not think, therefore, that the way to save the argument is to appeal to the claim that the dangerous person is responsible for his future actions because he is responsible for his character that makes them likely.

There may be other ways in which to show that we are responsible for our future actions, but I do not know what they are. Lacking any such argument, I would conclude, at least tentatively, that a dangerous person is not responsible for reckless endangerment either, and hence cannot be punished, or even restrained in self-defense. It does not follow, however, that he may not be detained. As in the case of necessity, it may be that he is called upon to allow the community to use his resources for the public good. If he is so called upon, however, he should be compensated. He may not be punished because he has not done anything that would justify punishment, whether the explanation be that he has not forfeited his rights, or that he does not deserve punishment. If he could be detained in self-defense, the intrusion would not interfere with his rights since he would in a sense be interfering with his own freedom by attempting to bring about harm that he is not entitled to bring about. Since neither of those two justifications fits the case, depriving him of freedom in a sense wrongs him. If it is justified nevertheless because of the great good it will do, then there ought to be compensation.[7]

7 The subject matter of this paper takes on a special relevance in the United States this year. The United States has decided to hear *Kansas v. Hendricks*, testing the constitutionality of a Kansas statute providing for detention of sexual offenders *after* they have served their criminal sentences.

John G. Francis and Leslie P. Francis, Salt Lake City, UT

Land Use In European and North American Communities: The Limits to Autonomy

Introduction

Environmental quality is a major value component of politics in advanced industrial societies on both sides of the Atlantic. From the protection of wetlands and watersheds, to limitations on land use, to promotion of air quality, environmental regulation has become a staple of political debate. When regulation limits economically valuable property uses, for example by restricting development in a fragile coastal zone or by requiring dedication of green spaces, property owners may claim that their rights of autonomy have been violated. A frequent legal response in the United States is to seek compensation as a condition of the regulation, through the doctrine of inverse condemnation. This strategy has become quite popular recently in the United States among landowners challenging governmental activities generally and environmental intervention particularly. Such inverse condemnation litigation, to the extent that it is successful, has the significant potential to curtail state efforts to realize environmental values, particularly in times of budgetary constraint.

In an age of considerable convergence in social and economic policy among the nations of North America and Europe, the policy and law of takings are notably divergent. In the United States, the underlying conception of property is individual rather than social. Demands for compensation based on the constitution have gained increasing legal recognition. In Europe, by contrast, property rights are more likely to be seen as socially embedded. Regulatory takings are more likely to be handled by negotiation and balancing than seen as constitutional absolutes. The result in Europe does not preclude, of course, sharp debates between land developers and conservationists, but it allows the discussion to remain in the context of public policy rather than being framed as a battle between state power and individual rights. This paper explores explanations for these differences and concludes that the ongoing American emphasis on individual constitutional rights has obfuscated important public policy debate on land use issues.

Compensation as Individual Right or Public Policy?

On both sides of the Atlantic, there is little opposition, either legal or political, to the principle that property owners should be compensated when their land is taken outright for a public purpose, such as the construction of a public reservoir. Where divergence begins is in the understanding of the basis and limits of the property right. In the United States, property is seen as a basic individual right, but in Europe, it is more likely to be seen as socially generated and constrained.

ARSP-Beiheft 67. Rex Martin u. Gerhard Sprenger (Hgg.)
(17th. IVR-Weltkongreß Bologna 1995, Bd. 1). © 1997 Franz Steiner Verlag Stuttgart

Even in France, where the revolutionary constitutional tradition announced principled opposition to the power of the state to take property, it is a long-established principle of civil law that the state may take property and is obligated to pay compensation when it does so. The essential understanding of this constitutional tradition is that ownership is signified by title and that when the state assumes title it thus takes over ownership just as any buyer would. It is then undisputed that the state must pay compensation when it condemns property for a redevelopment project or a new road. This is a quite limited understanding, however, and does not take a position on the constitutional significance of other governmental actions affecting land use or value, such as whether the government may require the land owner to dedicate portions of the property to a public right of way.

Property as Individual Right: The United States

In the United States, the Fifth Amendment to the Constitution provides that private property may not be taken for public use without just compensation. This federal constitutional requirement both establishes the government's ability to exercise the power of eminent domain and sets limits to that power: it may be exercised only for public uses, and it requires compensation for the individual rights thus lost. Beyond outright takings, answers to questions about the extent to which regulation requires compensation have been largely left to the courts as a matter of constitutional interpretation.

The touchstone of American inverse condemnation doctrine was Justice Holmes's open-ended observation in 1922 that when regulation goes "too far," it becomes a taking.[1] In the decades after Pennsylvania Coal, American courts were reluctant ever to find that state regulation constituted a taking and inverse condemnation litigation was comparatively dormant. On the other hand, when states took outright possession of property interests, even the minimal amount of space needed to lay television cable, compensation was regarded as mandatory.[2]

The extended drive towards environmental regulation in the United States, however, did not begin until the late 1960s and afterwards. The ultimate political result was significant opposition to an environmental regulatory regime seen as hostile to property rights, and renewed efforts to use constitutional doctrine on behalf of owners. This result has been defended by commentators who see individual property rights as foundational, and government activities as limited by and to their protection.[3] Opposition to government regulation has also led to the introduction of bills in Congress requiring compensation whenever regulatory activity significantly reduces property value; it is not at this point clear whether any of these bills will be enacted.[4]

1 Pennsylvania Coal Co. v. Mahon, 260 U.S. 393 (1922).
2 Loretto v. Teleprompter Manhattan CATV Corp., 458 U.S. 419 (1982).
3 Richard Epstein, *Takings: Private Property and the Power of Eminent Domain*, 1985.
4 Richard Miniter, "You Just Can't Take it Anymore: America's Property Rights Revolt," *Policy Review* 1994.

In the last few years, litigation seeking compensation for regulatory diminution of property value has achieved some noticeable success. The United States Supreme Court has held that conditioning a building permit on the dedication of public beachfront access,[5] or conditioning a redevelopment permit on open space and landscaping requirements, are takings requiring compensation.[6] These two cases might reasonably be categorized as involving governmental invasions on land on behalf of the public; however, the Supreme Court has also revisited the territory of Justice Holmes's pronouncement about the limits of regulation. In Lucas v. South Carolina Coastal Council,[7] the Court held that the state must also pay compensation when regulation deprives an owner of all economically beneficial use of land. Lucas was a developer who had purchased several beachfront lots in an area that was subject to intermittent erosion and unstable vegetation. At the time of the purchase, coastal zone regulation was under serious discussion. Shortly thereafter, the state included Lucas's lots in a protected zone in which building was prohibited. Lucas's suit argued that the state had deprived him of all economically valuable use of the property; the United States Supreme Court agreed, and concluded that compensation was mandated.

The Nollan, Lucas, and Dolan decisions have given increased impetus to efforts in the United States such as the "Wise Use Movement" to employ the constitution to block environmental regulations limiting land use. These efforts have taken place both at the federal level and at the state level, where constitutional provisions requiring the state to pay compensation for "taking or damaging" property are thought to give owners even more constitutional protection. It is a fair prediction that the constitutional understanding of individual property rights as paramount will significantly constrain both federal and state efforts at environmental regulation in the next few years.

Property as Socially Embedded: European Examples. In Europe, the issue has been framed quite differently from the individualist conceptualization in the United States. One illustration is the European Convention on Human Rights, Article I, which upholds property as an economic right, but subject to the right of state control in accord with the general interest. In interpreting this provision, the European Court of Human Rights has deferred to national constitutional understandings. Although the issues are of course complex, and doctrine is not uniform, these understandings are generally much more deferential to legislative process than current doctrine in the United States.

Current French land use planning legislation dates back to 1967 and 1976, and was significantly reshaped by the law on decentralization of administrative authority in 1983. In France, there are competing interests with respect to development and preservation of the countryside in areas sought after for vacation homes, such as the French Alps, or areas seeking economic development, such as the Southwest. These issues are ompounded by ambiguities over just who is responsible for planning in a context of

5 Nollan v. California Coastal Commission, 483 U.S. 825 (1987).
6 Dolan v. City of Tigard, 62 *U.S.L.W.* 4576 (1994).
7 112 S.Ct. 2886 (1992).

decentralization.[8] The underlying principle in French planning is that development is impermissible unless it takes place under a land use plan framed at the smallest unit of subnational government, the commune.[9] Although the initiative is left for the commune in developing a land use plan, a major issue in France is the role of the state in local land use plans, particularly when projects have national implications such as the location of motorways or the protection of areas of great historical significance. In general, land use regulation limiting development or requiring dedications for particular uses does not require compensation, although the obligation may be extended by statute.[10] The French debate, in sum, is framed in terms of values and institutional structures that ought to guide land use, and not as an constitutional exercise.

To take another European example, Britain has one of the more comprehensive land use frameworks in Europe. The Town and Country Planning Act of l947 incorporates both controls over usable lands and the design and form of built environments. A main feature of the Act is the provision that effectively nationalizes rights to develop land: if a property owner applies for permission for a new development of his or her property, and the permission is refused, no compensation is normally payable.[11] Nonetheless, in Britain since 1947 there have been sharp political debates over the aims and direction of land use planning. One of the more controversial subjects has been agricultural land. The l947 Act assumed the importance of farming, not only for preserving the countryside but also for supplying the nation with food. The Act therefore gave farmers considerable latitude to do with their land as they saw fit as long as agricutural yield remained the objective.

By the l970s and l980s, there was strong interest in some sectors of the political community to restrict what farmers could do in what were judged to be environmentally sensitive areas, and to open other economic activities up for consideration in rural areas. In the Town and Country Planning Act of l990, the Planning (Hazardous Substances) Act of l990, and the Planning Compensation Act of l99l, regulatory regimes that had been created for urban areas were extended to agricultural areas. Over the years, compensation packages were devised in some areas to provide farmers with subsidies to abandon practices judged harmful to the local environment. These packages are in effect state compensation, but they developed as negotiated legislative responses to the expansion of regulatory regimes, rather than as constitutional mandates.

To take a further example, there have been recurring debates in Britain over both the availability of housing and its affordability. The Conservatives have pressed for deregulation and greater reliance on market mechanisms to address the problem. Labour, operating within the context of planning, has in the past created state agencies to purchase land for housing development to address

8 Vivien A. Schmidt, *Democratizing France: The Political and Administrative History of Decentralization*, 1990.

9 See Chabason, "French land-use planning system," in Whitby and Ollerershaw, eds., *Land Use and the European Environment*, 1989.

10 Picard, "Expropriation in France," in Erasmus, ed., *Compensation for Expropriation: A Comparative Study*, 1990.

11 Simon Ball and Stuart Bell, *Enviromental Law*, 2d ed. 1994, pp. l79–l80.

problems of availability and cost. Both solutions have been problematic. For the Conservatives, a major problem was the rapid rise in housing costs; for Labour, it was the considerable expense to the Treasury of buying land.[12] But these controversies, too, have been seen as issues in public policy and the accommodation of conflicting goals, such as the respective values of farming, environmental protection, or affordable housing.

In Germany, the constitution provides for property rights but recognizes that property imposes duties and that its uses should serve the public weal.[13] Expropriation is permitted in service of the public weal, if compensation is paid; compensation is to be based on an equitable balance between the public interest and the interests of those affected.[14] There is a clear tension in this understanding of property in the German constitution: property is protected, but its protection is constrained by the public welfare. Property is thus understood in a dual fashion; claims to ownership do not preclude social claims to usefulness. Land use regulation is a significant characteristic of property ownership in Germany.[15] The structure of such regulation is quite elaborate and involves, in coordinated fashion, every level of German government, federal, state, and local. There is a national land use plan which provides special protection for the natural environmental and for agriculture. A feature of this plan, not found in the United States, is the commitment to universal standards for quality of life throughout Germany, regardless of local conditions. The impressive range of social constraints on property in Germany are simply how property rights are understood; the taking of property in an outright way, on the other hand, is what requires compensation.

In his dissertation, Ben Crum has analyzed a series of German judicial decisions concerning the respective rights of allotment garden tenants and owners of the property; these cases are a particularly apt illustration of the German social conception of property.[16] Since the end of the first world war, there has been recurring public policy interest in providing urban residents with garden plots. During the 1930s and the second world war, the German government looked for inexpensive sources of food, prompting state interest in urban farm plots. In 1942, for example, there was a decree calling for urban land to be placed in agricultural production. The decree strengthened the position of lessees who were using the land for gardens.

In the 1950s, under very different political and economic conditions, property owners, interested in urban development rather than urban gardens, began to challenge the prerogatives of the lessees. In the absence of legislation, initial court rulings tended to side with the property owners at the expense of the lessees' continued rights to use the garden plots. Over the following decades, however, there was a steady growth in the number, size, and political

12 Andrew Cox, *Adversary Politics and Land: the conflict over land and property policy in post-war Britain*, 1984.

13 German Constitution, Article 14 (1), (2).

14 German Constitution, Article 14(3), Article 15.

15 Hartmut Dieterich, Egbert Dransfeld, and Winrich Voss, *Urban Land and Property Markets in Germany*, 1993, pp. 56–104.

16 Ben Crum, "*Property in Germany*," dissertation draft 1995.

consequences of environmental groups in Germany.[17] During the 1980s, responding to the green movement, the federal Parliament passed legislation favorable to sustaining allottment gardens in urban areas. In turn, a new generation of property owners challenged the rights of the urban gardeners to renew their leases. The German constitutional court, in reviewing appeals of rulings by lower courts on the renewal rights of the lessees, sided with the allotment tenants.

Ben Crum describes the court's decisions as follows: "The justification that the government gives for the special status of stable allotments is not primarily driven from the need to protect the tenant but rather from administrative considerations."[18] Crum argues that the constitutional court was not driven in its consideration of the allotment cases by the basic right to individual property. Rather, it took as its obligation the defense of legislatively-enacted policies that sought to secure the public interest in maintaining allotment gardens. The difference between the earlier decisions that had sided with the owners, and the the later decisions, was the intervening actions of the Parliament. In short, the legislative understanding of the social uses of property became paramount in sorting out the competing claims of lessor and lessee in the allotment garden issue.

This discussion of property issues in Britain, France, and Germany contrasts rather sharply with the battles in the United States over wetland protection. In the United States, the broader social claim that wetlands might be endangered by the uses to which a property owner intends to put his or her property is trumped by the paramount recognition of individual claims to property as a right. The British and French cases provide examples of legislatively determined compensation. The German case demonstrates how a constitutional tradition can function by joining both individual and social claims to property through legislative enactment.

Property and Values

A number of different evaluative and institutional considerations have contributed to the distinctive American understanding of property rights and the takings issue. At the outset, it is important to understand the strong and pivotal role played by the American judiciary in the formation of the law of takings. Given the uniquely powerful role of courts in the United States, it is not unexpected for judicial action to have framed the renewed discussion of land use legislation as regulatory regimes that are a form of takings. When courts frame the issue, however, they do so in terms of their particular institutional competence – the protection of individual rights, rather than the achievement of political negotiation and compromise.

Attitudes towards government involvement are another major factor underlying the American understanding of the takings debate. Agreement on government

17 Eckhard Rehbinder, "Rethinking Environmental Policy," in Geoffrey Smith et al., *Developments in German Politics*, 1992, pp. 227–46.

18 Ben Crum, "*Property in Germany*," dissertation draft 1995.

involvement in resolving land use conflicts appears to be harder to achieve in the United States than in Europe. American ideology couples a tradition of great skepticism about the role of government with a view of property as a paradigmatic expression of individualism. To be sure, on both sides of the Atlantic there has been a rise in skepticism about the competence of government, compared to forty years ago. Nonetheless, Europeans began with a much higher level of acceptance of statist frameworks for solutions than did the United States, certainly in the area of land use questions.

American attitudes towards the importance of property rights are another critical difference. The ideology of property as foundational to American individualism is an ongoing theme in American political life. This ideology is mirrored in American economic life. The volume and level of turnover of real estate transactions is far more significant as a factor in the American economy than is the case in many European nations.

The values underlying disputes about environmental regulation also differ between the United States and Europe. On both sides of the Atlantic, quite similar environmental issues are advanced by environmental groups and governments, most notably air quality, water quality, opposition to nuclear power, and concern over hazardous wastes. But there are sharp thematic differences. In the United States, vast tracts of lands are still relatively undisturbed by human development. The notion of wilderness as the absence of human communities is an important theme in American environmental politics. For some, undisturbed nature is a celebration of a world that is enormously valuable because it is disappearing yet is critical to the health of the planet. With this understanding comes the recognition that nature has claims to be left undisturbed that are at least as weighty as claims that human development is necessary for the advancement of human society. A sharply contrasting interpretation of wilderness is found in the tradition of American individualism: cowboys on the range, adventurous miners striking it rich, and modern pioneers moving to the wilds to escape the problems of urban life and, by transforming the land, helping to build better lives for themselves and their families. In these images, the promise of economic achievement is conjoined with a moral critique of urban life.

The American land use debate has taken place at an ideological level not found in the environmental debates in Europe. In Europe, land use conflicts often arise between maintaining rural life, or at least village life in relatively less developed areas, and pursuing competing demands of economic development and recreation. The stakes are high, of course, but the debate lacks the sweeping conflicts over competing conceptions of the importance of the individual and the location of humanity within nature that are found in the United States.

Thus in the United States, unlike in Europe, both institutional structures and values have fed understanding of the takings issue as a matter of absolute, individual constitutional rights. Lines are drawn and entrenched: property is either taken or regulated; a regulation is either a taking requiring compensation, or it is not. The impact of this understanding is profound: land use policy is taken out of the range of public policy, accommodation, and compromise. American politics thus lacks resources that European polities can call on to deal with environmental issues.

American difficulties in handling wetlands protection are a good example of the problems created by this absolutist approach. Legislation protecting the ecological value of sensitive lands may make any kind of economic use of the land virtually impossible. Some American courts, reasoning that the land has not been taken outright, and the landowner retains some use, however minimal, have refused to find a taking under these circumstances.[19] Other courts have required full compensation for the highest and best use foregone.[20] The former cases may impose the costs of achieving important social values disproportionately on landowners unlucky in their topography.[21] The latter cases may make it almost impossible for governments to achieve environmental values in the face of existing structures of property rights.[22]

In Europe, by contrast, legislative accommodations of these kinds of conflicts are the norm. The German constitution's requirement that when compensation is to be paid it should be based on an equitable adjustment between the public welfare and the impact on affected landowners is an invitation to just this kind of accommodation. Recent legislative efforts in the United States, on the other hand, seek only to strengthen the hand of the individual landowner to receive compensation for reductions in the use value of the property. Although these legislative efforts are an effort to address the question of fairness to land owners, they do so with no effort to balance the impact of regulation on an individual landholder with concern for the public welfare.

Communitarian objections to the discourse of rights have been largely directed against personal rights such as reproductive liberty. These objections have typically ignored the economic sphere, where compromise is both more feasible and more desirable. Mary Ann Glendon's recent general critique of the absolutism of rights is to some extent an exception to this generalization, for Glendon includes individualist accounts of property in her critique.[23]

Yet even Glendon fails to appreciate the force of recent takings doctrine in the United States. Glendon views the Supreme Court as devaluing property rights in comparison to personal rights; we have argued in contrast that the current trend is towards a kind of absolutism of property rights not found in western Europe. Recent American treatment of the takings issue is an example of rights talk in a problematic context.

Moreover, it is rights talk with the potential for a deeply problematic future. The concern for fairness expressed in takings law is that individuals with reasonable and settled expectations not be forced to bear extensively disproportional costs of achieving an important social good, such as protection from environmental degradation.[24] As American law entrenches the right to

19 The best known example is Just v. Marinette County, 201 N.W. 2d 761 (Wis. 1972).

20 See, e.g., Loveladies Harbor, Inc. v. United States, 21 Cl. Ct. 153 (1990), aff'd, 28 F.3d 1171 (Fed. Cir. 1994).

21 For a forceful analysis of the takings issue that raises questions of fairness to individual landowners, particularly when local majorities seek to impose their values, see William A. Fischel, *Regulatory Takings: Law, Economics, and Politics*, 1995.

22 Eric Freyfogle, "The Owning and Taking of Sensitive Lands," 43 *U.C.L.A. L. Rev.* 77 (1995).

23 Mary Ann Glendon, Rights Talk, 1991.

24 The classic discussion of fairness is Frank Michelman, "Property, Utility, and Fairness: Comments on the Ethical Foundations of 'Just Compensation' Law," 80 *Harv. L. Rev.* 1165 (1967).

compensation when regulation reduces expectations of economic value to be gained from development, it ironically creates a vicious cycle. For compensation structures themselves create sets of expectations, which fairness demands in turn be considered for compensation. Where property is viewed as socially constrained, however, the cycle is cut at the outset. John Francis, Political Science Leslie Pickering Francis, Law and Philosophy[25] The University of Utah

25 Research for this paper was partially supported by a Faculty Summer Grant from the University of Utah College of Law.

Philippe Brachet, Paris

Les droits et obligations des usagers des services publics en France

Introduction

Ce rapport esquisse une problématique du changement dans le statut de l'usager de l'administration en France. À commencer par le changement d'appellation (administré –> usager), qui exprime un changement dans les représentations réciproques de l'administration et de ses usagers.

Sa démarche est celle de la sociologie et de l'histoire. Elle fait apparaître que la normativité co-substantielle au droit bloque souvent la compréhension par les sciences juridiques des conditions sociales de son application – de son effectivité, comme disent les Anglais.

L'exemple du décret de 1983 est significatif: si son article 5 (cf. note 9) a constitué une innovation effective, c'est qu'il oblige l'administration à l'appliquer en suspendant la validité de ses actes à la réception de l'accusé de réception. L'article 8 par contre (cf. note 7), plus innovant en théorie en faveur de l'usager, n'est en réalité pas appliqué.

Pourquoi? N'ayant pas fait l'objet d'un contentieux, il n'a donc pas créé un droit jurisprudentiel. Ceci parce que les ayant-droits potentiels n'en ont pas eu connaissance et que les services concernés ne le font pas connaître. Ils considèrent qu'ils n'ont pas reçu de directive explicite en ce sens, que «nul n'est censé ignorer la loi» et que la situation est de leur point de vue satisfaisante puisqu elle n'a pas généré de contentieux. Le cercle vicieux de la non-application est donc bouclé puisque si cet article du décret n'a pas généré de contentieux, c'est précisément parce qu'il n'est pas connu!

Cet exemple illustre la principale condition de l'effectivité dans l'application du droit des usagers de l'administration: qu'il soit considéré (et se considère) comme l'instrument d'une politique publique. Et que cette dernière institue un référentiel reconnaissant les principaux types d'ayant-droits comme acteurs à part entière de sa mise en œuvre.

Ce n'est pas le cas pour l'instant en France pour la politique de modernisation de l'administration car cela supposerait une volonté politique de reconnaître les usagers des services publics et leurs associations comme partenaires de cette politique. Même la politique de renouveau du service public n'est pas allée jusque là de 1989 à 1991. Et depuis, le volontarisme jacobin domine de nouveau tout en étant de plus en plus impuissant.

A) De l'administré dans le modèle bureaucratique centralisé à l'usager dans la théorie du service public

1. Ce *modèle traditionnel*[1] correspond surtout à l'État libéral réduit (en théorie) aux quatre fonctions régaliennes.

Le statut d'administré est là celui d'un assujetti, qui n'a pas de droits mais que des devoirs: s'arranger pour connaître la loi ("nul n'est sensé [l']ignorer"), s'exécuter et se taire.

Les principaux aspects de l'attitude de l'administration à son égard sont la distanciation, la rigidité, l'anonymat et le secret. Cette attitude est perçue par l'administré comme *arbitraire*, mais la puissance administrative, agent de la souveraineté de l'État l'oblige à se soumettre.

La relation est donc non seulement inégalitaire, mais de domination, et elle est voulue comme telle, au nom de la conception "jacobine" de l'État-puissance publique.

2. Depuis les débuts de la IIIe République, les théoriciens du *service public* (Léon Duguit, Jèze, Hauriou) ont fondé la légitimité de l'État sur l'"interdépendance sociale" des activités, qui caractérise de plus en plus la société: l'État a l'obligation d'assurer, de régler et de contrôler toutes les activités dont l'accomplissement est indispensable à la réalisation, au bon fonctionnement de cette interdépendance sociale.

Ce nouveau fondement du droit public doit respecter et concrétiser des *principes* qui découlent des valeurs de la République: l'*égalité* devant le service public et ses corollaires (la *continuité* du service et l'*adaptation* aux évolutions des techniques et des mœurs).

Ces principes codifient les droits d'usagers dispersés face à la production d'un bien collectif en situation de monopole. Leur respect vise à empêcher l'abus de position dominante (cf. le préambule de la Constitution de 1947) et à établir l'équivalent d'une situation de concurrence, du point de vue de l'optimum (économique et social) que l'on peut en attendre.

3. Depuis le début du siècle, l'État-providence qui a remplacé l'État libéral comme modèle d'intervention n'a pas *rompu* avec le modèle bureaucratique centralisé d'action administrative: il en a étendu le *champ* d'intervention plus qu'il n'en a changé les *modalités*. Les principaux acquits de la théorie du service public ont été réalisés sous la forme juridique d'administrations spécifiques (Poste, Éducation Nationale...) et surtout d'ÉPIC (Etablissement Public Industriel et Commercial. Les principaux sont EDF, GDF, SNCF, la Poste, France Telekom). Ce modèle a pourtant été affaibli: la puissance unilatérale de l'État doit désormais coexister avec l'utilité collective dans les représentations.

C'est la crise de l'État-providence, depuis vingt ans, qui a réactivé la nécessité démocratique et économique de définir, garantir et respecter les droits des usagers des services publics. L'extension de la sphère des services marchands, la montée des possibilités techniques (et des exigences) en matière

1 Cf. Jacques Chevallier *Science administrative* [P.U.F. – Thémis] 1976, pp. 311–349 (section I) et pp. 191–210, 391–425 (section II).

de communication, le rapprochement "matériel" des services que rendent les administrations des autres activités de service, la crise du financement du secteur public par les seuls impôts et taxes, l'ouverture (puis l'intégration) européennes: autant de facteurs qui agissent dans ce sens.

B) De l'administré-assujetti à l'usager: de la souveraineté au service public

1.a. *Les administrés* étaient en position d'assujettis quand ils n'avaient que des devoirs à l'égard d'un appareil administratif massif et compact, imbu d'être le détenteur de la souveraineté de l'État.

En réalité, la distanciation était sélective: maximum pour le grand public qui n'avait avec les services que des relations de guichet. Mais les décisions plus importantes (celles qui relèvent d'une manière ou d'une autre de l'investissement) étaient (et sont encore largement) prises en concertation avec les responsables administratifs, dans les "étages" et de manière moins procédurière et plus consensuelle. Et ces décisions concernent essentiellement les personnes dotées d'un certain statut social.

De sorte que l'égalité formelle de l'administration traditionnelle envers les administrés recouvre une inégalité de fait fonction des conditions sociales. Aussi bien retrouve-t-on naturellement ainsi le fait que l'origine de l'inégalité entre conditions sociales étant extérieure à l'administration est largement hors d'atteinte de son action correctrice.

b. Avec la diversification et l'extension de ses fonctions, l'administration a d'abord réagi sur le mode autoritaire. Cette attitude s'est traduite par l'extension des tutelles sur ses services extérieurs et les organismes publics, et par un renforcement des rigidités dans les rapports avec les administrés (procédures écrites, relations de guichet). Ce fut la phase tayloriennes dont l'inspirateur dans l'administration fut *Fayol* quant à l'organisation du travail administratif.

Pourtant, depuis le début du siècle, les théoriciens du service public, eux, concevaient déjà les administrés comme des usagers ayant des droits. Car les principes du service public tentent de codifier les obligations des services envers les publics. L'administration dépositaire (distante et secrète) de la souveraineté de l'État tend à faire place à une prestataire de services à la recherche d'un dispositif d'expression et d'évaluation des satisfactions équivalent au marché. Cette conception a connu un premier domaine d'application sous la IIIe République avec l'enseignement public et la Poste.

2. *Les premières innovations* dans les relations avec l'usager après guerre sont logiquement venues des services publics industriels et commerciaux.

Le *prototype en est EDF.*[2] Dans le silence de la loi de nationalisation (qui n'a pas défini ses missions, "évidentes" durant la période de reconstruction) EDF s'est engagé dès les années 50 dans un effort de définition de critères de rationalité économique et d'utilité sociale. La *tarification au coût marginal*

2 Cf. mon ouvrage, *Le partenariat de service public avec usagers, élus, professionnels,* [L'Harmattan] 1994.

implique une conception moderne de l'égalité de traitement: elle n'est pas uniforme mais varie en fonction du coût de la dernière unité produite parce que c est celle que son consommateur occasionne à la collectivité.

Ce principe l'incite donc à économiser ses consommations, en même temps qu'il sert d'indicateur à l'entreprise pour son programme d'investissements et sa gestion courante. Il permet donc d'optimiser l'arbitrage entre choix individuels et collectifs. En plus du respect d'une certaine éthique, cette attitude s'explique aussi par la nécessité d'économiser des ressources rares dans la période de reconstruction et de croissance des années d'après-guerre.

Encore proche du modèle traditionnel (la tarification est définie centralement et unilatéralement, elle s'applique uniformément même si le résultat ne l'est pas[3]), cette attitude d'EDF à l'égard de ses clients va évoluer en fonction du marché qui se rapproche d'une saturation relative et avec l'ouverture progressive des frontières au cours des années soixante: l'électricité est alors en concurrence croissante avec d'autres formes d'énergie.

À partir de 73, la contestation de son programme nucléaire amènera l'EDF d'une part à renforcer les exigences de sécurité de ses matériels et de ses centrales et d'autre part à négocier avec les communes les conditions de leur construction et leurs conséquences sur l'économie locale (protocole d'accord de la centrale nucléaire de Chinon II).

À partir de 75, la concertation est organisée avec les organisations de consommateurs quant à l'information, la tarification, l'examen des réclamations. D'abord nationale, elle est ensuite également départementale.

Enfin, à partir de 1984, l'EDF s'est lancée dans son *projet d'entreprise.* Consciente que le profit ne viendrait plus de l'augmentation quantitative de la demande (la règle du doublement de la consommation d'électricité tous les dix ans) mais désormais de l'amélioration de la *qualité de ses services,* elle a entrepris une réorganisation interne pour s'adapter aux exigences du "sur-mesure de masse": dé-hiérarchisation, déréglementation, contrats de résultats comprenant des batteries d'indicateurs définis après interrogation des besoins des clients, partenariat avec les clients et leurs représentants (indicateurs de qualité, intéressement...).

3. Cette évolution des EPICs fut à la pointe d'une évolution similaire de l'administration elle-même, suite à l'augmentation et la diversification des fonctions de l'État. L'attitude bureaucratique traditionnelle devenait d'un coût économique et social ressenti comme de plus en plus insupportable.[4]

Ceci d'autant que la représentation du modèle traditionnel d'action administrative s'effritait. Cette contradiction se traduisit durant les années 70 par le mouvement consumériste.[5]

3 En effet, les consommations sont aussi décentralisées que voulu.

4 Cf. mon ouvrage *Du commandement au management*, 1995, pp. 173–192, j'y analyse les politiques de modernisation de l'État en France depuis 1981.

5 Cf. *Le service public industriel et commercial dans la société française d'aujourd'hui,* Colloque de Rouen, 21–23 mai 1980, co-organisé par la Fondation des Sciences Politiques, Électricité de France (service national) et *Le Monde.*

4. *Pourquoi privilégier les "usagers"?* Pourquoi pas les contribuables, les consommateurs, les citoyens...? Parce que la qualité d'usager définit le moment où le service est rendu: son usage. L'usager de l'administration, c'est l'administré au moment où sa relation se concrétise à l'occasion d'un acte, d'une démarche. Cela lui donne donc une expérience directe de la qualité de la prestation de service.

A mesure que les services publics se rapprochent de plus en plus des services marchands, il apparaît que *tous* (qu'ils soient administratifs ou industriels et commerciaux) présentent (selon des proportions variées) *deux dimensions: réglementaire* (dont le cœur est la souveraineté de l'État) et *gestionnaire*, de reproduction standardisée de prestations qui les apparentent aux autres services.

Or la nécessité de modernisation de l'État suppose que la dimension "souveraineté" des actions de l'État, même là où elle est la plus forte n'obère pas *le droit du citoyen-usager à la qualité du service public.* Or ce droit, c'est *au moment de l'usage* qu'il se constate, se vérifie et peut se mesurer. C'est pourquoi la qualité d'usager n'est pas exclusive des autres (citoyen, administré, client, contribuable) *mais c'en est une dimension commune.*

Son importance, tant économique (efficacité) que politique (renouvellement de la démocratie) vient de ce que c'est au moment de l'usage que peut se vérifier la qualité du service public, selon des techniques et des méthodes appropriées. Les procédures de représentation des usagers dans les organismes de service public ont donc un double enjeu d'efficacité et de démocratie.

5. *Usagers ou clients?* Dans son acceptation moderne, le terme de "client" implique une relation marchande: quand la concurrence est effective, elle incite les entreprises à améliorer le rapport qualité/prix de leurs produits-services, sous peine de perdre leur clientèle.

Cette image d'efficacité a incité le Premier ministre Michel Rocard à souhaiter que dans l'administration aussi «ici ou là...on parle de "client" au sens du secteur privé où le client est roi, même si cela ne vaut pas pour la totalité des services».[6]

Mais il existe une différence de nature entre services administratifs et marchands: les premiers sont dans une situation de monopole qui interdit à l'usager de choisir et rend difficile toute relation entre leur mode de financement (impôt, taxe, tarif) et une sanction de la qualité du service. C'est pourquoi les services publics administratifs n'ont pas de clients à proprement parler. Mais tous ont un coût d'une part (qui doit être couvert, que ce soit par l'impât, une taxe ou un tarif) et tous sont susceptible d'une *évaluation* de leur efficacité, de leur qualité. Et cette dernière, pour être objective, doit confronter le point de vue des services et ceux de leurs partenaires extérieurs.

Ainsi, les principes du service public visent à constituer l'équivalent d'une situation de concurrence du point de vue de la satisfaction de l'usager, pour compenser la situation de monopole dans la production du service (au sens de "prestation") et les comportements d'abus de souveraineté qu'elle génère de la

6 Entretien au *Monde* daté du 23/2/1989.

part des “services” (au sens de “bureaux”). Car tout monopole quel qu’il soit a tendance à abuser de sa situation. Mais leur diversibilité n’est pour autant ni toujours possible, ni toujours souhaitable.

C) Les droits des usagers: principes et textes

1. *Les attentes sociales actuelles,* telles que les révèlent les enquêtes[7] et sondages, mais aussi les réactions de l’opinion à tel ou tel évènement, permettent de définir les principaux droits des usagers des services publics.

a. Droit à *l’accueil* et au *renseignement.*

Le principe «nul n’est sensé ignorer la loi» est susceptible d’une lecture moderne plus équilibrée que l’interprétation traditionnelle: les nécessités élémentaires de la communication montrent que l’information uniforme et centralisée est largement inefficace. Ce que l’usager attend, ce sont des renseignements personnalisés et donnés en situation.

L’accueil, c’est tout ce qui permet à l’usager de se repérer dans l’univers administratif, de formuler sa demande et de la traduire en démarches. Il est donc très lié au renseignement.

b. Droit à *l’explication*, au *recours*, à la *concertation.*

- Beaucoup de décisions administratives peuvent être différentes (voire opposées) selon que les agents ont (ou non) entendu à temps l’usager expliquer sont point de vue et lui ont (ou pas) expliqué à quelles conditions ce point de vue est recevable.
- Beaucoup de décisions “portant grief” ont leur origine parce que l’usager s’est mis dans son tort par ignorance. Et a laissé passer (là aussi par ignorance) les délais.

  Il s’agit donc de substituer à la répression la prévention.

c. Respect des *délais* raisonnables *par* l’administration, et opérationnels *pour* l’usager (c’est-à-dire qui soient connus de lui à temps pour lui permettre d’agir).

Or en général, l’irresponsabilité administrative se manifeste par l’absence de sanction à son encontre en cas de retard. Dans la jurisprudence des “T.A.”, il faut que le retard soit “abusif” (exemple des pompiers qui ne s’étaient toujours pas rendus sur le lieu d’un incendie trois jours après!) pour qu’il soit sanctionnable. A contrario, le “retard simple” (ex. de la carte de transport que son destinataire n’a jamais recu) ne l’est pas, et il avait tendance à couvrir tous les actes courants. En effet, la jurisprudence tient compte des difficultés de fonctionnement des services: sont sanctionnées les fautes qui vont au-delà - les fautes lourdes. Mais la définition de la “faute lourde“ évolue. Ainsi autrefois, le

7 Cf. L’enquête *Les usagers “particuliers”* et *le service public aujourd’hui* pilotée par l’Observatoire de la décision publique (O.d.p.), cofinancée par la SNCF, EDF, La Poste, France Télécoms et la Fonction publique (DGAFP) et réalisée par le cabinet E.M.C.W. devenu depuis What’s on 50 rue d’Hauteville 75 010-Paris.

fisc n'était condamné qu'en cas de faute lourde; maintenant, s'il s'agit d'une activité normative (qui ne présente donc aucune difficulté particulière) la faute simple suffit. Cette tendance se généralise (enfin!).

Pourtant,même depuis son nouveau statut de quasi-EPIC, La Poste n'est toujours pas sanctionnable pour retard (exemple du petit industriel du Nord qui a fait faillite parce que son mailing a mis trois semaines pour arriver – c'était en priode de grève – et qui n'a reçu aucun dédommagement).

Autre exemple: les immigrés qui attendaient des mois (voire des années) leur autorisation de séjour de l'OFPRA et qui, en attendant, vivaient en situation irrégulière (il faudrait vérifier si la situation a bien changé du tout au tout comme on nous l'affirme).

2. Il existe *quatre lois et décrets* qui constituent l'amorce d'une reconnaissance des deux premiers droits.

a. *La loi de 1973* instituant le *Médiateur* (devenu Médiateur de la République)

- *objet*: réclamations concernant le fonctionnement de l'administration, par l'intermédiaire d'un parlementaire ou d'une association (pas de saisine directe)
- *recommandations* aux administrations concernées (persuasion et non contrainte – sauf en cas d'inexécution d'une décision de justice – art. 11);
- *correspondants départementaux* sans moyens propres;
- *pouvoir d'investigation* étendus (art. 12 et 13);
- publie un *rapport annuel,* à la fois bilan de ses activités et propositions de réformes.

b. *La loi de juillet 78* sur le *libre accès aux documents administratifs* de caractère non nominatif

- consultation gratuite sur place et photocopies (art. 4)
- Commission d'accès aux documents administratifs (CADA) (art. 5) pour veiller à son application;
- le refus de communication doit être notifié et motivé (art. 6)
- toute décision individuelle n'est opposable à l'intéressé que si elle lui a été préalablement notifiée (art. 8)

c. La loi de juillet 79 sur la *motivation des actes administratifs*

- les intéressés ont le droit d'être informés sans délai des motifs des décisions administratives défavorables qui les concernent (art.1) ou celles qui dérogent aux règles générales (art. 2);
- la motivation doit être écrite et circonstanciée (art. 3);
- le défaut de motivation ne rend pas la décision illégale mais si l'intéressé en fait la demande, la décision doit lui être notifiée dans le délai d'un mois (art. 4)

d. Le décret du 28/11/1983[8]

- art.1: tout intéressé peut se prévaloir à l'encontre de l'administration des instructions, directives et circulaires en vigueur, comme des lois et décrets;
- art.5: l'*accusé de réception* (le délai ne commence pas à courrir pour l'administration tant qu'il n'a pas été reçu);
- art. 8: les décisions qui doivent être motivées doivent permettre aux intéressés de présenter des observations écrites et d'être entendus par l'agent chargé du dossier (ils peuvent se faire remplacer par un mandataire de leur choix).

Depuis la promulgation de ces textes de portée générale, de multiples textes d'application particuliers d'origine européenne ou nationale en précisent et renforcent la portée dans différents domaines (télécom, électricité. . .).

D) Des principes aux réalités: complexité des usages et inertie des mœurs

L'application effective de la réglementation dépend des mœurs, des coutumes plus qu'elle ne peut les faire changer.

D'une part parce que les gouvernements changent et que l'administration reste. Les lois et circulaires qui contredisent la volonté des services ont donc toute chances de rester lettre morte. Soit l'administration ne promulgue pas les décrets d'application d'une loi; soit elle campe sur l'interprétation restrictive de «nul n'est censé ignorer la loi» (ex. de l'article 8 du décret de 83).

8 Art. 5. - Les délais opposables à l'auteur d'une demande adressée à l'administration courent de la date de la transmission à l'auteur de cette demande d'un accusé de réception mentionnant:
1° le service chargé du dossier ou l'agent à qui l'instruction du dossier a été confiée;
2° le délai à l'expiration duquel, à défaut d'une décision expresse, la demande sera réputée, acceptée ou rejetée;
3° s'il y a lieu, les délais et les voies de recouurs contre la décision implicite de rejet.
Les délais visés au premier alinéa du présent article ne courent pas lorsque les indications que doit contenir l'accusé de réception sont incomplètes ou erronées et que l'intéressé se trouve de ce fait empêché de faire valoir ses droits.
L'administration n'est toutefois pas tenue d'accuser réception des demandes répétitives ou manifestement abusives par leur nombre ou leur caractère systématique.
Les dispositions du présent article ne sont pas applicables aux demandes dont l'accusé de réception est régi par des dispositions spéciales.
Art. 8. - Sauf urgence ou circonstances exceptionnelles, sous réserve des nécessités de l'ordre public et de la conduite des relations internationales, et exception faite du cas où il est statué sur une demande présentée par l'intéressé lui-même, les décisions qui doivent être motivées en vertu de la loi du 11 juillet 1979 susvisée ne peuvent légalement intervenir qu'après que l'intéressé ait été mis à même de présenter des observations écrites.
Toute personne qui est concernée par une décision mentionnée au premier alinéa du présent article doit être entendue, si elle en fait la demande, par l'agent chargé du dossier ou, à défaut, par une personne habilitée à recueillir ses observations orales. Elle peut se faire assister ou représenter par un mandataire de son choix L'administration n'est toutefois pas tenue de faire droit aux demandes d'audition répétitives ou manifestement abvusives par leur nombre et leur caractère systématique.

Mais d'autre part, les usagers eux-mêmes ont leur part de responsabilité dans la non-application de dispositions en leur faveur.

Une idée reçue aussi largement répandue que juridiquement fausse commande leurs mauvais rapports à la justice et à l'administration: ils croient en général que parce qu'ils sont dans leurs droits, les conséquences doivent s'appliquer d'elles-mêmes. Or le droit ne s'applique jamais spontanément, le juge ne pouvant pas se saisir lui-même: un ayant droit qui ne saisit pas la justice dans les formes et les délais finit par perdre ses droits. D'où des malentendus fréquents qui deviennent inextricables. Et finissent par entretenir le sentiment de méfiance de la grande majorité des Français à l'égard de la justice et de l'administration. C'est pourquoi les correspondants départementaux du Médiateur passent en fait la majorité de leur temps à expliquer à des administrés qui se sont mis dans des situations impossibles (le plus souvent par ignorance et/ou laisser aller) ce qu'ils doivent désormais accomplir à temps pour ne plus recommencer.

Souvent, des dispositions avancées restent lettre morte, soit parce que certaines parties prenantes ne jouent pas le jeu, soit parce que les usagers les ignorent ou n'osent pas en revendiquer activement l'application. Et cette passivité aussi fait partie de l'inertie des mœurs.

Ainsi de la loi sur l'affichage des prix, précisée par la circulaire Neiertz du 15 juillet 1989. Sur le Continent, l'affichage des prix est en gros respecté par les commerçants. Mais dans le cas contraire, si un client faisait une remarque, il y a tout à parier que les autres prendraient la défense du commerçant contre lui, alors même qu'ils ont les mêmes intérêts. S'il voulait persévérer, il devrait faire appel à un agent de police pour constater l'infraction: où en trouverait-il? Et en Corse… !

La circulaire Neiertz s'étend aux professions libérales (avocats, médecins, dentistes…) qui ont obligation d'afficher les bases de leurs tarifs dans leurs salles d'attente. Or pratiquement aucun ne le fait. D'une part leurs ordres et syndics ont traîné les pieds pour passer des accords d'application. Et d'autre part, imagine-t-on un patient qui poserait une question ou ferait une remarque à son médecin ou son dentiste sur ses tarifs? Avez-vous jamais eu l'audace de le tenter? L'idée vous en est-elle même venue? La relation de dépendance à son autorité est si forte qu'elle l'exclut et ce n'est pas la loi qui changera *seule* ce rapport de force.

En définitive, la part de non application de fait de la réglementation a son origine dans les comportements réciproques des agents et des usagers qui se confortent mutuellement en formant cercle vicieux. Quitte à ce que les conséquences de cette même non application produise un mécontentement diffus à l'égard de l'administration (ex. de l'affichage des prix et du mécontentement contre les hausses abusives des prix). Exemple: les mêmes consommateures qui n'osent pas protester après des commerçants contre le non-affichage des prix sont mécontents des hausses abusives de prix en général.

Comme quoi le droit est bien un rapport social.